MAPPING PSYCHIC REALITY

Mapping Psychic Reality is one of a series of low-cost books under the title PSYCHOANALYTIC **ideas** which brings together the best of Public Lectures and other writings given by analysts of the British Psychoanalytical Society on important psychoanalytic subjects.

The books can be ordered from:
Karnac Books
www.karnacbooks.com
Tel. +(0)20 7431 1075
Fax: +(0)20 7435 9076
E-mail: shop@karnacbooks.com

MAPPING PSYCHIC REALITY

Triangulation, Communication, and Insight

edited by
James Rose

KARNAC

First published in 2011 by
Karnac Books Ltd
118 Finchley Road, London NW3 5HT

British Library Cataloguing in Publication Data

A C.I.P. for this book is available from the British Library

ISBN: 978 1 85575 814 8

Edited, designed and produced by The Studio Publishing Services Ltd
www.publishingservicesuk.co.uk
e-mail: studio@publishingservicesuk.co.uk

Printed in Great Britain

www.karnacbooks.com

CONTENTS

ACKNOWLEDGEMENTS

I thank the *International Journal of Psychoanalysis* for permission to reprint the following:

Cavell, M. (1998). Triangulation, one's own mind and objectivity. *International Journal of Psychoanalysis, 79*: 449.

I thank the *Psychoanalytic Quarterly* for permission to reprint the following:

Britton, R. (2004). Subjectivity, objectivity and triangular space. *Psychoanalytic Quarterly, 73*: 47–61.

Hanley, C. (2004). The third: a brief historical analysis of an idea. *Psychoanalytic Quarterly, 73*: 267–290.

I thank *Neuropsychoanalysis* for permission to reprint the following:

Whittle, P. (1999). Experimental psychology and psychoanalysis: What we can learn from a century of misunderstanding. *Neuropsychoanalysis, 1*: 233–245.

I thank Nonin Chowaney for kind permission to reproduce a calligraphy of a haiku by Basho.

James Rose, PhD, is a Fellow of the Institute of Psychoanalysis. He has a private psychoanalytic practice in London. For many years, he has worked in the Brandon Centre, an inner-city charity specializing in the psychotherapeutic treatment of adolescents and young adults. He is past chairman of the British Psychoanalytic Council.

Introduction

Imagine a world without maps. When, long ago, man began to feel the need to move about on the earth, it seems that people found that it was helpful, not to say potentially lifesaving, to have a reliable map of the terrain to be travelled. *Cartography* (from Greek *chartis* = map and *graphein* = write) is the study and practice of making maps. Combining science, aesthetics, and technique, cartography builds on the premise that reality can be modelled in ways that communicate spatial information effectively. We have been doing it for at least 10,000 years.

One of the most important advances in creating reliable maps came about through discovering triangulation. Pythagoras' theorem and the beginnings of trigonometry enabled distances to be calculated accurately. Such advances not only enabled safe travel, but also would have radically changed our view of ourselves and others. Thus, the map sought to create an objectively accurate view of the external world. In doing so, it also inevitably influenced our view of our relation to the world and, thus, our subjective view of ourselves. It would have changed our internal world spatially. To this we have to add that the concept of travel over distance introduces a different concept of time. Thus, our internal world seems likely to have been influenced by the more consistent and reliable spatial and temporal dimensions needed to move safely in the external world.

In turn, these developments changed the way we could communicate between ourselves. In so doing, our view of ourselves would have changed in unexpected ways. Copernicus's revolution challenged our egocentric view of the world, but the efforts of the early map makers, for example, Herodatus, would have had just as radical an effect because he and others, such as Aristotle, challenged the prevailing view of the world as a plate. However, we cannot identify one single man among them to thank for discovering the vital fact that brought each individual insight into their place in the world. Map making (or triangulation), communication, and insight thus go together as ideas, for together they form a dynamic description of how we learn about ourselves and the world. When we are thinking about psychic reality, we are essentially thinking about our subjective view of the social and physical world in which we live. Subjectivity does not just involve perception, but also the lived experience we have as individuals and with those with whom we live.

This book is about how we can deepen our understanding of subjectivity through the use of the concept of triangulation. However, despite it being written from a psychoanalytic perspective, it is not primarily concerned with Oedipal processes. Fundamentally, this book seeks to address the question of how we can be objective about subjectivity. If psychology, as a *scientific* discipline, is concerned with the study of human experience, which is essentially subjective, then we are faced with the problem of how to apply the *scientific method, as it is commonly understood*. If experience is essentially unique to the experiencer, then there seems to be a basic incompatibility with the scientific method. As currently practised, this method searches for psychic phenomena, which can be validly and reliably measured, for example, intelligence, showing a range of individual differences. But this does not enable us to examine individual experience. An individual's *experience* seems to become impenetrable because generalization across different individuals' experience entails the loss of individuality in the generalization. Thus, in using the scientific method as it is usually understood, do we lose the very matter we are trying to study. This leaves us with the question of how we are going to advance our enquiry.

Let us begin with the experience of insight, which is indisputably a subjective phenomenon. One way of expressing what it is like to experience an insight is to describe it as an "aha" experience. When a child points to something and says "there", we know that the child is distinguishing himself from the something he points to and communicates something about what he sees. An "aha" implies seeing something in a new way; something we did not see before that moment.

Below is a haiku by Matsuo Basho, possibly his most famous one. Haiku capture an immediacy of experience in an uncanny way, which accounts for their lasting appeal to many people.

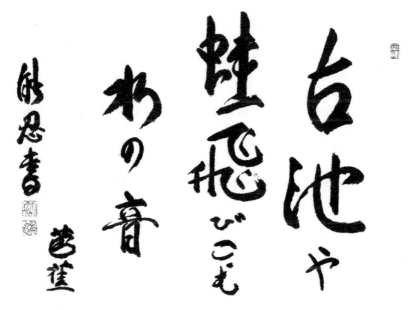

Four translations:

An old pond A frog leaps Then the splash	2. An old pond Leap-splash A frog
3. pond frog plop!	4. There once was a curious frog Who sat by a pond on a log And, to see what resulted, In the pond catapulted With a water-noise heard round the bog.

Below the Japanese calligraphy are given four possible English translations. The first two focus on different aspects of the experience that Basho seeks to capture: the first on the sound of the splash, while the second draws our attention to the fact of the frog, the cause of the impression of the sound of the leap-splash. The second two might be thought of as reductions that poke fun at the possibility of representing transcendental experience. There are many translations—essentially all equally accurate—emphasizing the subjectivity of experience. Some have said that this haiku seems to capture eternity in a moment. With the splash's immediacy in the timelessness of the old pond, we get a glimpse of the antinomy of time—the timelessness of eternity (the old pond) and its co-existence with the irreversibility of the arrow of time (leap–splash). This antinomy gives us an insight into the experience of the poet. My point is that the haiku communicates Basho's transcendental experience very effectively.

Another experience of an insight might be gained from the experience of "seeing" or understanding the solution to this prisoner's dilemma. This particular dilemma is taken from Lacan's (1945) explication of what he called "The theory of logical time". I do not intend here to examine this theory in depth. I ask the reader to have the experience of going through the process of solving the problem. You may see the answer straightaway. If you do, I ask you to put yourself in the individual prisoners' shoes and imagine the particular experience of being a participant. The dilemma is presented as a game.

The game is this: A prison warden has three prisoners selected and tells them that one of them is to be released. In order to choose the one to be released they will submit to a test. The warden has five discs—three white and two black—(which he tells the three prisoners). He tells them that he will fasten one of these discs to the back of each prisoner so that it is out of his own field of vision but not of the other two. The test is that the first to pass through a door and state the correct colour of the disc on his back will be released. This must be done by logic and not by probabilistic guesswork. The warden then fastens one of the three white discs to the backs of each of the three prisoners. The black discs are not used at all.

The solution to the problem works from the numbers of black and white discs. There are only three possible permutations of the three discs fastened to the backs of the prisoners—black, black, white (bbw); black, white, white (bww); and three whites. It is, therefore, possible that each prisoner can look at the discs on the backs of the others and realize that if he sees two black discs then he must be white. This *first possibility can be therefore excluded* because each person sees two white discs.

Lacan, then, from the logical solution to this problem, formulated three logical stages, which of course *have a temporal sequence*, but there is no necessary sense of *chronological* time implied by this sequence.

These were:

The instant of the look.
The time for understanding.
The moment to conclude.

In the first logical moment, or instant, of the look, all that happens is the exclusion of certain possibilities. Furthermore, in this time of pure perception no one knows who they are or if the others know who they are. Each is a stranger to themselves and the others. It is important to recognize that during this time all that happens is based on *the first person position*. It will be clear that if one prisoner saw black discs on the backs of the other two, he would instantly know he was white and would leave. As this does not happen, from the point of view of each prisoner the possibility of bbw is excluded.

In the secondary time for understanding, each prisoner can think (as a result of the preliminary exclusion of bbw as a possibility) "*if I were black, the other two whites I see would waste no time realizing they are whites*". Hence, in this phase, each must think of what the others are thinking. The answer for the prisoner to distinguishing the logical possibilities lies in the *inertia* of the other prisoners.

In the third logical time of conclusion, it is possible for each prisoner to think "I hasten to declare myself white so that these whites whom I consider in this way do not precede me in recognizing themselves for what they are". Hence, the moment to conclude represents an assertive judgement that the subject makes about themselves in which he or she emerges, from identification with the other, into the individuation of subjecthood. It is because the subject realizes that the others do not know what they are that the subject declares themselves to be white. In essence, it is a statement in the first person; that is, "I am white". While it is possible for each subject to think that he should declare himself white, there is not much that will help us predict which of the three will do so. Further, we do not know whether all three, in fact, equally want to leave the prison. But this is not to put oneself into the predicament of the prisoner: that is, the structure of each individual's experience.

I include this description of an experience to try to demonstrate to the reader that an insight may not concern simply an empathic response to another person's experience, as in Basho's haiku. This second description seeks to show that an insight may also occur as the result of thinking and reflecting on others' actions and experience. Insight, therefore, may be thought of as the result of a triangulation of what we ourselves see of a situation and what someone else sees of the same situation. Basho's haiku would be, in and of itself, inscrutable to those who cannot read Japanese. The wealth of possible translations shows us the depth and wealth of meaning of the haiku, which, to non-Japanese speakers, may seem more like a picture than a poem. To understand and gain something from reading the haiku so that one can "see what it means" *for oneself* needs the contribution of another's mind.

This is more obvious when it comes to the prisoners' dilemma. The solution requires attention not only to the discs, but the actions of the other prisoners. Thus, other minds are necessary for each prisoner to know who they are and some kind of communication is required. We seem to have a similar situation as we had in thinking about and appreciating the haiku. There is a situation shared by the participants, but for each to understand and in a sense "know their own minds" the contribution of others must be recognized and accepted. Thus, we have just seen two examples of a triangulation. What this book is fundamentally about is how triangulation as a concept can help us to understand the processes by which we, as individuals, can come to know our own minds.

Subjective experience and objectivity

How we can be objective about subjectivity? This problem has been with us from the moment that mankind began to study itself in a systematic way. Without a requirement for some kind of objectivity, one person's idiosyncratic view becomes just as valid as another's, and it is then hard to see how one can break out of one's own "first person view".

In the process of coming to know our own mind, we must start with the fact that our individual views of the world—material and social—are formed from our *active* individual perception of a world that *we*, as individuals, will deem objective. This inevitable *activity* means that our wishes and anxieties are partial determinants of our experience of that world. It is through discourse with others that we develop some sense of the objectivity—or reliability and validity— of our perception. Thus, our individual view *per se* can only be partially objective in the strict sense of the word. Hence, we live in an approximation to the real and not in full and direct confrontation with it, except—some might say—*in extremis*.

These matters are explored in the first paper reproduced in this book, which is by Paul Whittle (1999). He identifies what he calls a *fault line* in psychology between what he calls the sub-cultures of psychoanalysis and experimental psychology. These sub-cultures, each successful in their own ways, and in their own terms, now view each other with what he calls indifference or hostility. Each side perhaps loses something as a result, but in ways that may be hard for each side to see. There can be a sense that each says to the other "how can you possibly think like that?"

If psychology, as a scientific discipline, is concerned with the study of human experience and that human experience is essentially subjective, then we are faced with the dilemma of how apply the scientific method that we identified earlier. As a scientific discipline, psychology has responded in a variety of ways to this dilemma, ranging from the study of behaviour to the study of individual differences, rather than experience. In so doing, it has been possible to apply the scientific method and associated statistical models to the study of psychological phenomena, but many have felt that, as a result, something essential about subjectivity has been scotomized. This is not to say that there is no place and respect for detailed case studies of individual experience. But, the requirement of generalization seems to lead inexorably to a scotoma, and, thus, losing sight of individual experience as an object of study. We might say that a certain language, which would start with the phenomenon of mind, has been obviated. Each student of psychology has to come to some position on the problem of how the subjective can be made objective, or, at least, explored in terms that would satisfy those who believe that the first requirement of scientific endeavour is that it should be in some way objective, without which there is no knowledge.

In practical terms, this concerns the problem of describing experiencing in terms that could be called capable of verification. If something can be verified, then it can also be shown that the method of so doing is capable of showing that it cannot be verified. But, what happens when we enter a world in which verification and the notion of the negative are very problematical. One answer is to throw up one's hands in despair and beat a hasty retreat, but another might be to accept the challenge of describing something that cannot, by definition, be subject to the principle of verification, as, indeed, all experience is likely to be. This is because all experience is an individual reaction to circumstance and has an unconscious component and determinant.

My own first encounter directly with Whittle's fault line occurred when I was researching for my undergraduate thesis, which sought to show that the subception effect identified by Lazarus and McCleary (1947) resulted from a facet of their experimental design. Subception (a neologism coined from the idea of *sub*liminal per*ception*) was developed as a term to describe the apparent existence of perception at sensitivities beneath the normal level of everyday visual awareness. Lazarus and McCleary showed that, although a human subject might not be able to identify accurately a nonsense syllable when presented on a tachistoscope at very fast speeds, they could accurately discriminate these syllables, in terms of their galvanic skin response (GSR) to the syllable, once a conditioned response had been established between the nonsense syllable and a GSR. However, I showed that, when the amount of information (as measured in bits (binary units) of information) needed by the visual and GSR modes to discriminate accurately between stimuli was equalized, their effect disappeared. I then had to repeat Lazarus and McCleary's original experiment on my equipment to see if I could repeat their finding, which I succeeded in doing (Rose, 1968). At the time, I was rather pleased with my efforts because they were neat, watertight, and unambiguous—thoroughly nomothetic (of which see later).

But the experiential truth was that what stayed in my memory about the whole project were my experiences and observations of myself while I was seeking to establish a conditioned response to the nonsense syllables which would enable the GSR to be observed. This involved giving human subjects a very small electric shock when the syllables were presented. In case the reader has images evoked in their mind of experimental subjects vanishing in a blaze of electric current, leaving a smoking remain, I must emphasize that these were no more than tiny tweaks—noticeable, but definitely not painful. I remember being rather appalled by my zeal in establishing the GSR and felt, on reflection, that I might have been one of Stanley Milgram's subjects in his experiments on social compliance. These reflections were not included in my research report, but perhaps they should have been. Looking back on it, one might say that I was struck by my experience of myself. It was, perhaps, an unexpected introduction to Charles Hanly's notion of the Third (see later).

Now, it may have been that this experience was part of what eventually led me to psychoanalysis. The very concept of subception had captured my imagination because of the possibility that I was affected by, and reacted to, stimuli of which I was unaware. It perhaps placed me on one side of Whittle's fault line, but I did then go through something like fifteen years of a career in psychological, social psychological, and organizational research, and, subsequently, another five years in administration. I think in that time I came across several so-called fault lines that seem now to have one feature in common. It is quite a feat to get thought to flow back and forth across these fault lines, but, when one does, it can be quite fruitful.

The first of the fault lines I came across was the nomothetic–idiographic fault line discussed by Paul Meehl (1954). This sounds rather like Whittle's fault line, because the essence is to do with whether one is interested in a phenomenon that one learns about by taking a number of measurements of experience and then treats these as a sample of measurements which can then be subjected to statistical analysis (the nomothetic). Or, alternatively, is one interested in the phenomenology of experience (the idiographic)? Now, these two approaches have different research technologies and proponents of each criticize the other. On the one hand, the phenomenologists accuse the empiricists of imposing statistical models on experience, which ultimately come to distort understanding, whereas the reverse accusation by the empiricists is of irremediable subjectivity. This dilemma begins to look like a fruitless dichotomy.

Perhaps the answer to this dilemma is to seek to have a foot in both camps, which seems to be an antinomy. By antinomy, I mean the coexistence of apparently conflicting positions, each of which has a claim on the truth. Whittle's recommendation is that psychologists have to have a foot in both positions and, thus, a respect for each approach. As an example of how one can have a foot in both camps, I recall a time when I was working in the Greater London Council on the matter of the recruitment and training of firefighters. It had been identified that there was a consistent pattern of wastage during training, but the cause was not clear. Typically, training squads of between eight and ten men would lose one or two trainees half-way through their sixteen weeks' training. The pattern was too statistically consistent to be accounted for by random processes, but I wondered whether I could learn something from the trainees' experience of training that might explain this consistent pattern. So, I decided to follow a squad through their training by meeting them once a week for an hour to discuss their experience of going through the training. At the time, this was regarded as an extraordinary thing to do by the Fire Brigade training staff, but they acquiesced with a kind of amused detachment.

What I learnt in the course of this exercise was that there seemed to be crisis in the life of a training squad in which they seemed to wrestle emotionally with two questions. Please remember that this was in the days when firefighters were exclusively male. The first was whether the job of a firefighter was really a "man-sized" job because so much time was spent waiting for a "shout" (i.e., a callout) in proportion to the amount of time spent actually fighting fires. But the second question was who in the squad was not going to be "man enough" to do the job. The effect of these questions was that one or two trainees dropped out—they were not discharged. In other words, there seemed to be an unconscious "weeding-out" process in which certain individuals' lack of "height tolerance" became grounds for informally rejecting them, with the possible result that those who stayed felt confirmed in their manhood. Thus, it was possible to wonder whether I was observing here the development of an institutional defence against the anxieties of being a firefighter in the manner identified by Menzies Lyth (1988). The inevitable expectation of being in danger would be likely to create a fear of one's own anxieties and whether one would be "man enough" to do the job. If these anxieties were dealt with by projecting them into fellow trainees, it was easy to see how these probably unconscious "weeding out" practices would develop.

What was impossible to establish was the role of the training staff in this process, but it certainly seemed to be present in the squad. But, because wastage during training was a significant cost, steps were taken to deal with this by paying more attention to inculcating height tolerance during training, which did reduce wastage without the feared loss of standards, which was confirmed by the Fire Brigade Inspectorate of the Home Office. Now no one, least of all me, could claim that this is ground-breaking research that significantly pushes back the boundaries of human knowledge, but it was useful. It could be said that it could have been conducted as part of the normal process of managing the training of personnel. So, the question might then be: why did this not occur?

One might hypothesize that in any institution that reproduces itself by training its members, these training procedures will become institutionalized. They are, thereby, bound into an organization, becoming part of its traditions, which are then not open to question. The procedures will seek to contain anxieties, but, over time, become dysfunctional because of other technical changes. Without continuous review, these practices become part of an unquestioning tradition often rationalized by the belief that standards must be maintained. This phenomenon was by no means confined to the Fire Brigade. During our investigations, we learned that the selection processes of the British Army Parachute Brigade had put potential recruits through a quite unreasonably severe test of height tolerance, with the result that they had experienced great difficulty in recruitment. As a result, they changed their selection procedure such that recruits were given the chance to demonstrate whether they could learn to tolerate heights. As a result, the recruitment success rate markedly increased and the Parachute Brigade got the necessary recruits without the loss of standards that they had feared. But changing meant that they had to face the nature of their traditions and ask whether they were in support of something real, or were purely sentiment. This can be a painful process, by no means unique, and has been and no doubt will, of course, be observed in quarters much closer to readers' various professional homes.

My purpose in saying this is that it seems to me that "research" of this kind is not necessarily anything much more in itself but an expression of the ordinary, everyday process of questioning what we do and seeking feedback about our performance in the world. It is, however, an example of how the nomothetic (examination of wastage rates) and ideographic approaches (the exploration of the experience of training) can complement one another and enrich our understanding. Each approach puts a perspective on the other, giving a greater meaning to what is being studied.

Triangulation in coming to know one's own mind

How might we apply this approach to the problem of coming to know our own mind? Let us begin by proposing that when a psychoanalyst begins a psychoanalytic treatment with the objective of enabling an analysand to come to know their own mind, they create a learning system. This learning system comprises the two of them meeting on a regular basis in material, spatial, and temporal conditions, which to the outsider seem to vary as little as possible over time. This reliable setting enables the creation and then observation of a relationship between the two. Provided the psychoanalyst does not impose him/herself too much, the relationship that emerges will reflect the structure of the analysand's mind and the relationships that he/she creates in their life. Because the learning of the first session is fed into the learning of the second one, and so on until termination, this learning system can be called an iterative system. What it then can be possible to learn concerns the nature of the relationship between the psychoanalyst and the analysand in the context of the unchanging nature of the setting. This needs to take place in a reliable and unchanging setting, for this provides an objectivity in which the subjective experience of the analyst and analysand can meet. It is this that permits the seemingly impossible task of the subjective becoming objective to be achieved; in other words, the analysand coming to know him/herself with the help of the psychoanalyst. So far, I do not think there will anything mysterious or new in what I have said. Triangulation is a description of the analysand's internal world meeting their psychoanalyst in the context of an, objectively speaking, unchanging setting. The analysand's experience will, of course, not remain constant, but their experience will reflect what is going on their minds. But this experience is triangulated by the psychoanalyst and the setting making it more possible to reflect on this experience.

What I wish to explore in this book is how the concept of triangulation helps us to understand how certain features of this learning system work.

These include:

- How the psychoanalytic learning system functions such that private subjective experience—conscious and unconscious—can become something capable of being thought about, or, in other words, objective, or an object of study.
- How the psychoanalytic process functions in the temporal dimension, making it possible to think of it as a learning system.
- How the psychoanalytic learning system makes possible the understanding of psychic phenomena such as symbols or experience that cannot be easily described in words.
- How the psychoanalyst's unconscious can communicate with the analysand's unconscious and vice versa.

This book comprises ten chapters, following this introduction, divided into three groups. In the first group of papers is reproduced the paper by Paul Whittle (1999), referred to above. The purpose is to specify the fault line identified above more clearly, so that the relevance of the next two papers becomes apparent. The second paper is by Charles Hanly (2004), which concerns the idea of the Third. It seeks to trace the origins of this philosophical idea, which aims to make it possible to distinguish an object from the manner in which is described. In psychoanalytic terms, the concept of *nachtraglichkeit* uniquely captures this notion of the third that he seeks to explicate. This chapter is followed by Marcia Cavell's paper on "Triangulation, one's own mind and objectivity" (1998). In this paper, she puts forward the idea that coming to know one's own mind requires discourse with another mind about something external to both of them. Thus, the idea of a third is developed into the idea of triangulation, which is the topic of this book. The first section concludes with Ronald Britton's (2004) paper on "Subjectivity, objectivity and triangular space". In his introduction, he sets out his position succinctly.

This is that:

> The acknowledgement by the child of the parents' relationship with each other unites his psychic world, limiting it to one world shared with his two parents in which different object relationships can exist. The closure of the oedipal triangle by the recognition of the link joining the parents provides a limiting boundary for the internal world. It creates what I call a "triangular space", i.e., a space bounded by the three persons of the oedipal situation and all their potential relationships. It includes, therefore, the possibility of being a participant in a relationship and observed by a third person as well as being an observer of a relationship between two people. If the link between the parents perceived in love and hate can be tolerated in the child's mind, it provides him with a prototype for an object relationship of a third kind in which he is a witness and not a participant. A third position then comes into existence from which object relationships can be observed. Given this, we can also envisage being observed. This provides us with a capacity for seeing ourselves in interaction with others and for entertaining another point of view whilst retaining our own, for reflecting on ourselves whilst being ourselves. This is a capacity we hope to find in ourselves and in our patients in analysis. [p. 47]

This paper then goes on to examine the consequences to the individual of difficulties and failure to establish this structure.

In the second group of papers are two that look at triangulation in the temporal dimension. The first concerns the process of assessment and consultation in psychoanalytic psychotherapy and how the technology derived from the study of individual psychological differences can inform the process of exploring an individual's experience in psychotherapy. Thus, the exploration of individual experience can be shown to be enhanced by its comparison with others' experience, given properly developed instruments. This chapter is followed by one that explores the iterative feature of the psychotherapeutic process through the application of various ideas developed from chaos theory. These two chapters are a means of exploring Cavell's ideas about triangulation and the notion of iteration, which implies a *progressive triangulation because it occurs over time*.

The last group of chapters concern the application of the concept of triangulation, in the psychic dimension, as a means of exploring subjective experience. The first paper is concerned with how patients use the psychoanalytical setting to communicate their subjective sense of time. It is an exploration of how psychic time and space is distorted by the impact of anxiety and desire. The second paper considers the ability to symbolize and the facility it permits for managing the anxiety created by the continual need to adapt and change. In this paper, I explore Cavell's notion of triangulation in the process of coming to know one's own mind and how the psychoanalytic process permits this enterprise. I develop the notion of triangulation by introducing the idea of *progressive triangulation*; that is, a triangulation process that is iterative, which introduces a temporal dimension. The following two papers seek to explore the impact of what may, at first sight, seem to be an impossibly imprecise feature of the psychotherapeutic endeavour: the impact on the subject of first, absence, and second, the unrepresentable. They are clinical papers that explore the iterative features of the psychotherapeutic process.

The final chapter seeks to summarize and reflect upon the theoretical and technical implications of these papers. The purpose of this book is to show how the concept of triangulation can be used as a means of getting to a closer definition of how we can study experience. This definition means that we can develop our technology, as we will see in the chapters on consultation and assessment, and the understanding of the psychoanalytical encounter as a complex iterative learning system. This then leads to the possibility of thinking about how the psychoanalytic encounter permits the possibility of the unrepresentable becoming represented. One might say "Wo es war soll ich werden." This is commonly translated, following Strachey's translation, as *where id was, there ego shall be*. However, it can be perhaps more literally translated as *where it was, there I shall be*. Such a translation indicates a process of developing from an impersonal state where there is no such a thing as self and other to one in which the subject can address the other and truly speak in the first person.

References

Lacan, J. (1945). *Le temps logique et l'assertation de certitude anticipee.* Ecrits Paris: Editions du Seuil, 1966 [translated in *The Newsletter of the Freudian Field,* 2(2): 4–19, 1988].

Lazarus, R. S., & McCleary, R. A. (1947). Autonomic discrimination without awareness. *Psychol. Review, 58:* 113–122.

Meehl, P. (1954). *Clinical Versus Statistical Prediction: A Theoretical Analysis and a Review of the Evidence.* Minneapolis: University of Minnesota Press.

Menzies Lyth, I. (1988). The function of social systems as a defence against anxiety. In: *Containing Anxiety in Institutions: Selected Essays,* Volume 1 (pp. 43–85). London: Free Association.

Rose, J. S. (1968). A study of subception. *Papers in Psychology, 1(1):* 1–16.

Whittle, P. (1999). Experimental psychology and psychoanalysis: what we can learn from a century of misunderstanding. *Neuro-psychoanalysis, 1:* 233–245.

PART I

TRIANGULATION, COMMUNICATION, AND INSIGHT

Introduction

This part of the book brings together four papers exploring the relationship between triangulation as a concept and its relationship to the notions of communication and insight. The first is by Paul Whittle, who was an experimental psychologist. In this paper, he identifies and explores what he calls a fault line in academic psychology, which essentially concerns the split between the nomothetic approach and the ideographic (see above). He observes that psychologists seem to split around this fault line each implicitly asking those on the other side "how can you possibly think that that"? His conclusion is that this is an unhelpful split and he advises all psychologists to stand astride this fault line. The fact that there seems to be a split suggests that this is easier said than done.

This is followed by Charles Hanly's exploration of the philosophical and psychoanalytic notions of what he calls "thirdness"— of obvious relevance to the exploration of the psychic experience of triangulation. It is a discussion of a collection of papers published in *Psychoanalytic Quarterly* in 2004. In the paper, he makes the observation that the achievement of becoming a subject can seem to make the assumption of a capacity for intersubjectivity, which can be said to constitute another fault line in psychoanalysis.

This is followed by Marcia Cavell's paper on coming to know our own minds, in which she introduces a philosophical view of how we come to arrive at a sense of our own subjectivity and how we become "subjects". The link with the notion of triangulation is in her proposal that we come to know our own minds through discourse with another mind about something external to both of us. Cavell's proposal is seen by many to beg many questions, the answers to which are by no means clear. The reader is invited to think about these issues in the light of Hanly's summary and to explore how he or she implicitly responds, consciously or not, to these issues in their daily practice.

The question of a capacity for intersubjectivity is further explored by the last paper in this part of the book. This is by Ronald Britton, who approaches the matter from the point of view of his experience of treating narcissistic and borderline patients. He concludes by proposing what he calls a psychic atopia, or a kind of allergy to other minds. This presents many difficulties in psychoanalytic treatment. It is included to balance what might be thought by some to be Cavell's over-optimistic view, but, to my mind, it reinforces it because a refusal of another mind leads in many cases to the impossibility of achieving a sense of one's mind, and, thus, can be thought of as a confirmation of her proposal, even if it is thought by some to be in conflict with it.

References

Britton, R. (2004). Subjectivity, objectivity, and triangular space. *Psychoanalytic Quarterly, 73*: 47–61.

Cavell, M. (1998). Triangulation, one's own mind and objectivity. *International Journal of Psychoanalysis, 79*: 449–467.

Hanly, C. M. (2004). The third: a brief historical analysis of an idea. *Psychoanalytic Quarterly, 73*: 267–290.

Whittle, P. (1999). Experimental psychology and psychoanalysis: what we can learn from a century of misunderstanding. *Neuro-psychoanalysis, 1*: 233–245.

CHAPTER ONE

Experimental psychology and psychoanalysis: what we can learn from a century of misunderstanding*

Paul Whittle

This paper is a personal and informal ethnography of the subcultures of psychoanalysis and experimental psychology. It is a case study in incommensurability, and was written out of frustration with the incomprehension that each side displays toward the other. The two disciplines shared many common origins, but each now views the other, by and large, with indifference or hostility. I sketch some reasons why their relationship generates discussions, such as those concerning the scientific status of psychoanalysis, that are like trains passing in the dark. I make some tentative suggestions as to why we may always need such different styles of psychology, and for what different goals, and

---

*This paper was first presented to the Zangwill Club of the Department of Experimental Psychology, Cambridge University, in April 1994. Since it derives its structure and its liveliness from the occasion, it is being published as a record of the talk, with informal style and local allusions, rather than in more conventional journal-article format.

I read it to the audience from a finished text, contrary to custom in scientific seminars. This apparently small question of style was relevant to its substance. First, I needed the security of a text because I was talking in the gap between

personal and sociological reasons, we have developed them. I make even more tentative suggestions as to what, if anything, we should do about it.

Credit

In 1897, W. H. R. Rivers (1864–1922) was appointed to the first post in experimental psychology at Cambridge. He was a doctor, a physiologist (his 1900 encyclopaedia article on vision was "the most accurate and careful account of the whole subject in the English language"), a founding father both of the department and of British social anthropology. What is less often remembered is that he was also a major contributer to the spread of psychoanalysis in Great Britain, in two books stemming from lectures given here and based on his experience as a psychiatrist with First World War soldiers. Here he is writing in *The Lancet* in 1917:

> It is a wonderful turn of fate that just as Freud's theory of the unconscious and the method of psychoanalysis founded upon it should be so hotly discussed, there should have occurred events which have produced on an enormous scale just those conditions of paralysis and contracture, phobia and obsession, which the theory was especially designed to explain. . . . There is hardly a case which this theory does not help us to understand—not a day of clinical experience in which Freud's theory may not be of direct practical use in diagnosis and treatment. The terrifying dreams, the sudden

---

two subcultures. Second, it was an example of the subcultural differences I was talking about. Natural scientists like to talk with minimal notes, prompted by their visual aids, and often encourage interruptions from the audience. They believe they are reporting their interaction with nature, their words and diagrams being merely transparent media, and that their informal style testifies to their openness and honesty. In arts contexts or in psychoanalysis these assumptions are thought naïve, and "talks" are generally read from finished scripts. As a boundary-hopping scientist, I often feel excluded by this style. I can't keep up, and I often want to interrupt and query the assumptions. I miss the more open interaction of a scientific seminar. Nevertheless I found myself doing it. These different attitudes to language are a key to what is going on.

The paper was subsequently published in 2009, in *Neuropsychoanalysis*, 1: 243–245.

gusts of depression or restlessness, the cases of altered personality amounting often to definite fugues, which are among the most characteristic results of the present war, receive by far their most natural explanation as the result of war experience, which by some pathological process, often assisted later by conscious activity on the part of the patient, has been either suppressed or is in process of undergoing changes which will lead sooner or later to this result. [Rivers, 1917, pp. 912–914]

So, here we have another neurologist, probably a more careful and cautious scientist than Freud, reporting the same phenomena that Freud observed, but now of British soldiers not Viennese women, and agreeing with key components of Freud's explanation and treatment. I had read Rivers as an undergraduate, but forgot about him until reminded by an American feminist historian, Elaine Showalter, talking in the Department of History and Philosophy of Science. I think the roundabout route by which I relearnt the history of our department is also significant (Whittle, 1999).

One reason I start with Rivers is that he is so close to home. I could spend an hour telling you stories of other people whose lives link this department or Cambridge to psychoanalysis. In talking about psychoanalysis, we are talking about something deeply inter-woven both as practice and thought in British intellectual culture. Particularly in this department, in spite of appearances. Here, it is a cultural unconscious.[1]

Introduction

My topic is the fault line running down the middle of psychology. On the one hand we have experimental psychology as practised and taught in virtually all academic departments of psychology; on the other hand we have psychoanalysis, the Freudian tradition and its offshoots, which is much more influential in the culture at large. I shall take for granted, though with some elaboration shortly, that both traditions are alive and well and creative and in their own terms successful, and that the gulf between them is enormous.

It would give my talk a good resounding start if I could say with conviction that this split down the middle of psychology is an intel-lectual scandal. But I am not entirely convinced that it is. I have a sneaking suspicion that it may be a political compromise that allows a division of labour in which both sides can get on with their work without too much disturbance. In the 1990s, working political compromises are coming to seem increasingly attractive, even when one sees clearly that they also have serious costs.

In this case, there are two heavy and obvious human costs. The first is borne by students, who come to psychology hoping to learn about human nature, including their own, and find that the teaching institutions have been kidnapped by a particular style of thought. This is so in many subjects, but what makes it galling, and, I think, unjust, for those psychology students who are not uncomplainingly socialized into the tradition offered them, is first that experimental psychology has such a monopoly in universities,[2] and second, that it is obvious that there is another way of thinking about ourselves which is also called "psychology", which is adopted by large numbers of intelligent people, which has just as impressive a history and literature as the tradition they are taught, and which would probably tell them more about human nature, particularly their own. As well as this cost to students, another personal cost is borne by those who later depend on the services of these same students, if they become psychologists. They have been educated in only one tradition, and their clients' needs may sometimes be better met by the other one. Many would argue, having in mind, for example, the American experience of the dominance of psychoanalysis in psychiatry over the 1940s and 1950s, that this applies also to the clients of those who are trained in that tradition.[3]

That already gives ample justification for being concerned about the gulf. A further motive is intellectual. The people on both sides are talking about overlapping sets of difficult problems. It seems obvious to the point of banality that the perspective of each side must sometimes be helpful to the other, and it is easy to see many ways in which the perspectives of psychology and psychoanalysis complement one another. Another way to put it is to argue, as many have, that the mixture of ideas with which Freud started, one foot in neurology and one in interpretation (or however you like to describe the other place), was a fruitful mixture, even if it contained confusions. It clearly did bear fruit. The obviousness of this combining-perspectives argument is what does make some outside observers see the split in psychology as an intellectual scandal.[4] Yet, by now, after a century of history, to most psychologists this argument seems naïve. It is naïve in the form I have so far put it. I have spent years crossing to and fro over the gulf, unable to commit myself wholeheartedly to science or arts, yet I rarely find myself able to take suitable gifts from one side to the other. In general, neither side wants what the other side has, and when they do, or I think they do, they are put off by the wrapping. But this is puzzling, to put it mildly. If both sides are thriving and creative and their problems at least overlap, how is it that their subject matter and/or their methods have led to such a continuing separation? Even if we don't want to build bridges, we should surely at least be curious about the geology of the intellectual landscape.[5]

A final reason is the extraordinary *fin-de-siècle* replay, with a cast of thousands, of exactly the dilemma on which the early Freud was impaled: are memories of what we now call "child sexual abuse", but which Freud more gently called "infantile seduction", genuine or fantasy? This makes it harder than even ten years ago for psychologists to see psychoanalysis as old hat. I could add that while cognitive psychologists' interventions in this furore may have a useful calming effect, they might well be more effective if they had not cut themselves off from half the relevant literature.

That sketches the situation I want to talk about.[6] I now become somewhat more specific, and start by elaborating what I said I take as given. I proceed partly by an informal ethnography and history of the two subcultures based on my experience of crossing to and fro. I hope this won't seem too self-centred. I like to think that it is a graspable and unpretentious level. I think it is also an important level, because science is culture, and an essential preliminary to any philosophical treatment, which I am not particularly competent at and which leave many audiences cold.

What I'm taking for granted

First, the continuing achievements and creativity of both sides. Both are strong and vital intellectual traditions. I mean this in a quite superficial sense, as an observation that could be made by a Martian looking at the two institutions, attending their meetings, reading their literature, listening to their discussions, seeing how much demand there is for their services, and so on. In case there are those in this audience who need reassuring about the current vitality of the psychoanalytic tradition, I will mention, rather at random, three manifestations of it. One, the renaissance of psychoanalytic thought in France over the past few decades, where it has become the vocabulary for articulating much psychological and social and political thought, with lasting repercussions in feminist and in literary theory throughout the Europeanized world. To anyone in the English or Modern Language faculties in this university, this goes without saying. It is a symptom of what I am talking about that this may not be so in experimental psychology. Two, the fact that postgraduate courses in psychoanalytic studies are springing up by the dozen in British universities. Three, even closer to home, there is the growth over the past fifteen years in Cambridge of a community of psychodynamically orientated psychotherapists, now numbering around a hundred. These are just three out of many examples I could point to of its vitality. Only in the USA, where psychoanalysis suffered the fate of being for a time an orthodoxy, is it frequently asserted that it is moribund. I need even less to argue for the vitality of psychology. Situated in the overlap of cognitive science, neuroscience, evolutionary biology, and the social sciences, it cannot help but partake of the ferment in all those areas (particularly the first two).

This sort of vitality shows that a tradition is alive and well in what one might, since Foucault, think of as the domain of power–knowledge to indicate that it involves social and political components of practice as well as "knowledge". It does not mean that there are no major problems with either field; indeed, rather the opposite, since liveliness and problems often generate each other.

So, both are working subcultures. Any of us could be in either of them, but for chances of temperament and biography. In either, we would find criteria for explanation and truth that there would be no more and no less reason to question than there ever is. That's a fundamental premise of this talk. It's where I stand. You can gloss it in anthropological terms, seeing cultures as the prime influence on both practice and knowledge, or in Wittgensteinian terms as forms of life or language games, or postmodernist terms as different discourses. It is an injunction to strongly respect and notice cultural boundaries, but not, as I take it, to cease looking for common human characteristics.[7]

I also take it for granted that both traditions work in a somewhat less relativistic sense. Experimental psychology is, in its better exemplars, cumulative, and strong enough to support various kinds of technology, which is the most straightforward criterion of a successful natural science. Psychoanalysis increases personal insight. In what sense this insight is "true", and how much it helps to solve the problems that people bring to therapy, are other, and difficult, questions, but that people in psychoanalysis have many convincing "aha" experiences about themselves I do not think is worth disputing. Further, psychoanalysis provides concepts that are widely found useful in talking about ourselves and our lives. I mean both in ordinary life and in special domains such as social or literary theory. In most cases, these concepts were borrowed from ordinary ("folk") psychology in the first place, but psychoanalysis has refined and deepened them.

The third thing I take for granted is the magnitude of the gulf between the two traditions. The size of this split within what outsiders regard as a single subject is without parallel in any other academic discipline. Neither side reads the literature of the other. On the whole, they don't try to: it does not seem interesting or relevant. If they do try, they find it almost impossible. To each side, the literature of the other seems profoundly misconceived. Everything seems wrong; the obscure motivations of the writers, their impenetrable jargon, what they take to be appropriate method, and their criteria for truth and relevance. These come together in a powerful gestalt, so that the literature has so strongly the wrong feel to it that it becomes unreadable. To many on each side it seems so obvious that the other is trapped within particular ideologies, institutions, political stances that they shrug their shoulders and do not attempt debate. It is a gap between different subcultures, encompassing different belief systems, practices, and institutions, vocabularies and styles of thought.[8] It is comparable to the gap between the religious and the irreligious, and, just as that gap is commonly felt not to be a profitable subject for discussion after adolescence, this gap, too, is accepted and ignored, and those who, like Hans Eysenck, persist in reminding us of it, are felt to be showing bad taste or some psychological peculiarity.[9]

Of course, there are exceptions. There are psychoanalysts like Bowlby who would be at home in a department of experimental psychology; there are experimental psychologists like Keith Oatley who are at home in psychoanalysis. There are even some who, with striking though surely ill-founded optimism, are announcing the merging of the two traditions (Erdelyi, 1985; Horowitz, 1989). In social and in clinical psychology you can find many who draw from both traditions, and you can find many ideas and practices, such as cognitive therapy, which are deeply indebted to psychoanalysis but do not advertise the fact. These exceptions all exist, but they usually turn out on closer inspection to be exceptions that prove the rule; for example, in the case of the people I've mentioned, you find they are disregarded or thought of as "unsound" by one or both sides. The overwhelming situation is one of separation.[10]

Water under the bridge

I should say something of the standard history and philosophy of the relationship. I think of this as "water under the bridge". Given my title, you might well expect it to be my main topic. But my perception of the situation is that both sides are stuck on these issues. I need to summarize them to stop you wondering about this and that, but they have become boring. This is both cause and effect of the gulf. To get things moving, we need to go up a level, to try to get an overview. Hence my cavalier treatment of these issues over which blood has been split, and over which passions can still be readily aroused. (So, the boringness is defensive?) It is not only water under the bridge, but also a minefield strewn with dead horses. The last thing I want to do on these topics is to flog dead horses.

Both traditions share an origin in Helmholtzian physiology, the tradition from which experimental psychology springs, and in which Freud was educated.[11] Early relations between the traditions were cordial. For example, William James was in the audience at Clark University, Massachussetts, in 1908, an occasion that Freud called the first public recognition of his work, and said to Ernest Jones afterwards that "the future of psychology belongs to your work" (Jones, 1955, p. 64). Psychology's cultural revolution towards behaviourism ended this harmony. Interest in psychoanalysis became, and has remained, a minority interest in psychology.[12] It was sustained, and still is, outside psychology, notably in anthropology and psychiatry.

Attempts at "experimental verification" of psychoanalytic propositions. Overall conclusion equivocal (not negative). I come back to it shortly.

There are a few areas where there is more contact; for example, dream research in sleep labs. But again, early promise has somehow faded away. Why? One quite likely reason is that to progress, such work needs the intimate individual knowledge that psychoanalysis gives. Labov and Fanshel's (1977) study, *Therapeutic Discourse*, is another interesting example of interpretative psychology that found itself in that dilemma. But this demand for intimate knowledge breaks the conventional boundaries of laboratory research, and also becomes almost the same genre as psychoanalysis: individual interpretative studies with all their epistemological difficulties.

Developmental psychology is an area that still includes Freud in textbooks, but unassimilated. Here again, the story is of occasional forays (like Piaget's psychoanalytic period).[13] There would seem to be plenty of scope for interpretative laboratory studies of children's play (like Klein, or Anna Freud, or Erikson), but it hasn't much happened yet.

Another community of psychologists that has much of the openness that I admire in some psychoanalysis, and that partly overlaps with "human sciences", is constituted by those who work in a broad evolutionary–biological and perhaps developmental, and sometimes cultural, framework (like Freud). These communities act as a leaven, but for some reason that I don't understand they remain only a leaven within psychology, rather than transforming its substance. The obvious inference is that psychology is only half-baked, as many have suspected.

"Outcome studies." Does psychotherapy "work"? This literature is founded on the hope that states of human misery, arising, for example, from unemployment, incest, homelessness, years of loneliness, spiritual despair at the violence and heartlessness of the world, can be seriously helped by a few sessions of scientifically structured intervention by somebody with psychology training. If psychoanalysis fails the test, then so much the better for psychoanalysis. I hope that clinical psychologist colleagues will permit me a little rhetorical exaggeration, but that is one valid critique of that literature (which I borrow from a clinical psychologist, David Smail (1987, 1993)). Another weakness of this literature as a critique of the truth of psychoanalysis is that there is no logical connection between knowing the truth about your life and leading it more successfully. They may even be inversely related, as Freud himself suspected.

There is a whole different approach to which my conscience occasionally recalls me. This is to work like that by Malan (1979) to extract a consensus body of "low-level observations such as all (psychodynamic) clinicians use". The defence mechanisms of repression and projection would be prime candidates. These are observed daily by all therapists. There are thousands of descriptions in the literature (and in Shakespeare and . . .; they are folk psychology) which could, if you wished, be assembled into a boring but surely overwhelmingly convincing body of public evidence. If experimental psychology has difficulty replicating them in the laboratory, then so much the worse for experimental psychology. There is no shortage of good reasons why this might be so.[14] They may require real emotions, genuinely part of someone's life, not feelings such as can be called up by a supposedly unpleasant word on a screen in a laboratory. To distinguish regression from mere forgetting may require knowing a lot about a person, knowledge of a kind that requires time and trust, and, therefore, a relationship of a kind not readily obtainable in a laboratory, and there is the rub. These are indeed "low-level" observations for psychoanalysis, but they are not so for psychology. Far from being a body of knowledge that transcends the difference in subcultures because it is so obviously grounded in our common humanity (as many clinicians feel) it may, in fact, be the topic about which most argument has raged. By now it is another dead horse. To see why requires changing the level of discussion, as I am trying to do.

I imagine clinicians saying this can't be right. These things are so humanly obvious. But it is right, while people stay in their subcultures. To get them out of it you have, for example, to take an experimental psychologist by the scruff of the neck and put him or her in a situation where they have to start seeing differently. This happens in individual therapy, or is happening to some in their encounter with the child abuse furore. To get a psychodynamic psychotherapist to start seeing the need for public, conventionally scientific evidence, you perhaps have to put their jobs under attack so they have to justify themselves and their practice to administrators. (I'm not sure about that, there are too many other ways out.) But in both cases it will not be just individual opinions that will change. They will start seeing all sorts of things differently. Their "eyes will be opened". This is the force of talking about subcultures. Beliefs, attitudes, behaviour, percepts, come in packages.

I mentioned "the standard philosophy" of the relation. I cannot discuss this properly; I am taking a different tack. I will just mention it. The part that is standard in psychology departments is the well-known Popperian objection to psychoanalysis as unfalsifiable. It is both right and wrong.[15] It is another dead horse. The part that is standard elsewhere is the argument that is older than psychoanalysis, about the proper methods of natural and human sciences (Natur- and Geisteswissenschaften). Causes, reasons, agents, hermeneutics, Verstehen, etc. It helps in many ways, but it's not my approach just now. (For an accessible treatment, see Taylor (1971).)

Some of you may be thinking something like, "He's already conceded to Popper with all his talk about arts and science and so on. He admits psychoanalysis is not scientific." But I don't want to come out and say that, for a variety of reasons. First, we no longer know what science is. Second, there are ways in which psychoanalysis is more scientific (by anybody's definition) than experimental psychology; for instance, in its openness to the reality and subtleties of experience. Third, the statement is so loaded that it's another dead horse: it has succumbed under its load. Fourth, I think psychoanalysis is probably vital to psychology, but that the real challenge is to develop new categories for thinking about it (as probably for other topics we are stuck on, like consciousness).

I now go on to discuss why there is a gulf and what constitutes it: what are the contrasting aspects of the two subcultures that keep them apart?

What experimental psychology and psychoanalysis do

First, let me give a bald presentation of the different enterprises of experimental psychology and psychoanalysis (Table 1.1).

Table 1.1. The differences between experimental psychology and psychoanalysis.

	Experimental psychology	Psychoanalysis (clinical work)
Aim	Public science	Individual therapy and enlightenment
Method	Observation & experiment Impersonal & statistical	Personal relationship Interpretation & theory
Subject matter	General laws of behaviour and mental life (primarily the rational) Mental processes	Individuals (emphasizing the irrational) Mental "contents"

This is a table of emphases; of course, you can find exceptions to each item. It points to resources for explaining much of the gap. Each item brings with it moral, political, and institutional dimensions which are not explicit in my table, but interrelate with every cell of it, and are dialectically related both to the enterprises and to their separation. How we treat, and so think about, ourselves and each other. Keywords: technology, science, medicine, welfare, control, power, hegemony, sociology of knowledge.

Many of you may feel we could stop here. All right, they are very different enterprises. Of course there is a gulf, of course there are different cognitive styles, and so on. Why go on? Well, my enterprise is to persist nevertheless in trying to put perspectives together: an addiction to trying to see with the eyes of another culture. The moral imperative is "only connect" (E. M. Forster, *Howard's End*). Working in a department of experimental psychology and knowing many psychotherapists continually makes me feel this is quixotic. I gave reasons at the start for persevering, but we can now glimpse some of the reasons why we may not succeed. But the success of what? I wrote the last sentences back in the attitude that is natural to me of hoping for a single superordinate story that we might call psychology. But maybe connecting is possible, but not in that way. Maybe that is not how the pieces fit together.

One persuasive attempt at fitting the pieces into a single story has been offered by Stephen Frosh (1987, 1989) in two recent books.

He argues that psychoanalysis has given us the best psychology of individual subjectivity that we have. Its enterprise (see Table 1.1) makes this likely. Experimental psychology shies away from subjectivity and particularly individual subjectivity, the contents of individual minds. But, most people ask, how could that possibly not be of the highest relevance to understanding human behaviour and experience? If Frosh is right, and I think he is to a considerable degree, this is a most obvious way in which psychoanalysis has something vital to offer to psychology. Frosh, in fact, pursues this in detail through different topics from artificial intelligence to gender differences, suggesting in each case important questions, ideas, and explanations that psychoanalysis raises but psychology does not. A strong reason for "minding the gap", which is the subtitle of one of his books. He offers the most straightforward and fully worked-out answer to the question of what psychoanalysis has to offer psychology.

However, although Frosh is admirable and unusual in bridging the gap, my guess is that most psychologists would not much like the suggestions he makes. A major reason is that they come wrapped in too much theory. To cope with that problem, we need to get back to the ethnographic comparison of the cultures, to try to see what this theory is doing and how psychologists could (perhaps) learn to love it, or, at any rate, to stomach it.

The rest of this paper will be based on the assertion that the main tool or method in psychoanalysis is to fill gaps in self-narratives and self-awareness—the "talking cure", as Anna O, the first psychoanalytic patient, named it. That was its starting point and that is what it still does. We are aware of only fragments of ourselves (as experimental psychology also strongly holds). Many of the gaps can be convincingly filled by stories, using the psychoanalytic method. This is simply the common experience of people in therapy, that such stories can be convincing and sometimes helpful to them. They can be convincing also to others who know enough of the background. You can always ask for stronger criteria of truth, as psychologists or philosophers do. The questions are, "What for?" and "Are there any?"

This is the natural conception of psychoanalysis for our language- and text-centred era. To most analysts, however, it is superficial, because it ignores the structural changes in defences or personality that therapy aims at. Another radical qualification comes from thinking about the existential and moral dimensions of therapy. These are actually the heart of it. Therapy is not primarily talking about the patient and her life. Language is used more to show than to say (Heaton, 1968, 1972).[16] From this point of view, the descriptive psychology that the psychoanalytic literature is so full of is only a spin-off, not the main point at all, and may be even an escape from it. One answer to this comes shortly.

The different cognitive styles of the two sides

I want now to talk about the different cognitive styles of the two sides. I'm trying to give some feel for the experience of crossing to and fro between subcultures. Each side tends to be blind to the kinds of excellence admired by the other. This is important in maintaining the gap. I think the differences in style are an important part of it, and are not to be dismissed as "mere style". They embody cognitive habits that are crucial to the goals of the two subcultures.

I start with a quote from Adam Phillips, a psychotherapist who also publishes as a literary scholar. It is from his engagingly titled book, *On Kissing, Tickling and Being Bored*.

> One of the dramas that these essays try to sustain—and that is present in every clinical encounter—is the antagonism between the already narrated examined life of developmental theory and the always potential life implied by the idea of the unconscious. The conflict between knowing what a life is and the sense that a life contains within it something that makes such knowing impossible is at the heart of Freud's enterprise. So in one kind of psychoanalytic writing the theorist will be telling us by virtue of his knowledge of development or the contents of the internal world what a life should be like, however tentatively this may be put. And in another kind of psychoanalytic writing—which in its most extreme and sometimes inspired form pretends to ape the idea of the unconscious—there is a different kind of conscious wish at work: rather than informing the reader, there is an attempt, to echo Emerson, to return the reader to his own thoughts whatever their majesty, to evoke by provocation. According to this way of doing it, thoroughness is not inciting. No amount of "evidence" or research will

convince the unamused that a joke is funny. And by the same token ambiguity, inconsistency, or sentences that make you wonder whether the writer really knows what he is talking about, are considered to be no bad thing. I prefer—and write in these essays— this kind of psychoanalysis, but each is impossible without the other. Their complicity is traditionally underrated in psychoanalysis. [Phillips, 1993, p. xix]

First, note Phillips's style. Lovely subtle writing of a type unfamiliar and inappropriate in science. And he nicely describes, and admires, psychoanalytic writing of a more extreme kind. Lacan comes to mind, who took as his peers the Surrealist friends of his youth. Psychology comes out very differently that way from the way it does when you take medical textbooks as your model. Note the italicized passage. If you can't take that on board, you are not understanding how different psychoanalysis can be. Note also how he answers the problem I just raised, by pointing to the need for two kinds of language in psychoanalysis: descriptive and "inciting". This might also be our answer to the gap: the descriptive is scientific and the other something else. Unfortunately, the descriptive, for example Freudian or Kleinian developmental psychology, is doubtfully scientific in the judgement of most scientists, and still seems to function in psychoanalysis primarily as rhetoric, even though not of the "inciting" kind.

Understanding, in this subculture, often means to be able to discourse interestingly about something. To write a subtle net of language in which every sentence is compact with meaning sparks off free associations in several directions, and maintains an elusiveness and ambiguity that is true to life. Phillips exemplifies it. If understanding is to be able to speak evocatively about something, then this is understanding to the *n*th degree.

If understanding is to be able to "predict and control", then this is nothing. It offers no particular points of leverage, and such points are the *sine qua non* of technological action on something.

But, of course, the experience of psychoanalysis is that it is precisely such discursive understanding, the ability to speak in evocative ways, that does offer leverage on ourselves. Indeed, Richard Rorty (1991) goes so far as to describe it as a "Baconian" instrument in the human context. Contrast the style of experimental psychology. Wittgenstein's famous dictum (1918) is a good start: "What can be said at all can be said clearly, and what we cannot talk about we must pass over in silence" (*Tractatus*, preface). You say it clearly. You do not use teasing words like inciting or whatever their majesty, which work, if they work at all, the scientist feels, in indirect ways, and only for particular sensibilities. But note this is all acculturation. The person who can appreciate Phillips instantly may not be able to stomach an experimental psychologist talking about the same thing. She may be so aware of the number of begged questions and so put off by the crudity of the categories ("Is it cognition or affect?" Of course, it is always both, this is human experience we are talking about) that she can't hear it.

Here is another description of the style of scientific thought, taken from Nietszche:

> It is the mark of a higher culture to value the little unpretentious truths which have been discovered by means of rigorous method more highly than the errors handed down by metaphysical ages and men, which blind us and make us happy. At first the former are regarded with scorn, as though the two things could not possibly be accorded equal rights: they stand there so modest, simple, sober, so apparently discouraging, while the latter are so fair, splendid, intoxicating, perhaps indeed enrapturing. Yet that which has been obtained by laborious struggle, the certain, enduring and thus of significance for any further development of knowledge is nonetheless the higher; to adhere to it is manly and demonstrates courage, simplicity and abstemiousness. [Nietzsche, 1878, 1.3]

This catches beautifully, I think, the faith and cognitive asceticism of experimental psychology. The deliberate refusal or self-denial of understanding. Although psychoanalysis is also revolutionary in the type of understanding that it aims at, it doesn't at all have this asceticism. Rather the opposite. This kind of ascetism may be just what you need for experimental science, but just what you do not want if you are trying to fill gaps in a text or a life. For this interpretative synthetic enterprise, you need all the help you can get, all the concepts, all the associations, all the lateral thinking possible. Another obtrusive component of the cognitive style of psychoanalysis is its heavy use of theory.

The role of theory

The British are notoriously distrustful of theory. Newton was even, famously, distrustful of "hypotheses". Theory is continental. We think of it as Germanic, and heavy. We think of Hegel and Heidegger. Brits who get entangled in it, like Samuel Taylor Coleridge, or R. D. Laing, become incoherent substance abusers with marital problems. Psychoanalysis is full of theory. It has to be, because it is so distrustful of the surface. It could still choose to use the minimum necessary, but it does the opposite. It effervesces with theory, so infectiously that books of theory now bombard us from Paris, New Haven, Indiana, it sometimes seems from everywhere where there is a feminist, modern-language academic. This weight of theory is a major reason why experimental psychologists, who are the most deeply British–Empiricist culture that there is, cannot get on with psychoanalysis. How could they possibly? How could people whose habit of mind is to ask of every statement that might have empirical content whether (1) it is statistically significant, and (2), more interestingly, whether there might not be another, simpler explanation, possibly stomach these outpourings of prose, of sentence upon sentence of uncertain epistemological status?

But stop a moment. This theory effervesces. It is not Germanic and heavy.[17] It makes jokes (albeit somewhat esoteric ones), it is laced with jouissance, with sexual ecstasy. Teresa Brennan (1993) writes in the introduction to her most recent book, *History after Lacan*, that "Feminist theory is the most innovative and truly living theory in today's academies". A scientist who looks into such books and who is involved in, say, the creative excitement of molecular biology or computational vision, may think she is simply off her head, but she is not.[18] What you can find there, I know from personal experience of both books and seminars, is a unity of heart and creative mind that is indeed extremely unusual, in universities or anywhere else, and is to be valued most highly. So, what is happening here? What is happening, in a word, is play. This is theory as creative play. Playful theory. It is a way of exploring the connections of diverse aspects of our lives and experience, juggling them this way and that to see if they could be made to fit differently, making new concepts so that we can grasp certain configurations as wholes, and use them as tacit units in further thought. Imagining societies with different child-rearing practices, after which men might not hate women so much. Imagining different ways in which our psyches may be constructed: perhaps one of them will mesh with our experience sufficiently to be a useful way to think of ourselves (since we don't know how our psyches are constructed). Now, of course, it is not labelled as fiction or play. That would risk malign influences from the ambivalence of our culture to those forms. It would discourage some readers and theorists from taking it seriously, weakening the commitment required to grapple with such difficult thought. It is better to leave its epistemological status genuinely uncertain in the minds of all concerned. But I think that, nevertheless, it can usefully be seen as play, a form of play to which we bring the same schizoid blend of willingness to identify and emotionally commit oneself, with the suspension of many ordinary commitments, that we bring to stage plays or film or fiction. Which, incidentally, even psychologists are sometimes willing to admit are both more serious and truer to life than psychology is.

A play space

This notion of a play space is relevant in so many ways to what I am talking about. Psychotherapy provides it. Psychoanalysis itself needs it. I recently heard Mary Jacobus, a distinguished feminist literary scholar, talking about Melanie Klein's lengthiest case history, concerning a child called Richard. Psychologists who try to read this don't know what to make of it. Klein deluges her young patient with interpretations, so that anything Richard says or does is as much a response to them as a reflection of his own state. What is observation, what is interpretation, what is suggestion? But, treated as a work of literature, it immediately revealed all sorts of new facets, including psychological insights to which otherwise I would have been blind. It was the right intellectual space into which to take it. When I'm lecturing on psychoanalysis, I annually complain that Freud's concepts are ignored; psychology has not developed them in the way it has developed those of Helmholtz, Pavlov, or James, for example. This year I realized that I was look- ing for them in the wrong place. In a recent seminar in Cambridge, Elaine Showalter took up the rhetorical question "Where have the hysterics gone?", and jokingly answered, "They have gone into discourse" (because of the amount of feminist writing, both theory and novels, on hysteria). Where have Freud's concepts gone? They have gone all over the place, into ethnography, the ethnology and sociology of the body and emotions (vital background for understanding hysteria), feminist theory, literary criticism, and, in due course, some of them will come home again to psychology changed and deepened and ready for us if we need them, or choose to attend to them. Psychology did not provide the right culture for them. This is not necessarily an indictment of psychology, which was doing its own thing, fighting its own battles, and the resulting environment was not hospitable to these memes.

You may ask, but doesn't all creative work need this? How is it particularly relevant to psychoanalysis? (1) It is a model of the heart of the process. Provides space for the person. The therapist as court jester. (2) It is more explicit in psychoanalysis (and is open to misinterpretation as claiming to be something else: scientific findings; the misconception I was trying to dispel). The play theory is published and public. Maybe in science we need to give more space to "speculations", as we call them. I have often felt we need to give more space to "understanding", and that is a form of theory. We pride ourselves on the discipline that experimental methods provide. But maybe we resort to them too quickly and should play more. Here is another quote from close to home:

> Freud's strength [was] the most complete loyalty to facts as he observed them, an unshakable [belief] in his interpretation of the facts, a vast power of intuition or insight, and a great sweep of brooding imagination. In fact he raises in a most intriguing form the question of criteria by which a man is to be called a scientist. It may be that all the great scientists are people who work as artists in a field which everybody considers to be scientific. [Bartlett, 1955, p. 206][19]

Why human nature may need a bipartite psychology

We are this creature that constructs itself in culture from ideas, memories, and so on, often from narratives, which seem fundamental to our thought in so many ways (think of dreams). We do this from birth, at first in a highly confused way that we don't know how to describe. Hence, the individual tangles of ideas in our heads that are what psychoanalysis works on. These are the prime source of personal meaning. That is to say, all meaning that controls our thought and behaviour. But they are full of gaps.

Pluralism

One of the hidden themes of this paper is the notion of truth. In scientific work, "truth" is usually a workable concept. If I'm asked, "is it true?" I have ways of finding out. In psychoanalysis, I no longer know what it means.

Psychologists have argued a great deal about the truth of psychoanalytic interpretations, and students often find them hard to swallow, argue for this or that other interpretation, and conclude that this vagueness damns the enterprise.[20] Both assume that there should be a single true interpretation in the same way that scientists aim for a single true explanation (at a given level). This is also why the existence of many schools of psychoanalysis is thought scandalous. But is not a better analogy the multiple interpretations that a poem or other text allows? They complement each other, and allow a multi-dimensional, or multi-perspective view of the object. This does not mean that "anything goes". You can still argue, even "rigorously", about how valid a particular interpretation is, and you can hope that the different perspectives in some sense converge, and do the intellectual work to show how they do or do not.

Consider how easily you accept my two totally different metaphors for a certain body of work: "water under the bridge", and "a minefield strewn with dead horses". Two psychoanalytic interpretations for an item of behaviour or a dream might be equally different, but also both valid, that is to say, enlightening.

This seems a good analogy if the subject matter of psychoanalysis is like a text with holes in it. The different interpretations of a text create a new one like coral growing on some nucleus. That is what life is like; it is forward going. Each new interpretation changes the person. Who can tell what the original coral was like? Does it matter? The interest is in what the new organisms brought. Their behaviour was only in minor respects determined by what

they found. It depended also on their own nature and on the nutri-
ents that happened to be flowing by and many other factors. A
useful organic metaphor for mind? An ecological niche for memes.
The best way to know it may always be to see what lives in it. And
whatever lives in it changes it.

Two final quotes to help make such pluralism more attractive
(perhaps). You can relate them either to the coexistence of two types
of psychology or to the coexistence of alternative explanations
within psychoanalysis. One quote from Nietzsche again: "Truth is a
mobile army of metaphors". Another quote from one of the won-
derful books that Don Cupitt, our local radical theologian, produces
annually. Cupitt had in mind clearly contradictory interpretations
of God. But his remarks are equally applicable to possibly converging interpretations of the psyche. The problem of power is acute in
that domain too.

"But that is a horrific position to maintain!" it will be declared.
"You are saying you would rather keep the intellectual pleasure to
be got from contemplating the endless clash of opposed views than
discover one of them to be right. . . . You actually prefer pluralism
and intellectual aestheticism to salvation by the Truth?"

Yes indeed, because we are Westerners and not Muslims. My problem is—and perhaps it is yours too—that although I profess to love
truth I could not actually endure a One-truth universe, because
even as the angels ushered me into heaven I would still be nour-
ishing the suspicion that it was all trumped-up, an illusion generated by power. I . . . would rather contemplate the conflict of two
great truths and feel I had a choice between them, because that
possibility of choice disperses power a little . . . you are the same,
probably, so it sounds as if we Westerners actually prefer and have
chosen the nihilism that has engulfed us. We gave up Truth and
sold our souls, all for freedom's sake. [Cupitt, 1990, p. 114][21]

How psychology and psychoanalysis should cohabit: advice and problems

A psychology of individual subjectivity may always be as problematic as psychoanalysis. A century of history is enough to raise
this as a possibility that we should seriously entertain. It is not

popular in science to use history as part of our evidence, but maybe it should have some weight. You can't have any more certainty than in ordinary life. Epistemologically, psychoanalysis is folk psychology vastly developed (Gardner, 1993). By the same token, it is human understanding, and a lot of it. Something should also be said about personal temperaments and institutional constraints. Both are so important in maintaining the divide that the whole talk could be about them.

Personal temperaments: divergers, convergers (Hudson, 1966). Experimental psychology is dominated by convergent thinking, so, of course, psychologists have difficulty with a type of thought that is divergent in every respect, whose basic method, free association, is the paradigm of divergent thinking. But why is psychology so dominated by convergent thinking, even more so than other sciences? Is it really to the advantage of the subject? The divergent style that we see in theoretical physics is now found closer to us, in Artificial Intelligence. We often welcome it there, but why can't we nurture it ourselves? It is surely why experimental psychology is disappointingly less creative than one might hope, in the sense that it gets so many of its best ideas from outside (Shannon, von Neumann, Tinbergen, Chomsky, and so on) but has not yet generated ideas of comparable power for export.

Institutional constraints: no time to read; busyness; grant getting, not just for self but for department. These are currently of overwhelming importance in maintaining the cognitive styles and hence the gulf. This talk draws on years of random reading in fields not my own: professional suicide for a young scientist. Further, psychoanalytic training deeply involves and changes the whole person, not just his or her "knowledge". But to aim at that explicitly is counter to fundamental premises of university practice.

Do all psychologists have to bother about psychoanalysis? Of course not.

What psychoanalysis offers psychology

This is a large topic on which I can make only one or two remarks here. I have already suggested that psychoanalysis tells us more about "human nature", in the colloquial meaning of that phrase, than experimental psychology does. Psychoanalysis speaks much more directly to us as human beings. Its teaching is, of course, only the current version of a long tradition, as Ellenberger's monumental history brings out so clearly (1970). The immediately preceding versions were the nineteenth century "unmasking psychologies" of Schopenhauer, Dostoevsky, Ibsen, and Nietzsche.

I have already mentioned Frosh's work. There are many suggestions there that could help psychology towards its current goals. But psychoanalysis can also offer a critique of those goals, of the whole enterprise of scientific psychology, though that is another large topic that can only be mentioned here. For me, it offers an opening from psychology, in my teaching and reading, to all culture. One way of avoiding William James's complaint that "Psychology is a nasty little subject; everything one wants to know always lies outside it". What other topic would allow me to include in my lectures Hieronymus Bosch, Nietzsche, Hypnotism, Northwest coast art, Shakespeare, Dostoevsky, the nature of love, sex, the relation of social structure to childrearing, etc., etc., all in one course and while plausibly maintaining that I'm still doing psychology? Of course, psychoanalysis is not the only route to all these things.[22] Ethnography is another obvious one. But psychoanalysis cannot be ignored. It offers another perspective. Just two words, but it is all there.

Notes

1. "It is history which is the true unconscious" (Emile Durkheim, cited as opening quote in Bourdieu's *Homo Academicus*, 1984).
2. A situation that is at present changing fast, but not in psychology departments.
3. Good examples for both sides are conditions like dyslexia or stammering, for which the choice of level-of-explanation that exists for all behaviour is particularly open. Cognitive or neuropsychological analyses are relevant, but there will always be psychodynamics, too. In some cases, one level of understanding will be more appropriate, in others another.
4. It is an instance of a wider split that is often seen as scandalous. It is C. P. Snow's "Two cultures" split between arts and science. Psychology lies right on the fault line.

The arts–science split was personally very real to Freud.

I think there is a general enmity between artists and those engaged in the details of scientific work. We know that they possess in their art a master key to open with ease all female hearts, whereas we stand helpless at the strange design of the lock and have first to torment ourselves to discover a suitable key to it. [Letter from Freud to Martha Bernays, cited in Jones, 1953, p. 123]

5. I notice that fault line, gap, gulf, and chasm are the metaphors that come naturally to my mind. Not, for example, wall, river, or mountain range, which more commonly divide landscapes. What characterizes the gulf, etc., is that there is no ground to stand on. They are not habitable zones, or places where you can stand, float, or sit even uncomfortably (as in "sit on the fence"). Yet we must and do "go up a level" to resolve differences between incompatible cognitive frames.

6. I outlined a topic, but not at all an argument. An alternative sketch I produced is a list of propositions that at least point to arguments: (a) psychologists need help with their/our reader's block about psychoanalysis; (b) psychoanalysis provides our best psychology of individual subjectivity; (c) we must come to terms with its incorrigible pluralism. At any scale, from interpretations to schools. We must learn to actually value this, not just tolerate it. Then we can pare down, perhaps, to only a few interpretations. But at present our scientists' obsession with the one truth, with either/or thinking, hampers us; (d) the same for its predilection for theory?; (e) on some plausible and commonsense beliefs about human nature, the bipartite nature of psychology is to be expected and perhaps inescapable. This, too, suggests that we had better learn to love it.

   This talk is an essay, a discussion. I started with (e) as my thesis, but that has shrunk in importance. A more open discussion came to seem appropriate. A single thesis draws the fire, where what I want to do is to leave a lot of issues more open than they usually are.

7. It does not mean that we are locked in our subcultures—think of them as overlapping sets—or that we cannot compare one with another, or critique one from another, or look for universal features of human nature. Clearly, we can, and this talk is an example of it. What it does mean is that you should respect the boundaries, be prepared for strong context dependence of what goes on within them, and for surprises ("culture shock") if you cross them. It is opposed to the fundamental-

ist attitude, Christian, Islamic, scientific, or whatever, that we either have or are approaching the one truth, but not to the hope that we may find truths in common. As an attitude to understanding other people, it needs to be complemented by its opposite, the faith that there is a common human nature, just as empathy needs to be complemented by detachment.

8. I once lived in a house to which a young anthropologist returned after his first extended experience of fieldwork. He had lived with a small Amazonian people for a year or two. On return to Cambridge everything felt wrong. The noisy streets, the cars, the density of people and their strange dress and gestures and motivations and attitudes. It seemed to go deep. He had come to be drawn to plump shiny girls who could make good beer. Most of all, his allotted task of writing a thesis had become abhorrent: to objectify these friends with whom he had lived, to whom he had probably entrusted his life. Now he had to write of their "artefacts" and their "kinship systems" in black and white on clean paper to be bound and put away in the University Library. After a week or two he had got over his culture shock, and was working again on his thesis, attracted once more to fair-haired waillike girls.

The gaps between biological and social sciences are wide enough to produce comparable phenomena. Byron J. Good, a medical anthropologist writes,

> Early in the course of our study of Harvard Medical School, we came increasingly to understand that learning medicine is not simply the incorporation of new cognitive knowledge, or even learning new approaches to problem-solving and new skills. It is a process of coming to inhabit a new world. I mean this not only in the obvious sense of coming to feel at home in the laboratories or the clinics and hospitals, but in a deeper, experience-near sense. At times when I left a tutorial in immunology or pathology to go to an anthropology seminar, I would feel that I had switched culture as dramatically as if I had suddenly been whisked from the small town in Iran where we carried out our research back into Harvard's William James Hall. [Good, 1994]

The gap between psychology and psychoanalysis is even wider. I personally used to undergo minor conversion experiences each time I crossed. Now I can do it several times in a day, which is in itself suspicious. (One is no longer "sound": may give off a hollow or cracked sound if tapped unawares.) I digress into these things because they are one indication of the personal roots of attitudes that we sometimes pretend are "merely academic". We are constructed and maintained by culture. When we are touching on these things, which is always, we are not wholly rational, because so much of this cultural underpinning is unconscious.

9. Here are some cannon shots fired from one set of trenches into the other: "The Freudian scheme is a tissue of unverified and often unverifiable hypotheses, all oversimplified" (McCulloch, 1965, p. 289). "There will probably come a time when psychoanalysis is itself regarded as one of those curious aberrations of the mind to which man is periodically prone. Each age invents its own delusional systems" (Sutherland, 1976, p. 139). "Modern academic and experimental psychology is to a large extent a science dealing with alienated man, studied by alienating investigators with alienated and alienating methods" (Fromm, 1970, p. 69).

10. Organizing the talk around the fault line is a particular choice. I could choose to ignore it, and so can you. I could talk from a community of my own choosing, containing, for example, Rivers, Merleau-Ponty, Bowlby, Shweder, Oadey, Gilligan, Frosh, Erdelyi. That is to say, people who are at home on both sides, and whom one can see as belonging to a "human sciences" community. There is no shortage of them, past or present, and a surprisingly large number have been connected with this department. This would be a fine brave strategy and I like it. But it would be like a Bosnian Serb marrying a Bosnian Muslim or Croat ten years ago. Entirely admirable, but understood by only a few in their community, and ignoring a deep-seated split.

11. More mischievously, one can see another common origin in alchemy and cabbalistic mysticism. Scientists don't think too much about this background, which was inextricably intertwined with science up to the time of Newton, but cynics readily see it still alive and well in, for example, medicine's faith in the attainability of magic substances to cure deep-seated human ills. Analysts, too, don't often refer to David Bakan's delightful book, *Sigmund Freud and the Jewish Mystical Tradition* (1985), which argues most persuasively for this as one root of Freud's emphases on sexuality and on word play.

12. There was actually a good deal of sympathetic interest in psychoanalytic ideas on the part of American behaviourists in the 1940s and 1950s (for example, Dollard and Miller, 1950), but this took the form of an attempt to transfer ideas, for example on the nature of psycho-

logical conflicts, into the different framework of animal behaviourism. An interesting enterprise, and not wholly unsuccessful, but with somewhat the air of a takeover bid, of showing that the "speculations" of analysts could be verified by the laborious methods of science. I contrast it with, for instance, James's *Varieties of Religious Experience* (1902), which shows the intellectual flexibility of an earlier generation of psychologists, their willingness to adapt their method to the demands of the subject matter.

13. Piaget was analysed by Sabina Spielrein. Thereon hangs a tale, which relates to my main themes in various ways. Spielrein first appears on the psychoanalytic stage as a psychotic patient in the Burgholzli hospital where C. G. Jung worked. He cured her, and they had a passionate affair. She was training as a doctor and became an analyst. Jung's marriage was threatened and he behaved badly, though he kept in contact with Spielrein. She was a creative thinker and influenced Freud as well as Jung. She possibly originated the idea of the death instinct. She analysed Piaget, and then returned to her native Soviet Union and worked with and influenced both Luria and Vygotsky. In 1941, the Nazis took all the Jews of Rostovon-Don, including Spielrein and her two children, to the synagogue and shot them. So, here we have this beautiful, talented, crazy young woman, weaving in and out of the lives of five of the most important psychologists of the century in the shadows of the Russian Revolution and the Holocaust, and possibly feeding them some of their best lines. And what do we do? We forget her. We forget her story and remain ignorant of her writings. We embalm the five Dead White Males in textbooks and inflict their embalmed thoughts on psychology students—and our own minds—severed from any connection with this vivid life that linked them. When we do remember her, the most salient feature is often Jung's bad behaviour, as though the really important thing was "the ethics of mental-health professionals". A depressing example of the way we sterilize and distort the living body of thought that we call "psychology". No wonder it is less creative than we would like (Appignanesi and Forrester (1992), give the best short account of Spielrein's story).

14. Not to mention the argument that some everyday knowledge is more fundamental than scientific, because scientific procedure depends tacitly on the former at every turn.

15. See Cosin, Freeman, and Freeman (1971), for one of the most effective rebuttals of the Popperian argument. Norman Freeman was a graduate student here, working on animal behaviour.

16. John Heaton was a student in this department under Bartlett. He became an ophthalmologist and wrote a unique account of the phenomenology of ocular disease. Later he became a psychotherapist, and founded, with R. D. Laing, the Philadelphia Association. He recently published the Wittgenstein volume of the *Beginners Guide* series of cartoon books for intellectuals. The Philadelphia Association still runs one of the most interesting psychotherapy training courses, attending to philosophy as well as to the psychoanalytic literature.

17. Neither is Germanic theory necessarily so. Denise Riley (1994) told us in a recent Cambridge alumnus magazine that when she was an undergraduate in the 1960s, copies of Hegel's *Phenomenology of the Spirit* used to circulate "like the latest hot novel".

18. I ignore her possibly specialist use of the word theory. In this section, I slip between a number of different kinds of theory. My intention was not to eulogize feminist theory (some of which I indeed admire, but some of which I do not), but to suggest a fruitful attitude to theory in general. I am acutely conscious here of the gaps between subcultures and the impossibility of finding the right tone. To anyone at home in the kinds of theory I am talking about, my attitude and style will seem patronizing, primitive backwoods stuff. What wainscot is this man crawling out of? But to many of the scientists I know, most of this theory is either unreadable or beneath contempt or both.

19. Bartlett was the first professor of experimental psychology at Cambridge (1922–1952).

20. Forgetting William James's exhortation to psychologists to allow space for "the vague".

21. This is from a chapter entitled "A theory of God", which contains an appendix on Parallel Distributed Processing! Perhaps we are in a time when subcultures are converging rapidly. MIT can now offer a course on Heideggerian Artificial Intelligence.

22. I am often astonished, when I talk on this topic, by the need that some listeners have to classify me as a believer or not in psychoanalysis. I am not sure that I am a believer in anything. The kind of psychoanalysis I admire, for example, that of Winnicott or Marion Milner or Bion, is so heterodox that many would not at first recognize it as psychoanalysis. Psychoanalysis maintained as an orthodoxy—and it is strongly so maintained by some and some institutes—is as repellent as any fundamentalism. What is it about psychoanalysis that makes it necessary to say this?

References

Appignanesi, L., & Forrester, J. (1992). *Freud's Women*. New York: Basic Books.

Bakan, D. (1985). *Sigmund Freud and the Jewish Mystical Tradition*. London: Free Association Books, 1990.

Bartlett, F. C. (1955). Fifty years of psychology. *Occupational Psychology*, 29: 203–216.

Bourdieu, P. (1984). *Homo Academicus*. Cambridge: Polity.

Brennan, T. (1993). *History after Lacan*. London: Routledge.

Cosin, B. R., Freeman, C. F., & Freeman, N. H. (1971). Critical empiricism criticized: the case of Freud. In: R. Wollheim & J. Hopkins (Eds.), *Philosophical Essays on Freud* (pp. 32–59). Cambridge: Cambridge University Press, 1982.

Cupitt, D. (1990). *Creation Out of Nothing*. London: SCM Press.

Dollard, J., & Miller, N. E. (1950). *Personality and Psychotherapy*. New York: McGraw-Hill.

Ellenberger, H. F. (1970). *The Discovery of the Unconscious*. London: Allen Lane.

Erdelyi, M. H. (1985). *Psychoanalysis: Freud's Cognitive Psychology*. San Francisco, CA: W. H. Freeman.

Fromm, E. (1970). *The Crisis of Psychoanalysis: Essays on Freud, Marx and Social Psychology*. Harmondsworth: Penguin.

Frosh, S. (1987). *The Politics of Psychoanalysis: An Introduction to Freudian and Post-Freudian Theory*. London: Macmillan.

Frosh, S. (1989). *Psychoanalysis and Psychology: Minding the Gap*. London: Macmillan.

Gardner, S. (1993). *Irrationality and the Philosophy of Psychoanalysis*. Cambridge: Cambridge University Press.

Good, B. J. (1994). *Medicine, Rationality and Experience*. Cambridge: Cambridge University Press.

Heaton, J. M. (1968). Theoretical practice—the place of theory in psychotherapy. In: N. Bolton (Ed.), *Philosophical Problems in Psychology* (pp. 176–199). London: Methuen, 1979.

Heaton, J. M. (1972). Symposium on saying and showing in Heidegger and Wittgenstein. *Journal of the British Society of Phenomenol.*, 3: 42–65.

Horowitz, M. J. (1989). *Introduction to Psychodynamics: A New Synthesis*. London: Routledge.

Hudson, L. (1966). *Contrary Imaginations*. Harmondsworth: Penguin.

James, W. (1902). *The Varieties of Religious Experience*. New York: Longmans, Green.

Jones, E. (1953). *Sigmund Freud: Life and Work*, Vol. 1. London: Hogarth Press.

Jones, E. (1955). *Sigmund Freud: Life and Work*, Vol. 2. London: Hogarth Press.

Labov, W., & Fanshel, D. (1977). *Therapeutic Discourse*. New York: Academic Press.

Malan, D. H. (1979). *Individual Psychotherapy and the Science of Psychodynamics*. Boston: Butterworths.

McCulloch, W. S. (1965). *Embodiments of Mind*. Cambridge, MA: MIT Press.

Nietzsche, F. (1878). *Human, All Too Human*. Cambridge: Cambridge University Press, 1986.

Phillips, A. (1993). *On Kissing, Tickling and Being Bored: Psychoanalytic Essays on the Unexamined Life*. London: Faber & Faber.

Riley, D. (1994). My time at Cambridge. *Cam, Lent: 39*.

Rivers, W. H. R. (1917). *The Lancet, 189*: 912–914.

Rorty, R. (1991). Freud and moral reflection. In: *Essays on Heidegger and Others* (pp. 143–163). Cambridge: Cambridge University Press.

Showalter, E. (1985). *The Female Malady*. London: Virago.

Smail, D. (1987). *Taking Care*. London: HarperCollins.

Smail, D. (1993). *The Origins of Unhappiness*. New York: HarperCollins.

Sutherland, N. S. (1976). *Breakdown* (2nd edn). London: Weidenfeld & Nicolson, 1988.

Taylor, C. (1971). Interpretation and the sciences of man. In: *Philosophical Papers*, Vol. 2 (pp. 15–87). Cambridge: Cambridge University Press.

Whittle, P. (1999). W. H. R. Rivers and the early history of psychology at Cambridge. In: A. Saito (Ed.), *Bartlett, Culture and Cognition* (pp. 21–35). London: Routledge.

Wittgenstein, L. (1918). *Tractatus Logico-Philosophicas* (Revised English translation), 1961. London: Routledge.

CHAPTER TWO

The third: a brief historical analysis of an idea*

Charles M. T. Hanly

In what follows, I try to clarify historically the idea of the third in philosophy and in psychoanalysis. It is an account that has its own point of view, the evidential justification of which, of necessity, is only scantily presented. The exposition suggests an agreement and differences between the various philosophical thirds and the psychoanalytic thirds found in this issue. Even the agreement that emerges is at present controversial. I make no claim that this exposition of the topic escapes the influence of the controversy. My purpose is to provide background and to raise questions.

The third in philosophy

Charles S. Peirce

Peirce (1903) introduced the term the third into philosophy. Of itself, it has nothing directly to do with any psychoanalytic notions of thirds, of triadic relations, or of triangular "space". It is simply

---

* First published in 2004 in *Psychoanalytic Quarterly*. 73: 267–290.

the notion of meaning captured in general concepts, their nature, and their crucial place in knowledge.

Peirce was a realist in the tradition of the medieval scholastic philosopher, Duns Scotus (ca. 1270–1308), who was a "moderate", or Aristotelian realist, as opposed to a Platonic realist. For whatever reason, Peirce either was unaware of, or failed to appreciate, the devastating criticism that the empiricists (Bacon, 1620; Hobbes, 1651; Locke, 1690) and the rationalists (Descartes, 1641; Spinoza, 1673) had made of Aristotelian scholastic epistemology. Consequently, Peirce's notion of thirdness is epistemologically naïve, in so far as he—like Scotus, and before him, Aristotle—believed that the concepts by which we know, and the objects that we know, are co-natural (of the same substance).

Perhaps Peirce was influenced by the spirituality of New England transcendentalism. What is clear is that he could not entertain the possibility, for which there is plentiful pragmatic evidence (e.g., the effects on mental functioning of a blockage of an artery to the brain), that psychic life depends for its existence on the living matter of the brain and central nervous system. Instead, he believed that the universe is the sign of a self-developing God whose habitual thoughts are the laws of nature. Hence, Peirce could view ideas and things as co-natural. However, he stopped well short of a co-creation of nature by God and man. Nevertheless, as in Aristotle, Peirce's third, the general concept, simply abstracts what is inherent in the object of which it is a concept. Co-naturality applies to ideas about our own psyche—its organization, activities, and contents; for example, the idea of the instinctual unconscious is co-natural with its object, the instinctual unconscious. But the idea of any inanimate, material object is not co-natural with the object that the idea enables us to comprehend.

Concepts are general, but by means of them, we seek knowledge of objects that are particulars. Concepts are true when the properties, structures, dynamics, and relations they articulate are actually to be found in the objects to which they refer; when they are not, the concepts are artificial and false. The proposition that "man is mortal" is true, even though each person dies his or her own death in an individual way.

Peirce postulated a triumvirate of categories of concepts. Firsts are potential, uninterpreted, sensible qualities. Firstness is exemplified by a possible impression of a person's mood, facial expression, hesitation, discomfort, anxiety, or physical gait. Secondness is an actually existing object made up of qualities that engender a percept in the mind, such as a patient's entering briskly and cheerfully into a clinician's office. A percept is a sense-image or sensory representation (as in Locke (1690)) of an object ripe with the possibility of being known by means of concepts. Peirce, like his scholastic predecessors, and unlike Locke, uses the term percept to refer both to the sense-impression of an object and the object sensed. This usage leaves the door open for an idealist-type of metaphysics (one in which all things are mind). Peirce's concept of percept differs from Locke's concept of representation, although Peirce sometimes uses the latter term.

Thirdness is the concept by which we grasp what is general in a class of objects. The concept is real (and true as well) because it gains access to the reality of the object revealed by the percept. The concept, if correctly abstracted from the particularities of the object, can achieve generality on the basis of the observation of one individual—an Aristotelian notion. The concept is imbued with its reality and truth from the object via the percept of the object. A concept that is true of an individual will be true of the natural class of things of which the individual is a member.

Peirce proceeded to formulate a pragmatic criterion of meaning, truth, and reality. For Peirce, the third is an intellectual conception; a third is an affirmation or denial about the nature of an object. The meaning of any concept is to be ascertained by considering "what practical consequences might conceivably result by necessity from the truth of that conception; the sum of these consequences will constitute the entire meaning of the conception" (Vol. 5, paragraph 9). This crucial definition implies that concepts are real when and because they have a real external counterpart, some basic aspect of which is articulated by the concept. For example, the latent content of the dream is, in Peirce's definition, the referent in the object (dreamer) of the topographical theory of dreams. If the observations specified by the theory are forthcoming (e.g., wish-laden memories and fantasies in the analysand's associations), the latent dream is a real property of the dreamer, according to Peirce's definition of pragmatism.

Thus, Peirce's pragmatism requires epistemological realism: "The real is that which is not whatever we happen to think it is, but is unaffected by what we may think of it" (Vol. 8, paragraph 12). Objects, about which meaningful intellectual concepts can be constructed, are not altered by being observed; they are not co-created. An object is real, for Peirce, if—and only if—its nature is independent of how any individual happens to think it to be. Otherwise, an object is an artefact of experience, a phantasm of our subjectivity. Competent observers (those who have made themselves competent by divesting themselves of such personal idiosyncrasies as could only produce subjective impressions that reflect themselves and their individual beliefs) who perform similar experiments, or who make observations under similar conditions on a real object, will come up with similar results.

This concept of the competent observer can itself be evaluated pragmatically. Peirce's concept of intersubjectivity is that of science and common sense; it is diametrically opposed to the meaning of the term as used by psychoanalytic intersubjectivists. Observers, Peirce would say, who have been unable to divest themselves of idiosyncratic ways of experiencing objects will form subjective impressions that fail to correspond to the object as it is. It cannot be fairly said, however, that Peirce was a naïve realist, despite his Aristotelianism; his pragmatism implies fallibility. But neither was he a naïve subjectivist who believed that his perceptual field was only an expression of himself, leaving him unable to make experiential contact with independently existing, real objects, despite his idealist metaphysics. On the basis of Peirce's epistemological third, if psychoanalysts were irreducibly subjective, their knowledge claims would have to be considered meaningless.

Peirce's concept of thirdness is of interest to psychoanalysis because it is itself a third in a rather different sense, a sense that is found in other philosophies: it is an epistemological third. An idea, or at least a good idea, offers a perch, a prospect, a position from which we are able to better observe, become acquainted with and, hence, to better grasp or comprehend someone or something. Elsewhere, I (Hanly, 1995) have noted this function of ideas, drawing on Proust. It is something that abounds in Freud's thinking. For example, "We can say that the patient's resistance arises from his ego, and we then at once perceive that the compulsion to repeat must be ascribed to the unconscious repressed" (Freud, 1920g, p. 20). Peirce's idea of thirdness is itself, implicitly, an epistemological third.

Rene Descartes

This more specific, epistemological idea of the third is implicit in diverse philosophical ideas and arguments. The cornerstone of Descartes's (1641) systematic doubt is the idea of an all-powerful Malignant Deceiver. This idea permitted Descartes to take up a reflective third position that in turn enabled him to conceive of the possibility that his experience was irreducibly subjective—that he was alone with, and encased in, his sense-experience, memories, feelings, and thoughts. Descartes's cogito and his idea of God are rationalist, epistemological thirds that release him from his irreducible subjectivity.

John Locke

Locke (1690) used the idea of representation as a third. This offered him an ideational perspective from which to examine the nature of the relation between the perceiving subject and the object perceived. Locke accepted the testimony of our sense experience as reflected in common sense, natural science, and almost all philosophies (among them, Peirce's), specifying that the people and things that make up the world have a nature and existence independently of our experience of them or our ideas about them. Even Berkeley (1710), who believed that to be is to perceive or to be perceived, never seriously entertained the idea that there is no reality independent of our experience of it.

The answer to the old chestnut about the falling tree, mentioned by Gerson in this issue (p. 67), is that, in Berkeley's theory, when a tree falls, a sound occurs in the Divine Sensorium, whether or not an animal with auditory sensory apparatus is about. For Locke, for whom the universe is made up of physical bodies and forces, the fall of the tree causes sound waves that then cause the sound of the fall to be heard, and thus actually occur—if, and only if, there is an animal sensory apparatus in the vicinity to respond to sound waves; otherwise, the sound waves occur without the sound. Peirce would have said the same thing as did Locke, with different words; sound waves for him would be a potential sound. In either case, any curious animal in the vicinity could check out what caused the sound, if it were not already obvious from its pattern and volume (the swish of the branches descending, the crackles and snaps of branches breaking, and the thump of the trunk), by moving in the direction from which the sound came, and could see if a tree had actually fallen, without having to have it confirmed or disconfirmed by someone else.

From the vantage point of the third, was Gerson's patient making a "philosophical" point about the relational unconscious and the cultural relativity of meaning, or was he expressing an infantile, transferential dependency on the analyst, in order to reduce his anxiety about trusting the evidence of his own senses or his ability to make his own decisions? No doubt the patient received the benefit of an analytic interpretation of his dependency at the right time. Might one not wonder whether the patient reaped this benefit despite the hypothesis of a relational unconscious, rather than because of it?

Locke, who used the idea of perceptual representation as a third, differentiated the primary qualities of objects from their secondary qualities. The primary qualities of shape, mass, solidity, number, location, motion, and rest are intrinsic properties of physical objects. The secondary qualities of colour, sound, smell, taste, and so on, are subjective. The colours we see and the sounds we hear are intrinsic to our sensory experience of objects and guide us in our relations with them, but they are not inherent in the objects themselves. Intrinsic to objects is the power to cause our senses to generate the colours we see in them and the sounds they emit. These "sensible qualities", therefore, are irreducibly subjective, although also passive, normative, and unavoidable. Primary qualities are objective. However, Locke used the idea of representation to take into account the ways in which our perceptions of the primary qualities of objects can generate perceptual illusions under certain conditions—e.g., the apparent diurnal motion of the sun. The idea of representation enabled Locke to bring the implications of Newtonian optics into epistemology.

Like Descartes (1641) and other rationalists (e.g., Spinoza (1673), Locke (1690) considered self-awareness to be essential to the use of ideas as epistemological thirds. Consciousness is reflexive in the sense that, when we perceive objects, imagine them, have feelings about them, or think about them, we are aware that we are perceiving, imagining, feeling, and thinking. Self-awareness, for Locke and for Descartes, was not an automatic and necessary concomitant of consciousness, for we can and do "lose ourselves" in thought, imagination, observation, feeling, or action. However, we also "come back" to ourselves from reveries, even in instances when we cannot recall what had so occupied our thoughts. Psychoanalysis can help people—albeit with great difficulty—to get back from being lost in severely dissociated states. For Locke and Descartes, self-awareness was of fundamental importance to cognitive activities because of its attesting and correcting functions. And self-awareness was assigned a yet more fundamental importance in German idealism.

Immanuel Kant

In Kant's (1781) epistemology, the "synthetic unity of apperception" (pp. 155–157) becomes the ultimate ground of knowledge and objectivity. "I think" (pp. 152–153) must accompany every sort of propositional thought and representation. The reflexive nature of consciousness lays down certain conditions that any thought must satisfy in order to be a thought about objects. The "I think" imposes its own subjective categorical conditions of thought on our knowledge of objects. For example, we cannot think about an object unless we think about it in terms of substance and attribute and causality. These are subjective conditions that the mind imposes on knowing anything.

As a result, Kant drew the sceptical conclusion that we can only know objects as they appear, but not as they are in themselves—hence, his distinction between phenomena and noumena. The Kantian third—the idealist third—is made up of the reflexivity of consciousness and the categorical conditions it imposes on knowledge. Whereas Descartes (1641) and Locke relied upon the attesting, cognitive function of self-awareness, Kant assigned to it a legislative function in knowledge.

G. W. F. Hegel

Hegel (1807a) went much further: "The individual is the immediate certainty of himself and . . . he is therefore unconditioned being"

(p. 40). Psychoanalysis has taught us that self-knowledge comes only with labour and is seldom, if ever, certain. Perhaps Hegel is referring to a consciousness without content. But how could consciousness confer "unconditioned being", if there is such a thing, on anything, including itself? In Hegel, we find the third of absolute idealism.

Even this highly selective, abbreviated, truncated account of the epistemological third in philosophy presents a complicated picture. Self-awareness is of crucial importance for each of the philosophers considered here except Peirce. Peirce's pragmatic fallibility logically requires a philosophical third that includes self-awareness armed with the capacity to sustain self-criticism, self-approval, and self-doubt. Yet, Peirce denied individual identity. He thought of a person, and even of God, as a "bundle of habits", far removed from Kant's synthetic unity of apperception, Descartes's (1641) cogito, or Hegel's (1807a) grandiose notion of unconditional being. Peirce considered personal identity to be a "vulgar delusion".

Psychoanalysts who espouse theories in which relations are prioritized over individuals, and who claim that the failure to give primacy to relations results in an untenable one-person psychology, can find some support for their views in Peirce. However, Peirce cut the psychological ground from under his pragmatism when he eliminated the possibility of critical self-awareness of believing, which many feel accompanies belief. Self-awareness must be capable of distancing itself from a belief, in order to critically consider that belief or to adopt an attitude of scepticism toward it, or to treat it with impartiality and neutralize one's adherence to it as conditional upon being able to submit the belief to the pragmatic test. Peirce's concept of thirdness is not consistent with the ideas of co-created relational thirds of the sort proposed by Ogden and Benjamin in this issue, or by other intersubjectivists.

From a philosophical perspective, a third requires an idea. Otherwise, the functioning of self-awareness is limited to self-experience. An idea such as Descartes's Malignant Deceiver or Locke's representation is required to, as it were, "lift" self-awareness to a position from which the cognitive activities of the self can be scrutinized, analysed, and evaluated. The third can be the idea of a thing existing independently of the experience of it by human observers (Cavell, 1998). Such a third is to be found in philosophers as otherwise at odds as Descartes and Locke.

Benjamin, Gerson, Minolli and Tricoli, and Ogden tend to be critical of the idea that a third requires an idea (theory), let alone that a third requires an object independent of it (Descartes, Locke, Peirce). These analysts are concerned that a third in the form of an idea (knowledge, theory) at work in the analyst will have a detrimental effect on interaction within the analytic dyad by subordinating, derogating, or isolating the analysand in a variety of ways.

Britton, Green, Widlöcher, and Zwiebel recognize the importance of ideas in the work of a third. Philosophically, there can be no third without an idea. Since Peirce "eliminated" self and self-awareness, for him, a third is only an idea. However, other philosophers have recognized the need for both in the formation of an epistemological third. Wittgenstein (1918) treated philosophy itself as a self-eliminating third, a third that self-destructs as soon as it has achieved its purpose, a rational relation to reality. Philosophy does not yield an understanding of reality; it helps us to realize that science does so. "He [the philosopher] must, so to speak, throw away the ladder [philosophy] after he has climbed up on it" (Wittgenstein, 1918, p. 151).

Embedded in, or logically connected with, the epistemological third is some idea of truth and verification. For Descartes (1641), clear and distinct ideas warrant certainty no less in anatomy than in mathematics. For Locke, the truth of an idea depends on its empirical verification with the fallibility that attends it. For Peirce, ideas, however clear and distinct, require pragmatic testing of their consequences. Russell (1946) pointed out some of the difficulties with pragmatism as a criterion of truth.

We can say of the philosophical third that, typically (Peirce's views excepted), it is a function of self-awareness informed by an idea that differs in different philosophies.

The third in psychoanalysis

An idea of the third is also implicitly at work in psychoanalysis. In deriving and formulating this implicit idea and thus making it explicit, it is necessary to differentiate threesomes, triangular relations, and the use of the metaphor of "triangular space" or "triangulated space" from the third as such, although important linkages with them may be found. For example, Freud's (1905c) explanation of smutty humour requires a threesome, but it does not involve a third. Nevertheless, the third is at work and is an object of implicit inquiry from the beginning of Freud's work.

Freud (1895) plausibly described the psychological genesis of the third, as Peirce understood it, with the beginning of instinctual object seeking, reality testing, and subject–object differentiation. This genesis takes place in earliest infancy with the differentiation between the image of the satisfying object that does not satisfy and the object itself that does satisfy. At the heart of this experience is the first rudimentary awareness that images represent but do not duplicate, that they point beyond themselves to the needed, real, need-satisfying object. The rudiments of Locke's empiricist third are present in the structure, dynamics, and content of the primary infantile experience of need satisfaction, as Freud (1895) described it.

The Kleinian depressive position (Klein, 1935) is also a third. The depressive position is made possible by the infant's capacity to see the mother as a whole person, both satisfying and frustrating, who is good and bad, and to compare this real mother with the projections of the paranoid–schizoid positions. The third is an awareness of the difference between the largely subjective experience of an idealized and denigrated object and the more reliable experience of the object as it actually is.

There are innumerable dyadic parent–child situations in which a child becomes aware, while retaining self-awareness, that he or she is an object for another. An opportunity is provided for the child to gain a sense of how another sees him or her. These opportunities are building blocks for the child's evolving ability to objectify the self. However, seeing oneself with the eyes of another may either benefit or harm this inner capacity to be educated to reality. There are situations in which anxiety can cause a loss of self-awareness as a consequence of becoming an object for another. In these instances, the child feels overwhelmed, invaded, and taken over—consumed, as it were, by the object for whom the child has become nothing but an instrumentality. The result is a dyadic unity based on domination of the sadistic parent or surrogate and diminution of the self-awareness and identity of the masochistically surrendering child.

Britton (1987) and Feldman (1997), among others, have explored these sorts of factors in the transference and the role of the analytic third in the countertransference. In this issue, Benjamin describes situations of this sort in psychoanalysis. The differences observed between the point of view expressed in Britton's article in this issue, on the one hand, and that of Benjamin and others of the relational school, on the other, pose the question of whether clinical experience supports Kleinian and Freudian realism or relational, intersubjective idealism. Stated differently, which notion of the psychoanalytic third best helps the analyst to recognize, understand, and remedy these pathological situations and the analyst's involvement in them? It is my opinion that the radical revisions involved in the idea of Gerson's relational unconscious are not required to understand Jacobs's (2001) description of his becoming aware of a therapeutically disadvantageous countertransference. The same is true, I think, of what Arlow (1979), Loewald (1979), Bird (1972), and Boesky (1990) have to say along the same lines.

The preoedipal child has a benign, anaclitic reliance on both parents, especially on the parent of the same sex, as surrogate egos to test reality and to identify danger—a dependency that allows the child full enjoyment of his or her fantasy life. In this relation, the child becomes aware of the difference between the way in which a parent experiences an object and the way the child experiences the same object. The recognition of this difference invites the child to sufficiently detach from the narcissistically naïve self-evidence of his or her own experience to be able to question it, in Locke's terminology, and to treat it as a perceptual representation that may not be true of the object in this or that respect. In these ways and others, an education to reality takes place by pragmatic increments, made possible by a developing capacity for sensory and affective discrimination. The template provided by these early relations forms some of the psychological background for Cavell's (1998) argument concerning triangulation and objectivity. Fundamental to this process is primary identification.

Freud's increasing understanding of identification enabled him to clarify the psychological foundations of thirdness, that is, the preparation of the mental capacity for objectivity, and to advance his thinking on the role of identification in character formation and relations (Freud, 1917e, 1921c). He described how the strengthening of the child's identification with the parent of the same sex in the resolution of the Oedipus complex enables the child to internalize the position of the rivalled parent in relation to herself or himself, and, thereby, the parental prohibitions (Freud, 1923b).

This identification internalizes a crucial aspect of an indispensable object relation, and in so doing, deeply modifies both the child's relation to the parents and the child's ego. In this way, the child consolidates an improved capacity for critical self-awareness, for self-approval or self-condemnation, for a new measure of objectivity about self and primary objects (although at this point, the child cannot be expected to have an adequate measure of his or her parents). Whereas earlier, the child found her or his sense of worth primarily in the parent's love or withdrawal of it, sanctioned inwardly by shame, the child is now able to perform this function independently, sanctioned inwardly by guilt. The child has acquired a measure of moral autonomy and responsibility. The reflexivity of consciousness has been informed by a deontological morality.

But more than moral conscience is involved in this transformation as it proceeds. In the end, these developments provide for a fallible but reliable, self-critical, epistemic self-awareness, enabling us to objectify ourselves to some genuine extent (some more than others), in order to test our experience for its objectivity, to adopt measures to reduce its subjectivity, and to test evidentially the beliefs to which our experience gives rise. We feel a diminution of our self-esteem when we are caught by ourselves or others being logically inconsistent. In this way, psychoanalysis provides a psychological explanation of the origin and nature of the philosophical idea of a third position. This explanation is inconsistent with the Cartesian, Kantian, and Hegelian thirds, but consistent with the core of Peirce's third (see Green's article in this issue) and the empiricist third.

Freud's (1923b) focus was on the moral, behavioural, and relational consequences of Oedipal identification. Early on, Waelder (1934) noted the further implications of Freud's hypothesis: "What is common to these modes of super-ego attitudes [moral, humorous, cognitive] is self-observation, objectification of oneself, the attainment of a position above one's ego" (p. 104). This position "above one's ego" is a third in the philosophical sense. In addition, psychoanalysis provides Peirce with psychological grounds for classifying logic, along with morals, as a normative science, by setting out rules for valid reasoning and methods for empirical falsification and verification.

Rickman (1950, 1951) first introduced the idea of numbered psychologies (Hanly & Nichols, 2001). Having introduced the term two-person psychology, based on Freud's uncovering of transference and countertransference, Rickman detailed what he considered to be the limitations of a two-person psychology, among them that it is confined to the here and now and to the immediate interactions between analysand and analyst. A horizon upon the past in the present, essential to the genetic orientation of psychoanalysis, is lacking. The transference, after all, is only a sign, to use Peirce's semiotic definition (as distinct from de Saussure's signifier) of the analysand's past. The same is true of the analyst's countertransference. The transferential and countertransferential interactions of the dyad are but signs of these signs, which can only be read aright by a position that includes the past.

But analysis must seek out the past by means of free association. The horizon that opens a way to the past in the present requires the analyst to become aware of the analyst–analysand relation itself, by gaining a perspective or a position from which the relation can be objectified—that is, viewed for what it is. This position is made possible by the third person, either real or imaginary, of the Oedipal triangle. Rickman does not adequately formulate this notion because of his failure to grasp the importance and effect of Oedipal identifications and their profound influence on self-awareness (the reflexivity of consciousness, as philosophers would say).

Nevertheless, Rickman goes to the heart of the matter. According to Rickman, psychoanalysis, as Freud formulated it, is neither a one- nor a two-person psychology. It is a three-person psychology that requires the analyst to be able to observe the dyadic analytic relation from the position of a third person—or, more important, from the position of an observer who is sufficiently impersonal and unbiased so as not to be caught up in and confined to dyadic interaction. Freud set out how the analyst can function as the third in the analytic situation, as can the analysand. But given that the patient is debilitated by neurotic conflicts, and given the analytic contract, it is incumbent on the analyst to be able and prepared to facilitate the restoration or development of the function of the third in the analysand. The question arises as to whether or not and how, in this circumstance, a co-created third could serve this function.

This objectivity—in the sense of getting "outside" or "above" one's own subjectivity, in whatever form of complacency, partiality, dogmatism, preoccupation with self, or squeamishness that it may take, in order to become aware of it, to think about it, and disengage it (even partially) from the analysis—is psychologically grounded in the self-awareness made possible by Oedipal identification. This identification internalizes the observing function of the parent as auxiliary ego during the earlier, more anaclitic stages of development. The subsequent development of this function is in the direction of greater impersonality and impartiality—doing what is right rather than what one has been told to do; crediting one's senses rather than received opinion and belief; submitting one's observations, imaginings, and thoughts to the demands of reality, logic, and empirical testing.

This position "outside" the dyadic relation also opens the way to thinking about how the analysand experiences the analyst and his or her interpretations, as well as how the analyst experiences the analysand and his or her reactions to interpretations. There is nothing special about this analytic third; it belongs to common sense, science, art, and literature, as well as to everyday life. It is certainly not infallible, although experience, knowledge, and practice can improve it. In this respect, the analytic third, thus conceived, stands in opposition to the idealization of self-awareness found in the Cartesian, Kantian, and Hegelian thirds. Nor is this analytic third immune to psychopathology.

Britton (1987, 1998, and in this issue) traces the origins of the third position to the Oedipal triangle, which provides for being seen in a relation with another and seeing a relation between two others. This experience lays down a template for a "capacity for seeing ourselves in interaction with others and for entertaining another point of view whilst retaining our own, for reflecting on ourselves whilst being ourselves" (1987, p. 87). What is crucial about the Oedipal identification is that it internalizes these templates, drawing them from triangular relations. Nowhere else in this issue is there an explicit recognition of the contribution made by the resolution of the Oedipus complex to the cognitive use of thirdness. However, Green's, Widlöcher's, and Zwiebel's contributions appear to me to be compatible with Britton's insight and its relation to the philosophical, empiricist third.

Benjamin explicitly repudiates the Oedipal contribution to the psychoanalytic third when she takes Britton (1998) and Feldman (1997) to task for running the risk of "privileging of the analyst's relation to the third as theory . . . as well as to an overemphasis on the oedipal content of the third" (p. 12). Gerson also criticizes Britton's (1998) idea of the third for being insufficiently intersubjective. Minolli and Tricoli, as well as Ogden, adumbrate psychological theories in which the Oedipus complex and its resolution appear to have little part to play, if any.

A dialectical discussion

Some papers in this issue use the term dialectical without defining it. There are at least five different, serious uses of the term in philosophy: two by Plato (4th century bc) and one each by Kant (1781), Hegel (1807a), and Marx (1873).

One of the best known uses of dialectic is the Socratic dialectic of the Platonic dialogues. Often, the dialogues are searches for definitions of moral virtues, justice, love, the soul. The search is conducted dramatically by means of arguments in favour of some definition, for example, that justice is the interest of the stronger, or a compromise between what we most and least want, advanced by a character in the dialogue. Socrates then points out weaknesses in the definitions and eventually advances one favoured by Plato. Dialectic is the cut and thrust of the intellectual arguments. Plato (4th century bc) also used the term to refer to some undefined process of reasoning that was supposed to lead from the contemplation of the forms of natural kinds—artefacts, arithmetical and geometric ideas, virtues, and so on—to the form of all forms, the Form of the Good.

Plato's notion of dialectic as intellectual debate is scarcely of use in psychoanalytic clinical thinking because, although some analysands want us to engage in such disputatious exchanges with them, their treatments are not served by our going along with the wish to engage in intellectual combat. Psychoanalysis teaches us the futility of trying to reason a patient out of a neurotically caused belief.

Kant (1781) used the term dialectic to refer to the futility of trying to prove the immortality of the soul, the infinity of the universe, and the existence of God, favourite undertakings of metaphysics because, as Kant believed, the soul, the universe, and God are not objects of possible experience. This exercise of pure reason (i.e., the use of concepts without content), Kant tried to show, results in arguments with contradictory conclusions. He called this exercise the dialectic of pure reason.

Hegel (1816) sought to go beyond Kant with a dialectical logic in which contradictions generate higher truths in which they are overcome. Hegel believed that dialectical logic was at work in thought, in history, in the organization of society, and in the cosmic evolution of nature. For Hegel, dialectic was the logic of an ultimately unifying, self-actualizing, spiritual force he called Absolute Spirit.

Marx (1873) invented the fifth meaning of dialectic by substituting materialism for Hegel's idealism. Marx considered that Hegel had dialectic standing on its head. Marx turned it right side up by hypothesizing that economic forces are the fundamental causes of historical change. Marx thus took over Hegel's dialectical logic, leaving it otherwise unchanged.

Psychoanalysts who use the term dialectic should carefully define its meaning. They should consider whether there is a specific psychoanalytic meaning of the term that refers to something more than, or other than, psychic conflict (e.g., ambivalence, struggles between narcissistic libido and object libido, and so on). This semantic task is not trivial, as I shall now try to show.

Some further philosophical–psychoanalytic reflections and questions

Hegelian ideas make their appearance in several papers in this issue. Minolli and Tricoli make the most extensive use of Hegelian ideas, drawn from a sound translation into English by Baillie of Hegel's (1807b) *Phenomenology of Mind*. Suffice it to consider just one problem that cannot be avoided in formulating psychoanalytic findings in Hegelian terms. For Hegel, everything in developmental process is animated by conflict. Hence, on the surface, his idea of dialectics might seem to agree with the centrality of conflict discovered by psychoanalysis in individual psychic development. Unfortunately, it does not. According to Hegel, any and every process is dialectically conflicted; an initial state generates its opposite. This opposing second state stands in contradiction to the first. The conflict produces a resolution in a higher synthesis that overcomes the contradiction. These processes are teleological, irreversible, and progressive. Marx (1873) derived his utopianism directly from Hegel's logic. Two fundamental vicissitudes that psychic processes undergo cannot occur, according to Hegel's logic: fixations interrupt development and regressions reverse development. Moreover, needs and wishes cause individual and collective life to have purposes, but psychoanalysis does not view human life as the fulfilment of some cosmic teleology, such as the realization of Absolute Spirit.

To make Hegelian dialectic suitable for psychoanalytic theorizing, one would have to strip it of the logic peculiar to it or deny that there are fixations and regressions of needs, desires, and wishes. Why translate valuable psychoanalytic observations into a system of thought that runs counter to common sense? Marx's (1873) materialistic correction of Hegel's spirituality has not increased the credibility of dialectical logic. Any Hegelian definition of dialectic is incompatible with basic facts of human psychic life.

In his article, Ogden implicitly raises a fundamental issue. In understanding the analyst–analysand relationship, he states that:

> The task is not to tease apart the elements constituting the relationship in an effort to determine which qualities belong to whom; rather, from the point of view of the interdependence of subject and object, the analytic task involves an attempt to describe the specific nature of the experience of the unconscious interplay of individual subjectivity and intersubjectivity. [p. 168]

This recommendation is based on the assumption that, in addition to the two persons who make up the analytic dyad and their interactions, there is a third, more fundamental, relational reality—their intersubjectivity—which is an amalgam of the two persons. This amalgam is a "subjectivity that seems to take on a life of its own" (Ogden, p. 169). According to what one might call the Freudian/ Kleinian third, or the Oedipal third, when such a predominantly pre-Oedipal transference and countertransference develops, it falls to the analyst to sustain the analytic third in him or herself, so that the analyst may continue to observe the self, the analysand, and the interplay between them in the sessions, in order to enable the analyst to assess the therapeutic efficacy of their relationship.

Such conflicting assumptions currently divide psychoanalysis. There does not appear to be any way to reconcile them. The otherwise very different philosophical positions considered earlier agree that individual self-awareness is essential to thirdness (except Peirce's). To be sure, self-awareness is not sufficient in and by itself; an idea is necessary to inform it and give it direction, but there are no philosophical precedents for intersubjective relational thirds, apart from individual consciousness—which is, of course, a consciousness of both self and others.

In the philosophical third, in one way or another (depending on the philosopher), the function of the third is to organize and direct the mind to take cognizance of itself in order to be better prepared to observe and understand both the self and the world. It is readily apparent how closely psychoanalysis agrees with—and enriches and improves the prospects of success in—this broad philosophical project, which Bacon (1620) traced back to the ancient Greeks. Perhaps Hegel could be made out to be an exception, despite the primacy he gives to individual self-awareness, but any attempt to use Hegelian ideas runs into the problem of the dialectical logic by means of which he derives the other from the subject.

Of course, conscious and unconscious relations of fundamental importance to the analysis are established between analyst and analysand. The analyst, by means of empathic trial identifications, needs to be able to feel, imagine, and think something (hopefully to a sufficient degree) of what it is like to be the analysand. But the analyst may feel him or herself drawn into a fusion with the patient, in which the analysand comes to feel disorganized and enmeshed with the analyst. The same experiences may occur in the analyst. An analysand, for example, may feel drawn into a fusional bond with the analyst that is focused on the soothing sound of the analyst's voice. But does the revival of such infantile experiences, and others like them, warrant the inference of a third entity that exists independently of the different transferential, countertransferential, and reality-bound relations formed by one member of the analytic dyad with the other?

If we follow Peirce back to medieval philosophy, we find William of Ockham, of the school of Scotus—who, with his now-famous razor, declared that entities should not be unnecessarily multiplied. Perhaps, upon further reflection by analysts, such entities as inter-subjective thirds, the relational unconscious, and others will, like Platonic forms, fall under the cutting edge of Occam's razor—or perhaps not. Yet, in science, as in philosophy, the simplest theory to comprehend the phenomena will be most serviceable for the advancement of knowledge and more likely to turn out to be true.

Philosophy, as indicated by the foregoing all too brief survey, is almost universally committed to epistemological realism. Even philosophers like Peirce and Hegel, who were metaphysical ideal-ists, were epistemological realists, as were Plato and Aristotle. Epistemological subjectivism is an unusual doctrine—espoused, perhaps, by Protagoras, but by few others. Some intersubjectivists, at least, adhere to the idea of irreducible subjectivity, a highly ambiguous notion (Hanly & Hanly, 2001). If its meaning is psycho-logical, it signifies only that each person's feelings, motives, experi-ences, thinking, and so on are his or her own and no one else's. Objects can be shared; experiences can be verbally shared; but my experience of the object is mine and yours is yours. They are psychologically irreducibly subjective because each individual is the owner of her or his sensory apparatus.

This statement says nothing about our capacity to have the same experiences, however, or to know that we have different experiences of one and the same object; nor does it say anything about our abil-ity, by means of sense perception, to become aware of the existence and nature of objects that exist apart from and independently of our own subjectivity—as Peirce and Locke, but also Descartes (1641) and Berkeley (1710), philosophically affirmed. But if the meaning of irreducible subjectivity is cognitive, and, hence, epistemological, it means that our perceptions, thoughts, and so on must inevitably fail in making us aware of the existence and nature of objects that exist apart from and independently of our own minds. No method of investigation, no correction of perceptual illusion, will serve. Our minds are inevitably locked into their own subjectivity.

Thus, if the notion of irreducible subjectivity is implied by inter-subjectivity, and if the notion of irreducible subjectivity is taken as an epistemological one, rather than merely as the assertion of an elementary psychological and neurological fact, we are each located in our own worlds, as contrived by Descartes's Malignant Deceiver. Most authors, in fact, treat irreducible subjectivity as a cautionary notion—not an epistemological premise, but a warning against naïve realism. These warnings are obviously helpful. However, the concept as often used carries the implicit, false implication that all realists are naïve realists. It is true of Aristotle or Plato, perhaps, but not of Locke or Peirce, or of Galileo, Harvey, Newton, Einstein, Darwin, or Freud.

That psychoanalysis is a process, who could doubt? That it is greater than the conscious volition or detailed comprehension of analyst or analysand need not be in doubt either. But these facts do not require a special ontology of the primacy of relations. What can be doubted is that there is a third participant making up the process, a co-created subjectivity of some sort, with some kind of life of its own. Aristotle's classic third-man critique of Plato's forms would appear to apply here. It is an infinite-regress argument. Since the analyst and analysand co-create a first relational third, the analyst will have to form some kind of relation with this third. But this relation will co-create a second relational third, and so on, *ad infinitum*. The same will apply to the analysand.

I can understand that psychoanalysts might not be as impressed as philosophers by the problem posed for theories by infinite-regress arguments. They do indicate serious logical and conceptual flaws in theories when they apply. In any case, would it not be adequate, as well as simpler, to assume that the analytic dyad is made up of two persons with separate identities, needs, characters, and motives, who relate to each other according to their respective needs, characters, and motives, one of whom is in need of help and one of whom is there to help?

Platonism survived Aristotle's critique until Scotus, William of Ockham, Aquinas, and others paved the way for the replacement of scholasticism by modern scientific thought.

References

Arlow, J. (1979). The genesis of interpretation. *Journal of the American Psychoanalytic Association*, 27: 193–206.

Bacon, F. (1620). *Advancement of Learning and Novum Organum.* New York: Willey Book Co, 1944.

Berkeley, G. (1710). The principles of human knowledge. In: M. W. Berkeley (Ed.), *M. W. Calkins* (pp. 99–216). New York: Charles Scribner's Sons, 1929.

Bird, B. (1972). Notes on transference: universal phenomenon and hardest part of analysis. *Journal of the American Psychoanalytic Association, 20*: 267–302.

Boesky, D. (1990). The psychoanalytic process and its components. *Psychoanalytic Quarterly, 59*: 550–584.

Britton, R. (1987). The missing link: parental sexuality in the Oedipus complex. In: J. Steiner (Ed.), *The Oedipus Complex Today* (pp. 83–101). London: Karnac.

Britton, R. (1998). Subjectivity, objectivity and potential space. In: *Belief and Imagination.* London: Routledge.

Cavell, M. (1998). Triangulation, one's own mind and objectivity. *International Journal of Psychoanalysis, 79*: 449–467.

Descartes, R. (1641). Meditations on first philosophy. In: E. S. Haldane & G. R. T. Ross (Trans.), *Philosophical Works of Descartes, Vol. 1* (pp. 144–199). New York: Dover Press, 1955.

Feldman, M. (1997). The dynamics of reassurance. In: R. Schafer (Ed.), *The Contemporary Kleinians of London* (pp. 321–344). Madison, CT: International Universities Press.

Freud, S. (1895). Project for a scientific psychology. *S.E., 1.* London: Hogarth.

Freud, S. (1905c). *Jokes and their Relation to the Unconscious. S.E., 8.* London: Hogarth.

Freud, S. (1917e). Mourning and melancholia. *S.E., 14.* London: Hogarth.

Freud, S. (1920g). *Beyond the Pleasure Principle. S.E., 18.* London: Hogarth.

Freud, S. (1921c). *Group Psychology and the Analysis of the Ego. S.E., 18.* London: Hogarth.

Freud, S. (1923b). *The Ego and the Id. S.E., 19.* London: Hogarth.

Hanly, C. (1995). Ideas and facts in psychoanalysis. *International Journal of Psycho-Analysis, 76*: 901–908.

Hanly, C., & Hanly, M. A. F. (2001). Critical realism: distinguishing the psychological subjectivity of the analyst from epistemological subjectivism. *Journal of the American Psychoanalytic Association, 27*: 193–206.

Hanly, C., & Nichols, C. (2001). A disturbance of psychoanalytic memory: the case of John Rickman's three-person psychology. *Philosophy of the Social Sciences, 31*: 279–301.

Hegel, G. W. F. (1807a). *Hegel, Texts and Commentary*, W. Kaufmann (Trans. & Ed.). Notre Dame, IN: University of Notre Dame Press, 1977.

Hegel, G. W. F. (1807b). *The Phenomenology of Mind*, J. B. Baillie (Trans.). London: George Allen & Unwin, 1971.

Hegel, G. W. F. (1816). *The Science of Logic*, A. V. Miller (Trans.). London: George Allen & Unwin, 1969.

Hobbes, T. (1651). *Leviathan*. Harmondsworth: Penguin, 1974.

Jacobs, T. J. (2001). On unconscious communications and covert enactments: some reflections on their role in the analytic situation. *Psychoanalytic Inquiry, 21*(1): 4–23.

Kant, I. (1781). *Immanuel Kant's Critique of Pure Reason*, N. K. Smith (Trans.). London: Macmillan, 1950.

Klein, M. (1935). A contribution to the psychogenesis of manic-depressive states. In: *The Writings of Melanie Klein* (pp. 262–289). London: Hogarth, 1975.

Locke, J. (1690). An essay concerning human understanding. In: J. A. St. John (Ed.), *The Philosophical Works of John Locke, Vol. 1*. London: George Bell & Sons, 1898.

Loewald, H. (1979). Reflections on the psychoanalytic process. In: *Papers on Psychoanalysis* (pp. 372–383). New Haven, CT: Yale University Press, 1980.

Marx, K. (1873). *Capital*, Preface to the Second Edition, S. Moore & E. Aveling (Trans.), F. Engels (Ed.). London: William Glaisher, 1909.

Peirce, C. (1903). *Complete Papers of Charles Sanders Peirce, Vols. 1–8*, C. Hartshorne & P. Weiss (Eds.). Cambridge, MA: Harvard University Press, 1966.

Plato (4th century BC). *The Republic*, B. Jowett (Trans.). Cleveland, OH: World Publishing, 1946.

Rickman, J. (1950). The factor of number in individual-and-group dynamics. In: *Selected Contributions to Psychoanalysis*. London: Hogarth, 1957.

Rickman, J. (1951). Number and the human sciences. In: *Selected Contributions to Psychoanalysis*. London: Hogarth, 1957.

Russell, B. (1946). *History of Western Philosophy*. New York: Routledge, 1996.

Spinoza, B. (1673). Ethic. In: J. Wild (Ed.), *Spinoza Selections* (pp. 94–400). New York: Charles Scribner's Sons, 1930.

Waelder, R. (1934). The problem of freedom in psychoanalysis and the problem of reality testing. In: *Psychoanalysis: Observation, Theory, Application*. New York: International Universities Press.

Wittgenstein, L. (1918). *Tractatus Logico-Philosophicus*, D. F. Pears & B. F. McGuinness (Trans.). London: Routledge & Kegan Paul, 1961.

CHAPTER THREE

Triangulation, one's own mind, and objectivity*

Marcia Cavell

Some psychoanalysts now hold that an intersubjective model of the mind and of the analytic situation renders the ideas of truth, reality, and objectivity obsolete. Arguing from a position of sympathy with this model, the author contends that nevertheless both a real, shared, external world and the concept of such a world are indispensable to propositional thought, and to the capacity to know one's own thoughts as thoughts, as a subjective perspective on the world. Without the idea of an objective world with which we are in touch and which we attempt to be more-or-less objective about, any so-called intersubjectivist model collapses into the one-person paradigm. The author traces a certain developmental line in twentieth-century philosophy that supports an intersubjective view, a line that shows the place of the normative ideas of truth and falsity, right and wrong, in the advent of mind; it attempts to disentangle the concept of truth from an authoritarian view that was implicit in Descartes; it points out connections, and a difference, between the view of triangulation that it argues for

---

* First published in 1998 in *International Journal of Psychoanalysis, 79*: 449–467.

and the views espoused by a number of psychoanalysts. Some implications of this intersubjectivist position for psychoanalytic practice are considered; for instance: the interrelations between the analyst's third-person knowledge of her patient, and the patient's developing understanding of himself; and what the concept of unconscious fantasy presupposes.

Until recently, we conceived the mind as essentially monadic, containing entirely within itself much of its content as well as the rudiments of its structure. In recent years, however, a number of psychoanalysts and philosophers have begun to view the mind as constituted by an interactive, interpersonal world. (The new discovery that connections in the infant brain are made through the infant's earliest interplay with responsive adults is a graphic neurological correlate of this thesis.) We think of the observational stance as within an intersubjective field (Mitchell, 1988), and hold that knowledge is achieved through a process of dialogue in which every person's contribution is necessarily partial. I will refer loosely to these and kindred beliefs as the Intersubjective view of the mind, aware that in both psychoanalysis and philosophy there are important differences among the view's various proponents.

It is a shift with enormous clinical implications, affecting how we think about resistance (Spezzano, 1993), the unconscious (Stolorow & Atwood, 1992), psychic change (Hoffman, 1983), and, of course, the analytic relationship. The "neutral" analytic observer, situated somehow outside the analyst–analysand pair where he or she has privileged access to the truth, has disappeared; between analyst and patient, we recognize, interpretation goes two ways (Hoffman, 1983).

I think that, in general, the intersubjectivists are on the right track. All the more reason for protecting their position against some mistaken inferences they themselves occasionally draw that actually undermine it. The following passages from recent psychoanalytic writers, with all of whom I am generally in sympathy, represent the sorts of mistakes I have in mind: (1) "'Reality', as we use the term, refers to something subjective, something felt or sensed, rather than to an external realm of being existing independently of the human subject" (Stolorow & Atwood, 1992, pp. 26–27). (2) The idea of analytic "objectivity", Fogel and colleagues suggest, is "an intellectual remnant of the one-person psychology paradigm". They continue,

Might reducing the object of analysis to the "interaction" between patient and analyst not mislead us, if it predisposes us to imagine that there is an objective reality, "out there" between analyst and patient, that one can be "objective" about? [Fogel, Tyson, Green-berg, McLaughlin, & Peyser, 1996, p. 885]

(3) "If an observation or measurement could establish a truth, that truth could never become untrue. Yet this happens all the time in science" (Spezzano, 1993, p. 30). Each of these passages says something important. The first and second insist that the only "reality" we can investigate, know, deceive ourselves about, must be within the realm of someone's potential experience. So Kant said, and on this point few philosophers would disagree. But it does not follow that reality is subjective. On the contrary, in the absence of a distinction between what I "subjectively"—or even we, putting our "subjectivities" together—believe to be the case (a belief which itself is as much a part of reality as the chair I am sitting on), and what is the case, however that is ascertained, the concept of reality loses its sense. In what follows, it will emerge, I hope, that objective reality is a concept indispensable to human affairs.

The third passage warns that what we take to be a truth can always be called into question at another time, or under other circumstances; that our claims to truth must always be provisional; that a truth claim is always that, a claim, requiring support; that between the best evidence and what is the case there will always be a gap; that a justified belief and a true belief are, unfortunately, not necessarily the same; that talk about "the truth", especially "sincere", self-righteous talk, is often a way of dignifying one's own blind-spots; that the conversational move which says "you're wrong" or "that is not true" is often a conversation-stopper (this last is more a question of tact than fact, however).

Yet, it is what we hold true that changes, not truths themselves. The shift from the widely held twelfth-century idea that the earth is flat to the fifteenth-century idea that it is round is not a change in truth but in belief. We now hold that our ancestors had very good reasons for believing what they did about the shape of the earth, indeed little reason for believing anything else. Their beliefs were amply justified, yet wrong. We suspect, furthermore, that if these ancestors were here now and knew what we do, they would agree with us; that between us and them there would be room for dialogue.

So, what is truth? We might think, confusedly, that answering this would deliver all the particular truths there are. But as I understand it, the question seeks a clarification of the concept of truth, and this clarification will not tell us which particular propositions are worthy of belief. In short, we cannot give a definition of truth that will allow us to pick out just those propositions that are true. That would be a bit of magic. Nevertheless, we can say clarifying things like the following: truth is a property of sentences, beliefs, propositions, such that if a person's belief that the earth is round is true, the world is round. (Philosophers put it this way: "P" is true if and only if p. For example: The sentence "Miriam is Adrian's sister" is true if and only if Miriam is Adrian's sister.) I will call this idea that truth depends on the way things are, not on how people think they are or wish they were, the homely view of truth. (It is because of this dependency that some philosophers have viewed truth as correspondence. The trouble with this view, however, is that it does not even begin to explain truth; for there is no way of carving out just that part of the world that makes a belief true. This is where coherence comes in. We cannot say that truth just is coherence either, for coherence is only one constraint on rationality. A system of beliefs might be perfectly self-consistent, yet inconsistent with another system. To this, coherentists sometimes respond that any coherent system of beliefs must be appropriately responsive to the way the world is, a response that returns us to the homely idea of truth. For a fuller discussion of truth, correspondence, and coherence, see Cavell, 1993, Chapter One.) Of course, to investigate the truth of any belief or sentence we must first know its meaning, which is constructed by us. Meaning is constructed; so are theories. Furthermore, the meaning of a belief or sentence is constrained by its place in a network of other sentences in the language, or beliefs in the person's mind. But truth is not constructed.

Truth is objective in the sense that the truth of a sentence or belief is independent of us; what is true about a particular matter may be different not only from anybody and everybody's opinion about its truth, but also from its utility: a belief that works for me, even for us, may turn out to be false. (When pushed on this point, pragmatists often retort that "useful" must take in the longest possible run, and everything we will ever know, a retort that collapses "useful" back into "true".)

Here is my claim: subjectivity, in a certain key sense of the word to be defined later, goes hand in hand with intersubjectivity, but also, a concept of intersubjectivity that floats free from the ideas of objectivity and truth is no intersubjectivity at all. This is because of what I see as necessary conditions for the mental. Many psychoanalysts have been saying in different ways that the "space" within which thinking can occur is triangular in character. (I return later to some of these authors.) So I say also; but the space I see is triangulated by one mind, other minds, and the objective world, discoverable by each of them, existing independently of their beliefs and will, a world they share in fact, and which they know they share. The argument I am going to work out is that two minds can know each other as minds only on the same condition. Take away this third point of the triangle, the objective world, and we are left with no minds at all. Give up the idea of an objective reality, "out there" between analyst and patient that we can be more-or-less objective about, and what we are left with is "the one-person psychology paradigm". Forego the idea that analyst and patient share a common world, despite the differences in their experiences of it, and we make the idea of interpretation unintelligible; for interpretation requires that there be public things, like the words we say, the things we do, the common room that patient and analyst inhabit, to give a common reference from which interpretation can get started, a ground for either agreement or disagreement. I cannot disagree with you about the shape of the earth, for example, unless I know more or less what you mean by "the earth", and believe that we are talking about, more or less, the same thing. If we are not, then we are not disagreeing but talking past each other. The separateness of analyst from patient that is an essential aspect of the psychoanalytic situation is a function of the fact that there is an objective world out there, larger than the two participants, to allow them a perspective beyond their own.

In Sections I and II, I elaborate a certain shift that has taken place in twentieth-century philosophy from what I will call a subjectivist view of meaning and mind to an intersubjectivist view, and I argue for the latter. We find versions of the first in philosophy from Plato, on whom I touch briefly, through Descartes, my central focus, all the way to the contemporary philosopher, John Searle. My discussion of subjectivism attempts to make clear that it is only the Cartesian view of truth from which we need to distance ourselves.

For versions of the intersubjectivist view, I single out George Herbert Mead, Vygotsky, Ludwig Wittgenstein, and Donald Davidson. Psychoanalysts familiar with other philosophers who might seem equally well to deserve consideration here, for example, Husserl, Gadamer, Habermas, or Putnam, may wonder why I omit them. I do so for the sake of brevity, and because my view of intersubjectivity is tendentious. The philosophers I discuss are en route to the following specific ideas that I think are crucial: (1) the concept of mind can be elucidated only by reference to the normative concepts of truth, objectivity, and reason. This, of course, does not mean that all thought, even of a propositional sort, is rational; much is not. It means, first, that a creature lacking these concepts altogether could not be said to have any thoughts of a propositional sort; it means, second, that so long as there is a mind at all, that mind must be rational to some extent. I will not be arguing the second claim here. (2) When a child can be said to have propositional thought, she has made a qualitative leap from the on-the-way-to-thought child that she was before. The leap describes her, and also our vocabulary for understanding her. (3) To make this leap, the child must have been in communication with other (thinking) creatures. This is the sense in which the mind is constituted by an interactive, interpersonal world.

Considerably shorter, Sections III and IV discuss unconscious fantasy and some problems facing psychoanalysis now. The theme of truth threads through all four sections.

I should make three things clear at the start. First, when I talk about thought, I have in mind desires and emotions as well as beliefs. Second, my concern is specifically with the capacity for thought that is symbolic and propositional in character. Of course, much goes on in the infant prior to the development of this capacity that affects what sort of thinker the child will be. Third, I take for granted that many thoughts, even of a propositional character, are unconscious, and that we all have many thoughts that cannot be captured in words.

The subjectivist view

Plato was struck by the fact that whenever we make a judgement about something—as we do, for example, in believing that this is a table—we use predicates that are general in character. Words and particular ideas mean what they do, Plato thought, by invoking the corresponding general Forms, which transcend material reality and which antedate all human minds. Plato was struck also by the fact that a judgment says something that is in principle true or false. When we know for certain which it is, then apropos that judgment, and only then, Plato thought, do we have knowledge; and certainty, like meaning, points to our acquaintance with the transcendent world of Forms. Thus Plato accounts for meaning, truth, and knowledge by appealing to a realm of being that is perfect, timeless, and from which our very corporeality distances us. One important source for the later Christian ideas of original sin, and of atonement (at-one-ment) as requiring an act of divine grace, is here in Plato. (Read "the spatio-temporal body" as what deprives us of godly knowledge.) Nietzsche's famous attack on Truth was fired in part by his belief that the idea of truth is inevitably linked to subservient self-loathing and a denigration of the "merely" human.

Some of Plato's view is discernible in Descartes: for example, the ideas that any knowledge worthy of its name must be certain, and that certainty is underwritten by a transcendent order of reality, which for Descartes was God. But whereas Plato envisaged knowledge as a relation between Mind and the Forms, Descartes substituted a relation between individual mind and its inner ideas or objects.

Descartes asked: given that we are often mistaken in our beliefs, how can we be sure we know anything at all? A part of his answer is that knowledge is guaranteed so long as I claim to know nothing more than the immediate contents of my consciousness. I may be mistaken in believing that the room is hot or that the table is red; I cannot be mistaken in thinking that I believe the table is red. For to know what I believe I only need turn my mental eye inwards and discern the mental objects that are there, for instance, the idea "the table is red". I will refer to this as the ocular model of self-knowledge. Descartes conceives the mind on the analogy of a theatre, a theatre that only the person whose mind it is can enter. Therefore, that person and she alone is in a position to see at first hand what is happening on the stage. But whereas my physical eye sees a table in the material world, normally the same table that you see if you are in the right position, my mental eye sees a thoroughly private, subjective object. These ideas, not the things they supposedly represent, are the only things with which the mind can be acquainted. With Descartes, subjectivity in its modern sense is born, the sense in which our knowledge of our minds is presumably not connected in any essential way with the external world, and in which knowledge of other minds is either impossible or mysterious. (It would be interesting to see how Freud's concept of "das Ich"—"the ego"— implicitly relies on a Cartesian view of the self, even as Freud attempts to change it radically.)

Descartes's picture seems to be in accord with some important phenomena of our mental life, and because it is, the view continues to appeal both to common sense and to some philosophers. It is true, for example, that I can often know what I am thinking about without looking outside myself. So it may seem that the content of an idea is entirely contained within it.

Nevertheless, there are a number of overwhelming problems with the subjectivist paradigm. I will mention a few.

Scepticism: Since it claims that all that we are directly acquainted with is our private, internal representations, the paradigm inevitably leads to scepticism about the very existence of the external world and other minds. (How indeed can we even call these ideas "representations"?) Descartes's escape hatch is God, who presumably warrants our knowledge claims if we arrive at them in the right way. Thus, in His goodness, God can close the gap for us between justified belief and true belief. We should note, in passing, that the Cartesian knower is just that "neutral" observer of which many psychoanalysts are now rightly so sceptical, the observer who presumably sees things free of human taint, just as they are, and who can therefore sometimes pronounce with the authority of God.

Meaning and mental content: By the content of a thought I mean what it concerns or is about (I believe this is what Freud meant by "quality", 1895). Descartes's view of meaning is "internalist" in the sense that he thinks there is no necessary connection, anywhere in the network of a person's thoughts, between mental content and what is outside his mind, between what one means by his words and the external world. The problem here with Descartes is this: if we have no direct acquaintance with the external world but only with our own thoughts, then what entitles us to describe them in a language of material things? What entitles us to say that a particular thought is a world-is-round-sort-of-thought? How can we even speak of our ideas as representations? (To know that one thing represents another, one must have had some experience of both.) Kant might seem to have got around Cartesian scepticism in arguing that there must be a fundamental compatability between mind and world, and that it is this compatibility that makes knowledge possible. But the distinction Kant draws between the conceptual scheme (imposed by us) and some raw, uninterpreted Given, on which this scheme is imposed, leaves the gap between (subjective) experience and (objective) reality as great as it ever was. To close this gap we need to say, not that we can never know reality perfectly, but that it is reality we apprehend. (For a fuller discussion of representation, "the myth of the Given", and the scheme–content distinction, see Rorty, 1979.)

Historicity: The Cartesian view does not make room for an idea that comes to seem more and more important in the latter part of the nineteenth century, that all knowing is historically situated, necessarily partial in character, the achievement of individuals who are limited by their particular places in space and time. Knowledge is never certain, we now think; and it grows not by transcending partiality altogether but through a dialogue over time.

Language: It is clearly a public phenomenon. The subjectivist begins with the private, internal and the intrinsically subjective, and will have to account for the publicity of language by somehow matching public words to private states or objects. But since on his view these states are thoroughly internal, it is hard to see how any such matching can take place.

To be sure, there are philosophers who think these problems can be solved in very different ways from the ones I suggest. I cannot argue with them here. My aim rather is to sketch an approach to mind and meaning that to many of us looks very promising, an approach that starts with public phenomena like people doing things with each other, and works its way "inward" to mind.

Before leaving subjectivism, I should point out that Freud unquestioningly accepted the Cartesian ocular model of self-knowledge (somewhat modified by Kant), together with its scepticism about our knowledge of the external world. Freud writes, "Consciousness makes each of us aware only of his own states of mind" (1915e, p. 169). And also,

> behind the attributes of the object under examination which are presented directly to perception, we have to discover something else which is more independent of the particular receptive capacity of our sense organs and which approximates more closely to what may be supposed to be the real state of affairs. We have no hope of being able to reach the latter itself . . . [1940a [1938], p. 196]

And again: "[psychical reality] is as much unknown to us as the reality of the external world, and it is as incompletely presented by the data of consciousness as is the external world by the communication of our sense organs" (1900a, p. 613).

The intersubjectivist view and the normativity of the mental

One of the first thinkers to put forward an intersubjectivist position was G. H. Mead. Influenced by Darwin, Mead attempted to give a naturalistic account of specifically human thought by tracing it to lower, simpler orders of communication (Mead, 1934). At the same time, he insisted that our symbolizing activity is categorically different from any form of communication from which it evolves. The (impossible) problem he set himself was, in effect, to reduce the irreducible (more about reducibility later).

Mead distinguishes three levels of meaning. The first he calls a conversation of gestures, seen among the higher vertebrates. The second is the signal-language level at which a single word like "fire", for example, acts as a stimulus to behaviour. The third level is fully articulated propositional thought in which symbols, which are not context-dependent, replace signals that are.

In a conversation of gestures, the evolutionary starting point, two animals respond to each other reciprocally, the behaviour of each acting as a stimulus to the other. In a dog-fight, for example, the behaviour of Fido prompts a second dog to act in a way that in turn modifies Fido's behaviour; and so on. The two dogs are interacting in a way that resembles human conversation, but we do not think their "gestures" are accompanied by ideas in their heads; it is we, the observers, who ascribe meanings to animal behaviour on the basis of what function it has within a group: searching for food, defending against predators, finding a mate, and so on.

An essential difference between a mere gesture and gesture at the symbolic level, Mead holds, is that the latter is accompanied by an idea, an idea that is virtually the same for both creatures. (The patient says "I am feeling depressed", and if the analyst catches his meaning, she thinks something like "He is feeling depressed".) To explain how symbolic communication evolves from the conversation of gestures, Mead posits an identificatory act that he calls "taking the attitude of the other". The basic idea is that a gesture of the first creature, A, takes on a meaning for a second creature, B, who responds to A's gesture; in so doing, B interprets A's gesture in a certain way. A did not intend his gesture to have such a meaning; he did not intend anything at all. Yet, if A can now take B's attitude towards his own gesture, he becomes his own interpreter; his gesture acquires for him a meaning like that it has for B. I have cast the process Mead envisions as if it took place in the life of a single individual; but Mead thinks of it as spanning species and generations. At the end of this process, he thinks, a creature with symbolic thought has evolved.

With the ideas of "internalizing" and "taking the attitude of the other", Mead hoped to have located a particular bit of behaviour that would explain the rise of symbolic thought, while preserving his insight that it is irreducible to anything less complex. But it is a pseudo-explanation; for either A's taking the attitude of the other is just the very thing to be explained, an act of interpretation that presumes symbolic thought, or else there is nothing yet to distinguish what A does from mimicry or imitation, and we have not left the conversation of gesture. Nevertheless, in launching an investigation of meaning from two creatures interacting in a shared world, Mead's argument moves in the right direction. By implication, Descartes's investigation was wrong-headed, both because it made the solitary individual its starting point, and because it took reflection rather than purposive, wordly action as the paradigmatic expression of human thought.

During roughly the same period of time, the Russian psychologist Vygotsky was developing an idea similar to Mead's. Vygotsky also held that the individual mind emerges from a more rudimentary and collective form of life, and that the crucial turn is a kind of internalization of the other. Critical of Piaget, who held, following Freud, that first there are deeply personal, subjective, autistic mental states, which under the pressure of socialization finally yield to "social thought", Vygotsky traced a developmental scheme that proceeds from social communication, to egocentric thought, and finally to full-fledged mental states (Vygotsky, 1962). Vygotsky writes, "the process of internalisation is not the transferral of an external activity to a pre-existing internal plane of consciousness; it is the process in which this internal plane is formed" (quoted in Wertsch, 1985, p. 64). For example: the child reaches unsuccessfully for an object, and the mother comes to get the object for the child. Over time, what was at first a gesture that had no significance for the child but only for the mother, becomes, through that interaction, a gesture with which the child means to point.[1] By this route, eventually the child as well as the mother can point to the apple with the idea in mind, "Here is an apple". Daniel Stern's use of the idea of feedback loops in parent–infant interactions might suggest a similar process (Stern, 1995).

Like Mead and Vygotsky, the later Wittgenstein thought the traditional subjectivist picture was fundamentally wrong-headed in isolating thought from action, private thought from public speech, mind from body, and one mind from other minds. The Platonic idea that individual words or concepts have meaning all by themselves begins its investigation of meaning in the wrong place, for words come to have meaning only through the activities of actual speakers who are doing things with words in the course of carrying out communal enterprises (Wittgenstein, 1953). Attention to the ways language is actually used in daily life will free us from the temptation to hypostatize language and meanings, as Plato did in positing a heaven of Forms. There are not meanings, but people meaning things by what they say and do.

To see how a view about meaning might take us to the intersubjectivist claim that the mind is constituted out of its interactions with other creatures, recall Descartes's ocular view of the mind, that each of us knows what she thinks (what she means)—when she does—by looking inwards. The presupposition here is that the meaning of an idea is written on its face. Ideas have the content they do through representing something else. But, Wittgenstein points out, the concept of representation does not help in explaining how words and ideas acquire meaning; for what a sign represents is not something the sign itself can tell us. Even a portrait of Marilyn Monroe that is very faithful to her can be taken to be her portrait only by someone who knows something about Monroe. And, of course, many representations are not isomorphic with the things they represent. For a representation of an apple, say, to be a representation of an apple, the person for whom it represents an apple must intend it to do so, must know its meaning already. So the idea of representation leaves unexplained the very thing it was meant to elucidate, how signs, words, ideas, thoughts, come to have the meaning they do.

To take another tack: supposedly our inner life is what we most intimately and, sometimes, most surely know. This is the datum from which Cartesianism begins. But how does a child ever learn the concept of pride, for example? How does it begin to learn that it feels proud, and to be able to say to itself "I feel proud"? There must be intrinsic connections between behaviour and concepts like belief, desire, anger, sadness, pride, if a child is able to acquire such concepts. My pride is known to me in a peculiar way, but it also has an objective aspect, transforming me as an object for others. If this were not so, no one could ever learn the language of mind. The more interesting argument—I think it can be made but will not attempt it here—is that the child learns not merely to name pride but to feel it through social interactions. (Anxiety and rage are among the emotions that in their most primitive form are not constructed through interpersonal interactions.)

Wittgenstein is not denying that my experience of pride, or sadness, or pain, is peculiar to me, nor that we can sometimes keep our pains and thoughts to ourselves, two ideas that the concept of subjectivity captures. He is insisting that unless the child were in communion with other creatures who had pains, who sometimes expressed them in their behaviour, and who recognized that the child has experiences similar to the adult's, the child could not learn the concept of pain. She could not even think the thought, "I am in pain", or "Mama is in pain". We use the word "subjectivity" in many ways; in some, it is attributable to infants and creatures other than ourselves. But in the non-Cartesian sense of "subjectivity" that

I am singling out, subjectivity exists only where there is the having of thoughts, some of which one knows as thoughts, and as his own thoughts. In this sense, about which I will say more shortly, subjectivity is not a condition into which we are born, but one we slowly enter through our interactions with the world and with other persons in this world.

When one already has a mind of one's own, it remains the case that others can sometimes know us in a way we cannot know ourselves; this is one implication of the concept of unconscious mental processes, and one reason why other persons can play an important role in the acquisition of self-knowledge. If I am a patient in analysis, the only truths about me that will do me any good are truths I myself possess. But sometimes a first step in my knowing, for example, that I am sad, and being able to link up a feeling with the thoughts that make it comprehensible to me, may be somebody else's pointing out to me that I seem to be sad. Modell writes of the ways in which "the growing child requires the confirmation of the other to claim possession of her affect", and remarks that the analyst does something analogous for his patient (1990, p. 72).

Wittgenstein does not investigate in detail the personal interactions leading to subjectivity; but he implies that such an investigation would include the ways in which other people's responses to the child shape his emerging sense of himself, and so the understanding that he brings to his eventual first-person thinking. These are just the sorts of interactions that, because of its essentially interpersonal character, the psychoanalytic dialogue can bring to light. For example, Winnicott tells the story of a male patient who knows himself to be male, but who talks as if what he were feeling were penis envy. Winnicott says to him:

> I am listening to a girl. I know perfectly well that you are a man but I am listening to a girl, and talking to a girl. I am telling this girl, "You are talking about penis envy". After a pause, the patient responds, "If I were to tell someone about this girl I would be called mad".

Winnicott claims the madness as his—that is, as that of the mother who had wanted this boy to be a girl—and goes on to say: "This madness which was mine enabled him to see himself as a girl from my position" (Winnicott, 1971, pp. 73–74).

I have said that learning a mental vocabulary presumes interaction with other people. Yet so far, Wittgenstein's argument does not obviously unsettle our (Cartesian) assumption that language is merely a (public) tool with which we attempt to communicate thoughts, many of which are intrinsically private. Wittgenstein does have a more general argument, which unfortunately is extremely elusive, and much debated. As I see it, the argument begins with the assumption that only behaviour that is guided or informed by concepts can be said to be "minded". It goes on to say that one grasps a concept only if one knows how to follow a rule that tells us how to apply the concept, and that the measure of knowing how to follow a rule is being able to go on applying it as other creatures do. As Wittgenstein puts it: "it is not possible to obey a rule 'privately'; otherwise thinking one was obeying a rule would be the same thing as obeying it" (1953, par. 202). If the argument worked, it would indeed show that no creature can have concepts, or thoughts of a conceptual nature, in the absence of communication with other creatures. It would show that a child whose physical needs were taken care of but who was raised without communication with others could not know its own mind because it would not have a mind to know.

But why should we invest the ability to follow a rule with this significance? What does Wittgenstein mean by "following a rule"? Clearly, something other than the mere disposition to do as others do; for bees and lemmings and indeed all other creatures are so disposed, yet we can describe their behaviour without ascribing to them concepts. Nor does discriminatory behaviour, by itself, indicate the presence of concepts, for in their absence, sunflowers can turn toward the sun, thermostats register degrees of heat, bulls be enraged by the colour red.

The relationship between being a creature that can follow rules and being a creature whose behaviour is guided by concepts becomes clearer if we say this: having concepts (in the sense Wittgenstein is trying to capture) presumes the creature's understanding that some things are correctly included under the concept and some things are not, that some applications of it are right, and some wrong; for this would begin to explain the link Wittgenstein sees between having concepts and the ability to follow a rule. An infant might wave its hands in a particular way only when it is handed a rattle; but many of us would not want to say that therefore the infant has the concept of a rattle. So I read Wittgenstein as making the following suggestion: let's speak of the child's having the concept of a rattle not only when it responds selectively to rattles, but when it can think something like "this is a rattle" and also "that is not a rattle". Wittgenstein is suggesting that concepts—and the sort of thinking that uses concepts, propositional thinking—come along only with the normative concepts of error, correct and incorrect, right and wrong. Like "subjectivity", "concept" too can be defined in many ways. But the concepts Wittgenstein has in mind presumably emerge only in specifically human contexts, through engagement in those worldly forms of life of which he so evocatively speaks. Both the claims that thinking has an essentially normative character, and that only a social situation can provide a field in which this normativity arises, are more clearly argued in Davidson. It is in his light that I have presented Wittgenstein. Before turning to him, we should ask: why is propositional thought so important? Because only thought of a propositional sort has implications, makes assertions, sometimes contradicts itself makes promises and reneges on promises, commits the thinker to certain conclusions (whether he accepts them or not), is open to doubt, challenge, question, reflection. Only propositional thought makes a place for dialogue that is both personal and intrapersonal: I can wonder what I mean by what I said, and I can also ask you what you mean by what you said. It is only thinking of this sort that can be either rational or irrational (as distinct from a-rational): self-deceptive, or foreclosing reflection, or repressing what one knows, or dissociating some thoughts from others. What is involved in having belief that is propositional in character, Davidson asks? The answer goes something like this: to believe that "p" just is to hold that "p" is true. Of course, you can know that it might be false, can be doubtful of its truth, and so on; the point is that the concepts of belief and truth, evidence, and reason, are necessarily linked. So, if you have a belief of a propositional sort (the beliefs we may attribute to other animals than ourselves are presumably not propositional in character) you must have a grasp of the distinction between how you think things are and how they (truly) are, between right and wrong, correct and incorrect, true and false, since belief is, by definition, a state of mind about the world; it is the sort of thing that, by definition, can be true or false (even though one may never know in a particular case which it is), and for which one adduces evidence and reasons. (Whatever conditions provide for the possibility of belief, provide also, on my view, for the possibility of fantasy, if by fantasy we mean a mental state ascribable only to a creature that has some beliefs.) The goal, then, is to say what we can about how a child might get hold of the distinctions between the false and the true, between how things seem and how they objectively are.

There must be a kind of triangulating process, as Davidson calls it (1989, 1992), in which child and adult communicate—at first, not in words on the child's part, of course—about an object in the physical world they share. To see how triangulation works, Davidson sketches a primitive learning situation. The mother hands the child an apple, saying "apple" as she does. Mother and child are together interested in the apple, and interested also in each other's response to it. The child babbles, and at some point, in this or a similar transaction, the child hits on a sound close enough to "apple" so that the mother rewards the child—with a laugh, intensified interest, more play, or any of the other kinds of responses that infant observers have described. In time, we can give content to the mother's saying that the child is responding specifically to apples. The mother has in mind the apple when she says "apple", and apple is what she means by the word.

The question, however, was the point at which we can say that "apple" is what the child himself means, and so far, there is nothing to distinguish the mother's response to the child from an observer's response to a trained dog. So, our story about the child needs a more complex form of triangulation than the one we have yet described. What it needs is a very particular sort of interaction between child and mother, in which they can observe an object in common, and observe also each other's responses to that common object. The child must be responding to a specific object, and he must know that the mother is responding to that same object. Over time, the child can then correlate the mother's responses to the object with his own. (Winnicott's writings about the transitional object are on to a similar idea. The concept of reality is constructed for any child, Winnicott suggests, through her triangular interactions with some loved external object and a loved other person who is responding both to her and to that same object. Such an object can then become symbolic, say of the breast. Winnicott writes, "When symbolism is employed, the infant is already clearly distinguishing between fantasy and fact, between inner objects and external objects, between primary creativity and perception" (Winnicott, 1971, p. 6). Yet, while Winnicott thinks that before this time there are inner objects, I want to say that only when there are, for the child, objects that are truly public can there also be "objects" that are truly inner in a subjective, inner world.)

So the object must be something public, discernible by both mother and child, to which, furthermore, they can give a name that will allow them both to refer to it even in its absence. They must be responding to the same object in the world; they must be responding to it in similar ways; and they must both observe that they are. In such a situation it will sometimes be the case that mother and child respond to the same thing—something they can both see to be the same thing—differently. The questions can then arise: Who is right, she or I? What is the object really like? What does she see that I don't? Or, What do I see that she doesn't? It is this sort of situation that makes room for the normative concepts of error, right and wrong, true and false, "my view of things" versus "hers", "my view" versus "the way things (objectively) are". (It makes room for these concepts; it does not fully explain them, a caveat I return to in a moment. And at some point this child may learn that there is no such thing as a view of the object from nowhere). Such an interaction not only allows the mother, or any interpreter, Sarah, to say of John, "he is seeing an x"; it allows John to say of himself, as it were, "I am seeing an x" (or "I want an x", or "I am thinking about an x".) The belief that there is an apple on the table draws a line from oneself to the world. But what fixes the terms joined by the line? If we say, "I and the thing itself", there is nothing to give me the idea of it as an object external to me that can be seen from different perspectives.

This picture of what is needed for concept formation begins with the claim, which many philosophers in this century have made, that mental content is partly constituted by the events in the world that are its cause. (This is not something that Descartes maintained. Whatever the causal relations between external and internal world, they are, on his view, not in any way intrinsic to the content of that internal world.) But events in the world have causal impact on sunflowers and lemmings, without this impact taking the form of concepts. So the question is, what is needed to begin to bridge the gap between mere causal relation and an object or event in the world that the child can conceive as such? What is needed to allow the cause—say the rattle, or the apple—to enter into what Wilfred Sellars called "the space of reasons"? What allows the stimulus—light from an apple on the table reaching my eye—to become a belief, a perception of the form "I see that there is an apple on the table"? What is needed to baptise this cause with a name, and a name, furthermore, that has meaning for the two players—where meaning, as we have seen, is itself a normative notion? This is the question to which the triangulation picture suggests a partial answer. As Richard Rorty recently wrote,

> The key to understanding the relation between minds and bodies is not an understanding of the irreducibility of the intentional to the physical but the understanding of the inescapability of a normative vocabulary. For the inability by an organism to use such a vocabulary entails that that organism is not using language at all. [Rorty, 1997]

My own triangulation argument differs from Davidson's in claiming that the child needs not just one but two other persons, one of whom, at least in theory, might be only the child's idea of a third. To have the distinctions between true and false, thought and world, the child must move from interacting with his mother to grasping the idea that both his perspective on the world and hers are perspectives; that there is a possible third point of view, more inclusive than theirs, from which both his mother's and his own can be seen and from which the interaction between them can be understood. One prerequisite for this is the experience of sometimes being responded to in an appropriate way, as Wittgenstein also suggested. Another prerequisite is observing disagreement between other persons.

The grasp of this third possible point of view is also part of what allows for such perplexing adult attitudes as self-forgiveness. One can experience forgiveness if she is forgiven by the person she feels she has wronged. But if he does not forgive her, or if he is dead, then forgiveness can come only from oneself, which seems to present the insurmountable problem of getting outside one's own skin. A solution is in sight when one becomes able, imaginatively, to occupy a position beyond herself from which her actions do not appear as isolated "bad" fragments, but as interactions with another person, each with complex wishes and needs. One needs to see not only oneself as a whole, but also the relationship between oneself and the other. In having such a third-person perspective, the analyst can help her patient begin to discover one like it.

Now I can say more about that sense of subjectivity that I am urging comes only with intersubjectivity. A creature has subjectivity in this sense when it knows some of its beliefs as beliefs, and as its own beliefs. This means, as Wittgenstein and others have argued, that it is able to make attributions of mental states to others (see Strawson, 1963, Part III, and Evans, 1982, Chapter Six); it understands that the mental states of another are available to him in a way they are not to one's self, as one's own thoughts are accessible to one's self in a way they are not to others. Such a child, as Fonagy puts it (following Premack and Woodruff), has "a theory of mind" (Fonagy, 1989); and only such a creature can distinguish, some of the time, between playing and reality, fantasy and fact. (I would say, furthermore, that only when that distinction is in place does the concept of fantasy have any clear meaning, but I am not arguing that here.)

Of course these knowings that characterize the very having of a mind, a mind that is one's own, are fragile, vulnerable, easily disturbed. We do not always recognize a fantasy for what it is (that we do not is one of the defining characteristics of fantasy in its specifically psychoanalytic sense); particularly if we are children, we confusedly fantasize that our own minds are transparent to others, and we confuse wishing something were so with making it so. But these are vicissitudes of mind, not the natural condition of a particular sort of (disturbed) mind. As Fonagy writes:

> Although borderline patients' capacity to differentiate self and other is legitimately described as impaired and "boundaries" between the two can be said to be blurred, those descriptions do not do justice to the complexity of the mechanisms involved. Even frank psychotics know that the person they are talking to is a separate person. [1989, p. 109]

But what about—one will rightly ask—the subjectivity of children for whom all of this is not yet in place? Can we not ask what the world is like for them? And may not the answer bear on the sort of thinking, reflective, self-aware persons they will become? Of course. Fonagy, Stern, Emde, and others who have observed infants, have asked these questions and begun to suggest some interesting answers. From these writers we have learnt that early infant–parent exchanges have a great deal to do, for example, with whether the child begins to feel that he can, or cannot, make himself understood; that he has or does not have something valuable to say or to give (a child who is not noticed, not listened to, may come to believe, by way of defending his parent, and himself from catastrophic anger toward her, that he is not worthy of being understood); that he is more or less at home in the world, or, dangerously omnipotent, at its edge. But I would describe all this as a matter of habits of attention or avoidance, of response and the evoking of response in others, of perception and feeling, that have a lot to do both with how the child will come to sense himself and the world, and with how reflective and thoughtful a person he will become, but that are set up prior to thought *per se*.

There are obvious similarities between the concept of triangulation I am urging and those of a number of psychoanalytic writers. Thus, Ronald Britton (following Bion) writes that the child's acknowledgement of the parents' relationship with each other creates "a triangular space" in which thinking can occur (Britton, 1989). Green writes that Winnicott's "transitional object" describes not so much "an object as a space lending itself to the creation of objects" (Green, 1993, p. 285). Ogden develops a concept of "the analytic third", according to which the analyst gives voice to the experience of the analysand as experienced by the analyst (Ogden, 1994, Chapter Five), thus providing, as I think of it, a third perspective from which the analysand can see himself. My picture of triangulation differs from Britton's and Green's in insisting not only on the presence of persons besides the child, but also on a real external world, common to them both. Furthermore, language has a central place in triangulation as I conceive it, for it is through language and language-learning that triangulation takes place. Child, mother, and world interact in such a way that concepts, belief, propositional thought, come into being for the first time.

Some "knowledge" of syntax may be innate, as Chomsky and others have argued. But no one has successfully shown that mental content is innate. Language is not a robe that the child casts over his thought, but the medium through which he engages with others and the world in the way that begins to constitute mental life.

It is important to point out that the triangulation argument gives only a necessary condition for thought and not its necessary and sufficient conditions, which is to say that a creature might inhabit the situation that triangulation describes and yet not develop thought. This is one of the reasons for my saying that thought is irreducible to any of the prior conditions that we can specify for it, without covertly including thought itself among them. The search for something more, for necessary and sufficient conditions, is very tempting: since mind obviously cannot come into being unless all the physical properties and worldly conditions necessary to sustain it are present, one might hope to identify mind with these conditions or some subset of them. The present interest in consciousness seems to be motivated by such a hope: surely there must be, some philosophers, psychoanalysts, and neurologists think, some particular set of neural connections that will explain consciousness so thoroughly that we can say, this is consciousness. But mind, subjectivity, thought, consciousness, truth, and so on, all confront us with what Polanyi calls "emergent properties" (Polanyi, 1958), properties that in a developmental process arise spontaneously from elements at the preceding levels and are not specifiable or predictable in terms of them.

When we can attribute propositional thoughts to a child, I have argued, we must also be attributing to it the concepts of "the objectively real", "true" and "false", "my perspective" and "your perspective", all of which concepts arise only within the language of mind; and for none of these concepts can we supply necessary and sufficient conditions in some other language. In this sense, all these concepts arise together; in particular, it is not the case that the child first grasps the concept of himself and then the concept of other person. (Daniel Stern's claim (1984) that there is from the beginning a sense of self is ambiguous: a "sense" of self is not necessarily the recognition of oneself as an "I", with all that is involved in knowing the use of the first-person pronoun. In any case it is a claim that Stern acknowledges he cannot substantiate.) Wittgenstein wrote

(1972, par. 141): "When we first begin to believe anything, what we believe is not a single proposition, it is a whole system of proposi-tions. (Light dawns gradually over the whole.)" By the time the whole over which the dawn comes is fully lit, the child has made a quantum leap.

Mead descried a categorical difference between a conversation of gestures and one that can be adequately described only in the language of mind. He hoped to bridge the gap with an act of identification or internalization. But as I pointed out earlier, he begged the question by answering it with the very thing to be explained. This must be the fate of all attempts to specify an emer-gent property in terms of things at a lower level. For this reason, if Bion's project (1962) is to trace a continuous line from primitive "thoughts" to thinking, it fails: either we have abstracted these thoughts from something that is already a thinking process, or they are so distant from it that thinking itself cannot provide a bridge. It is true that all of us are unable to think about some of our thoughts; but they occur in a mental setting in which we can think about some. We cannot extrapolate backward from fantasies or thoughts, unrecognized as such, to a time of thoughts before there was any thinking.

Nevertheless, though it does not fully explain propositional thought, the triangulation argument illuminates it in the following ways: it works against the subjectivist view of the mind in telling us that the child comes to have thoughts about the world or to make judgements about it only as he comes to be an interpreter of others; and it indicates that such acts of interpretation require a shared world and the concept of objectivity. Mead's deep insight was that there is an intrinsic connection between being interpreted by another and being an interpreter oneself, between interpretation and symbolic thought. Neither interpreting others nor thinking for oneself could exist in isolation. Since reason is a parameter of any conversation between creatures who think, I will call it a dialogue to distinguish it from a conversation of gestures. Unlike the latter, dialogue creates and presumes a shared conceptual space in which something of common interest can be talked about together; and only a dialogue is genuinely intersubjective in the sense that each participant knows himself as an "I", a subject who can think of him-self as a self, and knows the other as a subject, an "I" for himself.

Towards the beginning of this paper I said that the concept of reality loses its sense in the absence of a distinction between how things seem to me or to us, and how things are, and I promised to say why we need such a concept for our human lives. The answer is that a creature who could not grasp this distinction, in principle (though not always in a particular case), would necessarily lack the idea that another's experience of the world is different from one's own, so lack both the idea of subjectivity and that capacity for empathy which takes for granted the uniqueness of every person's perspective. Such a creature could not recognize its beliefs as beliefs, rather than simply the way the world is. So it would lack also the concepts of evidence and reasons, the capacities for reflection and for dialogue.

Here is how things look on the intersubjectivist account I am presenting. The concepts of right and wrong, true and false, do not enter our minds from some Platonic or Judaeo-Christian heaven, but emerge from within an interpersonal, worldly situation. This does not mean that truth is just a convention, or what the majority holds true; it is perfectly possible for the majority to be mistaken on any particular issue. On just this possibility the distinction between things as they appear to me, or to us, insists. A convention is a practice we can change, or can imagine changing; but there is no imaginable alternative to the concept of truth that will do the job we human creatures need to do—argue things out, assess evidence, look for reasons, disagree with each other, find a consensus, question our own convictions, and so on. Which beliefs we hold true, of course, differ from person to person; so also our ways of discovering the truth, and what we count as evidence. But the concept of truth does not. Both the proverbial Trobrian Islander and the speaker of Standard American English implicitly understand that a claim about what is calls for evidence and reasons (they may differ about whether a particular reason is bad or good, or whether a particular test captures evidence that is relevant to the issue at hand). In short, both believers share roughly the same methodology. Then, having come into a condition of dialogue with the other, the anthropologist might even discuss with his informant whether his beliefs are true, just as the psychoanalyst may also with her patient. This is not necessarily a dead-end question, since an ongoing conversation in which you and I come to understand better what each of us believes may, in fact, lead to a change of mind. It is in just this way that changes in what we hold to be true come about.

The seventeenth-century ideal of scientific objectivity posited an observer who does not affect or intrude upon the object of his investigation. We have abandoned that ideal. But another, to which I think all analysts do hold fast, asks us to try to distinguish between fantasy and reality and to take the viewpoints of others into account. With Aron, we might now view analytic neutrality as "the analyst's openness to new perspectives, a commitment to take other perspectives seriously, and a refusal to view any interpretation as complete, or any meaning as exhaustive" (Aron, 1996, p. 28).

Our developmental picture looks something like this: from the very beginning, infants make sounds and gestures that their caretakers take as signs of the infant's wants and needs. But the infant only gradually becomes able himself to mean something by what he says and does. The implication is not that before the infant has propositional thoughts and intentional states nothing at all is going on in its head. Infants have feelings, emotions, sensations, purposes, instincts; they communicate, perceive, and learn. Once again, infant research is useful here in showing how patterns of inter action between infant and care-taker can very early establish habits of response that later might be expressed as core beliefs such as "I had better not let on that I know what I know", or "I deserve every bad thing that happens to me", or "I am [or am not] able to cope with new tasks", or "the world is a fearful [or an exciting] place".

The practices of interpreting another, asking him and oneself for evidence and reasons, pointing out that this remark or this judgement is not consistent with others, mark the very space of reasons the child enters, and must enter, in learning how to think. Of course, the interpersonal relations that initiate the child into it are not coolly rational, but fraught with other lessons about loving and losing, abandoning and being lost, wanting and not having, and these lessons often fetter one's thinking ability. Psychoanalysis very well describes our initiations into thought, not by picturing a space alternative to that of reasons, but more of what the space of reasons is like.

Fantasy and the foreclosure of thinking

I have said that subjectivity in a certain specific sense—my having thoughts that I sometimes know as thoughts and as mine—comes along with some understanding of the world as public and shared, which we interpret in some shared ways. I now want to distinguish this general sense of subjectivity from another. The first words the child learns are public; the language she grows up speaking is also sufficiently public for her often to make herself understood. But, because no two people are alike, any concept quickly acquires resonances that are unique to the child; so at the same time as she learns to mean something by her words and communicate that meaning to others, the child is acquiring an idiolect, a way of thinking, that is hers alone. Some of this is unconscious.

The trouble with that part of the inner world which is neurotic is that dialogue, intersubjective testing, even reflection by the agent herself, are foreclosed. This is the status with neurotic fantasies: they are fixed, frozen in time; apparently (so they seem to the person herself) among the givens of the world, like the objects that we find there. We do not recognize them as our thoughts about the objects that we find. (Whether one accepts Melanie Klein's account of the infant's inner world, it aptly depicts the way in which unconscious fantasies can strike the person herself as things embedded in the mind, or as the lining of the mind, rather than as the mind's own thoughts.) As distinct from fantasizing, thinking allows for self-reflection and for appraising one's own thoughts as true or false, realistic or unrealistic, and so on. We think with thoughts, about things, and we cannot think about these things unless we recognize our thoughts about them as thoughts. Someone gripped by a fantasy has for the moment put aside the possibility that what he thinks might be false, or a case of wishful thinking, or just a partial view of things. He has put aside questions of evidence and reasons. One of the therapist's tasks is to engage him in such a way that what was a fantasy can become instead a belief, and as such, subject to reflection and doubt; to free important other persons in his world from their frozen status in fantasy so that, in Loewald's memorable image, ghosts (haunting the patient's mind) can become ancestors (in the real and public world).

The goal may be accomplished partly through the way in which, in transference, the patient attempts to plug the analyst into the world as he, the patient, has unknowingly constructed it. The analyst feels, through countertransference, something of what the patient wants from her; at the same time, she is learning his idiolect through listening to his dreams, images, and associations. So the analyst both learns to speak in a way the patient can understand, and refuses to play the role that she is asked to play in his fantasy world. The analytic process is sometimes described as giving the patient more choice. Before, he did not know what he was doing; now that he does, he can, for the first time, choose whether to go on doing it. But, as Jonathan Lear (1993) points out, this misdescribes the process: when one sees that what one had taken as just the way things are is instead one's own way of looking at the world, "just the way things are" can no longer survive as simply that. This world collapses. It is replaced by a space for thinking about the way things are.

The claim that all experiences are equally subjective—though trivially true—has the effect of flattening, for the analyst, the distinctions she needs between the publicly available and the privately constructed. The claim can also lead to confusions about the nature of empathy, which I understand as the ability, temporarily, to experience the world more-or-less as another does, not by forgetting the other's particular vantage point but precisely by having a good sense of it, at the same time as one holds on to one's own perceptions and one's own methodology for testing them, a methodology that in the broadest sense is the same as the patient's. The patient's fantasies are fantasies because he does not, or refuses to, query them in the way we query, at least when the occasion arises, our fully conscious belief and desires. If the analyst treats all the patient's convictions as having equal validity among themselves, and with her own, she, in effect, colludes with him in keeping his fantasies untested (Grossman, 1996); she is in no position to point out that some of his convictions conflict with his own beliefs, and also with his own understanding of what gives a belief validity, which is not its actual truth (this is always open to question) but his having submitted it to dialogue, with another or himself. These are ways in which analyst and patient share a common methodology.

There are, of course, other forms of irrationality than unconscious fantasy; and all of them make sense only linked to the concepts of truth and falsity. Self-deception, for example, sometimes consists in allowing oneself to hold on to a belief in one part of one's mind, so to speak, that in another one thinks is false. Resistance sometimes consists in holding at bay a perception one fears may be true.

Where we are now

Why would anybody deny the homely view of truth, as the pragmatists Peirce, James, Dewey, and, recently, Rorty, have seemed to do? And why would many psychoanalysts, particularly those who count themselves as "relationalists" or as "intersubjectivists", have jumped on the pragmatist bandwagon? My remarks on the history of philosophy were an attempt to answer the first question by saying that the pragmatists were reacting to a view of meaning that ignores its roots in human interests, and holds that reason, divinely guided, can find certainty. We can call this truth with a capital T. Rorty, in particular, thinks we have to turn our backs on the philosophical tradition that thought of truth as correspondence with something outside the mind, something to which we do not have direct access. Showing how a theory of mind can banish truth as correspondence, and how that very theory must hold on to the concept of truth as defining the concepts of belief and mind, is something that cannot be done here. I hope to have given some idea of the lines the argument would take. (For a longer answer, see Davidson, 1984.)

The second question has to be set in the context of the very difficult problems now facing psychoanalysis. Viewing therapeutic change as to some extent brought about by new, collaborative constructions in the present rather than by accurate reconstructions of the past, seeing insight as a creating as much as a finding, psychoanalysts are confronted with some philosophical puzzles about what the self and self-discovery are. And in the course of questioning many of the hypotheses Freud thought definitive of his "science" (among them, drive theory and the centrality of the Oedipal complex), psychoanalysts have generated a plurality of theories, some of which are clearly incompatible with each other. In thinking about the important question, "what is it this particular patient is warding off?", for example, the analyst has to make some choices, as she does also in sorting through the various competing theories, both about the mind and about how it can change through therapy.

In his discontent with the imperfections of human knowledge, Descartes turned away from the external world. He replaced external objects and real other minds with internal objects that we can know, he thought, for sure. The "two-person" psychology of the intersubjectivists is at war with old-fashioned (Cartesian) authoritarianism. It insists that what matters to us is not some timeless other world, but the human here-and-now. Yet, interestingly, to say that "reality" refers only to something "subjective" is just the "about-face" that Descartes made. And it suggests, with Descartes, that if we play our cards right, we need no longer be troubled that another person, or the future, may prove us wrong.

If we cannot get rid of truth, then we cannot abandon the sorts of questions that a concern with truth asks, like: What evidence is there to think that a particular theory is true? Is it compatible with something else we hold true? Are you and I perhaps both deluded, or thinking wishfully? As Glen Gabbard has recently pointed out (1997), the question of analytic "objectivity" is not without its clinical implications. My guess is that in their practice, most psychoanalysts honour the distinctions between justified belief and true belief, also between what works and what is the case. These distinctions call, however, for a different account of truth than the one some psychoanalysts have championed, often in the name of openness to other points of view. There is talk now of the way in which analyst and patient "co-construct reality". Each of us constructs a picture of reality. Reality is what keeps pulling us back to the drawing board.

Note

1. Ferenczi was on to a similar idea in "Stages in the development of the sense of reality" (1956). In the third, he says, the infant learns that some of its wants will be answered if it makes the right signals. Putting Ferenczi's point in another way: what is initially a cry without meaning to the crier becomes meaningful to him in part through the behaviour it produces in another.

References

Aron, L. (1996). *A Meeting of Minds, Mutuality in Psychoanalysis.* Hillsdale, NJ: Analytic Press.

Bion, W. R. (1962). The psycho-analytic study of thinking. *International Journal of Psychoanalysis, 43:* 306–310.

Britton, R. (1989). The missing link: parental sexuality in the Oedipus complex. In: J. Steiner (Ed.), *The Oedipus Complex Today* (pp. 83–101). London: Karnac.

Cavell, M. (1993). *The Psychoanalytic Mind. From Freud to Philosophy.* Cambridge, MA: Harvard University Press.

Davidson, D. (1984). *Inquiries into Truth and Interpretation.* Oxford: Clarendon Press.

Davidson, D. (1989). The conditions of thought. In: J. Brandl & W. L. Gombocz (Eds.), *The Mind of Donald Davidson* (pp. 193–205). Amsterdam: Rodopi.

Davidson, D. (1992). The second person. *Midwest Studies in Philosophy, XVII:* 255–267.

Evans, G. (1982). *The Varieties of Reference.* Oxford: Oxford University Press.

Ferenczi, S. (1956). Stages in the development of the sense of reality. In: C. Newton (Trans.), *Sex in Psychoanalysis* (pp. 213–239). New York: Dover.

Fogel, G. I., Tyson, P., Greenberg, J., McLaughlin, J. T., & Peyser, E. R. (1996). A classic revisited: Loewald on the therapeutic action of psychoanalysis. *Journal of the American Psychoanalytic Association., 44:* 863–924.

Fonagy, P. (1989). On tolerating mental states: theory of mind in borderline personality. *Bulletin of the Anna Freud Centre, 12:* 91–115.

Freud, S. (1895). *Project for a Scientific Psychology. S.E., 1:* 283–398. London: Hogarth.

Freud, S. (1900a). *The Interpretation of Dreams. S.E., 4–5.* London: Hogarth.

Freud, S. (1915e). The unconscious. *S.E., 14:* 159–204. London: Hogarth.

Freud, S. (1940a [1938]). *An Outline of Psycho-analysis. S.E., 23:* 141–208. London: Hogarth.

Gabbard, G. O. (1997). A reconsideration of objectivity in the analyst. *International Journal of Psychoanalysis, 78:* 15–27.

Green, A. (1993). *On Private Madness.* Madison, WI: International Universities Press.

Grossman, L. (1996). Psychic reality and psychic testing. *International Journal of Psychoanalysis, 77*: 508–517.

Hoffman, I. Z. (1983). The patient as interpreter of the analyst's experience. *Contemporary Psychoanalysis, 19*: 389–422.

Lear, J. (1993). An interpretation of transference. *International Journal of Psychoanalysis, 74*: 739–755.

Mead, G. H. (1934). *Mind Self and Society, Vol. I.* Chicago, IL: University of Chicago Press.

Mitchell, S. A. (1988). *Relational Concepts in Psychoanalysis, An Integration.* Cambridge, MA: Harvard University Press.

Modell, A. H. (1990). *Other Times, Other Realities.* Cambridge, MA: Harvard University Press.

Ogden, T. H. (1994). *Subjects of Analysis.* Hillsdale, NJ: Jason Aronson.

Polanyi, M. (1958). *Personal Knowledge.* Chicago, IL: University of Chicago Press.

Rorty, R. (1979). *Philosophy and the Mirror of Nature.* Princeton, NJ: Princeton University Press.

Rorty, R. (1997). Davidson between Wittgenstein and Tarski (unpublished).

Spezzano, C. (1993). *Affect in Psychoanalysis, A Clinical Synthesis.* Hillsdale, NJ: Jason Aronson.

Stern, D. (1984). *The Interpersonal World of the Infant: A View from Psychoanalysis and Developmental Psychology.* New York: Basic Books.

Stern, D. (1995). *The Motherhood Constellation: A Unified View of Parent–Infant Psychiatry.* New York: Basic Books.

Stolorow, R., & Atwood, G. (1992). *Contexts of Being.* Hillsdale, NJ: Analytic Press.

Strawson, P. F. (1963). *Individuals, an Essay in Descriptive Metaphysics.* New York: Anchor Books.

Vygotsky, L. S. (1962). *Thought and Language,* E. Hanfmann & G. Vakar (Trans.). Cambridge, MA: MIT Press.

Wertsch, J. V. (1985). *Vygotsky and the Social Formation of Mind.* Cambridge, MA: Harvard University Press.

Winnicott, D. W. (1971). *Playing and Reality.* New York: Basic Books.

Wittgenstein, L. (1953). *Philosophical Investigations,* G. E. Anscombe (Ed.). Oxford: Blackwell.

Wittgenstein, L. (1972). *On Certainty,* G. E. Anscombe (Trans.). Oxford: Blackwell.

CHAPTER FOUR

Subjectivity, objectivity, and triangular space*

Ronald Britton

T he author reviews his ideas on subjectivity, objectivity, and the third position in the psychoanalytic encounter, particularly in clinical work with borderline and narcissistic patients. Using the theories of Melanie Klein and Wilfred Bion as a basis, the author describes his concept of triangular space. A case presentation of a particular type of narcissistic patient illustrates the principles discussed.

The acknowledgement by the child of the parents' relationship with each other unites his psychic world, limiting it to one world shared with his two parents in which different object relationships can exist. The closure of the Oedipal triangle by the recognition of the link joining the parents provides a limiting boundary for the internal world. It creates what I call a "triangular space", that is, a space bounded by the three persons of the Oedipal situation and all their potential relationships. It includes, therefore, the possibility of being a participant in a relationship and observed by a third person as well as being an observer of a relationship between two people. . . .

* First published in 2004 in *Psychoanalytic Quarterly*, 73: 47–61.

If the link between the parents perceived in love and hate can be tolerated in the child's mind, it provides him with a prototype for an object relationship of a third kind in which he is a witness and not a participant. A third position then comes into existence from which object relationships can be observed. Given this, we can also envisage being observed. This provides us with a capacity for seeing ourselves in interaction with others and for entertaining another point of view whilst retaining our own, for reflecting on ourselves whilst being ourselves. This is a capacity we hope to find in ourselves and in our patients in analysis. [Britton, 1989, pp. 86–87][1]

Treatment of borderline and narcissistic disorders

The theorizing that underlies these comments came from my experiences with borderline patients, from whom this capacity had been missing for long periods of time. Green (1997) sees borderline disorder and hysteria as distinct, and also makes the point—with which I agree—that borderline disorder is not a larval psychotic state. As will be evident from this paper, I regard the borderline syndrome as a particular form of narcissistic disorder, one that I characterize as hypersubjective or "thin skinned" (Rosenfeld, 1987, p. 274). It has gradually become evident to me that what is missing in these cases is the third position described above.

I came to realize that my efforts to consult my analytic self were detected by such patients and experienced as a form of internal intercourse on my part that corresponded to parental intercourse. This, they felt, threatened their very existence. The only way I could find a place to think that was helpful and not disruptive was to allow an evolution of my own experience within me, and to articulate this to myself, while communicating to the patient my understanding of the patient's point of view. The possibility of my communicating with a third object was unthinkable, and so the third position I refer to was untenable. In such cases, the third object could be my theories, links with colleagues, or the residue of previous analytic experience.

As a consequence, it seemed impossible to sufficiently disentangle myself from the to-and-fro of the interaction to know what was going on. Any move toward objectivity could not be tolerated.

Analyst and patient were to move along a single line and meet at a single point; there was to be no lateral movement. A sense of space could be achieved only by increasing the distance between us, a process such patients find impossible to bear unless they initiate it. In such situations, what I felt I needed desperately was a place in my mind that I could step into sideways from which I could look out at things. If I tried to force myself into such a position by asserting a description of the patient in my own terms, violence would follow—always psychically, and sometimes also physically.

Triangular space

The crucial importance of the three persons of the psychic triangle has been emphasized by psychoanalysts of other schools and in other countries, particularly in France, notably by McDougall (1971), Chasseguet-Smirgel (1984), and Green (1997). In America, also, it is addressed by some of the writers on intersubjectivity. That ideas derived from psychoanalytic practice based on the theoretical background of the British Kleinian school could lead to similar preoccupations and illuminations as those from the French school and from the USA encourages me to think that we might be addressing a clinical reality that transcends country, culture, and theoretical framework.

The influence of primary relationships

I personally arrived at the idea of triangular space and the third position from particular clinical experiences, and my theorizing was based essentially on Klein's (1928) concept of the early Oedipal situation and Bion's (1959, 1962a,b) theory of containment. Bion described the consequences for some individuals of a failure of maternal containment as the development of a destructive, envious superego, which prevents them from learning or pursuing profitable relations with any object. He made it clear that the inability of the mother to take in her child's projections is experienced by the child as a destructive attack by her on the child's link and communication with her as the good object.

I suggest that the idea of a good maternal object can then be regained only by splitting off the mother's perceived hostility to linkage and attributing it to a hostile force. Such a force was represented in various religions of the ancient world by "chaos monsters": in ancient Egypt, it was Apophis, who was "an embodiment of primordial chaos. He had no sense-organs, he could neither hear nor see, he could only scream. And he operated always in darkness" (Cohn, 1993, p. 21). Apophis continually threatened *ma'at*, the female personification of order in the world. Mother as the source of goodness, like *ma'at*, is now precarious and depends on the child's restricting his or her knowledge of her. Enlargement of knowledge of the mother as a consequence of development and of the child's curiosity are felt to menace this crucial relationship. Curiosity discloses the existence of the Oedipal situation. The hostile force that was thought to attack the child's original link with the mother is now equated with the Oedipal father, and the link between the parents is felt to destroy her as a source of goodness and order.

I am suggesting, therefore, that the problem has its origins in the relationship to the primary maternal object in cases where there is a failure to establish an unequivocally good experience of the infant—mother interaction to contrast with the bad experience of being deprived of it. Instead of the natural, primary split of predepressive development, there is confusion. To arrest the confusion, an arbitrary split in mental life is imposed to enshrine the notion of good and to locate and segregate the bad. The essential structure of the Oedipal situation lends itself to splitting of this kind. This can give rise to the misleading appearance of being a classical, positive Oedipus complex based on rivalry with mother for the love of father. The transference tells another tale. The familiar, split nature of the positive Oedipal configuration—usually used to separate love and hate—in these cases provides a structure to segregate desire for subjective understanding and love from the wish for objective knowledge and a shared intellectual identity. I have come to regard these as the characteristics of narcissistic and borderline disorders.

Subjectivity and objectivity

Here I am using subjective to mean the first-person point of view and objective as the third-person point of view. The philosopher

John R. Searle (1995) distinguishes objectivity used as third-person description, which he calls ontological objectivity, from the use of the word to denote dispassionate judgement, which he calls epistemic objectivity. In this sense, it is the integration of ontological subjectivity with ontological objectivity that for some patients provokes catastrophic anxiety.

Rey (1979) described narcissistic syndromes as "a certain kind of personality disorder which defied classification into the two great divisions of neurosis and psychosis. We now know them as borderline, narcissistic, or schizoid personality organization" (p. 203). What sufferers of these various syndromes have in common is that they cannot, at least initially, function in analysis in an ordinary way, because they cannot form an ordinary transference relationship. Some remain aloof and detached; others are adherent, clamorous, and concrete in their transference attachment. But in neither of these is the analyst experienced as both significant and separate.

It was Abraham (1919) who discovered that some individuals who were not psychotic or manifestly unco-operative were extremely difficult to analyse because they did not, or could not, use the method of free association, nor could they expose their subjective experience. Rosenfeld (1987) described such patients as "thick-skinned narcissistic" individuals, in contrast to "thin-skinned narcissistic" ones. In a book published just after his death, he wrote that there are those patients

... whose narcissistic structure provides them with such a "thick skin" that they have become insensitive to deeper feelings. ... To avoid impasse these patients have to be treated in analysis very firmly. ... When interpretations at last manage to touch them they are relieved, even if it is painful to them. ... By contrast ... the thin-skinned patients are hypersensitive and easily hurt in everyday life and analysis. Moreover, when the sensitive narcissistic patient is treated in analysis as if he is the thick-skinned patient, he will be severely traumatized. [p. 274]

What I have suggested (Britton, 1998) is that these two clinical states are the result of two different relationships of the subjective self to the third object of the internal Oedipus triangle. In both states, the third object is alien to the subjective, sensitive self. In the hypersubjective, the self seeks to avoid the objectivity of the third object and clings to subjectivity. The hyperobjective patient identifies with the third object and adopts a mode of objectivity, renouncing subjectivity.

What is quickly revealed in both cases is that analysis is a major problem for such a patient—and for the patient's analyst. Being in analysis is a problem-that is, being in the same room, the same mental space. Instead of there being two connected, independent minds, there are either two separate people unable to connect or two people with only one mind. These two situations could not be more different from each other in analysis. What patients in both situations have in common, however, is the inability to function in an ordinary way and terror of the integration of separate minds.

In one group, the other is treated as of no significance; in the second group, the patient cannot commune without making the significant other an extension of him- or herself. In the first situation, the analyst cannot find a place within the psychic reality of the patient, while in the second, the analyst cannot find a place outside it. The first is hyperobjective, with narcissistic detachment, and the second is hypersubjective with narcissistic adherence.

Hyperobjectivity and narcissistic detachment:
thick-skinned patients

A case presentation follows in which the analyst was an outsider, that is, outside the subjective interaction with the object of desire and identified with an objective observer. The patient, Mr B, was a successful writer who sought psychoanalysis after a period of marital therapy, at the suggestion of the marital therapist and with the prompting of his wife. After telling me this, he added with disarming frankness that his problem was intimacy: "I am no good at intimate relations, my wife tells me, and I'm sure she's right." He also let me know in the consultation that he suffered from depression of a kind in which he would awaken sick with a sense of terror and despair about his own uselessness and life in general.

When Mr B was young and still religious, he had believed that he was damned and beyond redemption, and that the usual religious remedies of confession, contrition, and so on would not work for him. When I suggested that he might feel the same way about analysis, he quickly agreed that he could not imagine its helping or changing him in the slightest—"but I have to try it if you are willing to have a go," he added.

The problem of shared analytic space quickly asserted itself when Mr B arrived for his first session. We had agreed on a time, and he accepted the analytic convention, as he saw it, of lying on a couch for fifty minutes. But he conveyed that he could have co-operated equally willingly if I had suggested that he stand on his head for fifty minutes. "Enduring things," I suggested, "is something you know you can do without their having any effect on you." He agreed with this, offering several convincing examples from his childhood of his fortitude's having protected him from being changed by regimes inflicted on him.

Once we got underway, the problem was mine. Although I could understand him without too much difficulty, I could not find a means of sharing Mr B's mental space, of getting into contact with him. I was the outsider in this analysis. The patient would claim that he was not really involved in the analysis; he sympathized with me for having to endure such an unappreciative patient, when presumably, I would like to be thought important and to have my ideas appreciated. My needs, therefore, were worth his consideration, but he could not do anything about them. Pity was what he offered me as a decrepit old man whom he once described as the "West Hampstead worm".

I was not empty minded, however, outside the realm of his attention. Mr B had a gift for communicating to me what difficulties faced him and what anxieties troubled him, so that I was vividly aware of his very real suffering. If I drew attention to these, he politely scoffed at me for taking them seriously. He would then leave the session on an upbeat note of "Begone, dull cares," and with a wave, would say, "See you tomorrow." I was left, in other words, holding the baby.

This applied also to the patient's memories: to his recollections of cruel experiences, his revelations of painful humiliations and considerable deprivation. He treated my opinion that he had suffered an unhappy childhood as eccentric. If I then reminded him of recollections he had disclosed in the previous session, he would quickly say that he had a terrible memory and forgot everything from one day to another. So I was the only one who now knew of the existence of the suffering child.

My patient had gone missing. When I suggested to Mr B that he had emptied his experiential self into me and then left the two of us behind, he responded by describing a story he had written. Although it had another title, he said that it "could have been entitled 'The Story of a Missing Person'." In the story, someone was exploring a residence and could not establish whether anyone lived there or not. An outline of the missing person's life and attendant details were visible as traces left behind, but there was no presence. The essence of the story was that of emptiness shaped by absence, the shape of a missing person.

In analysis, as in his marriage, absence appeared to solve the problem of presence for Mr B. However, it required a place from which to be absent. In order to be an absentee husband, one needs a wife; to be an absentee patient, one needs an analyst; to be a runaway, one needs a home to run away from. And to have a missed session, one needs to have a session arranged.

Largely through the use of my countertransference as a source of information about my missing patient, we were able to get some idea of the problems that led to Mr B's psychic retreat to the periphery of his life. I found that, although I retained my usual analytic position of receptivity and enquiry, I could not achieve my customary sense of significance. I would be tempted to insert myself into my patient's field of psychic vision by assuming a role already assigned to me, often that of a coach or friendly critic. The price to be paid in the countertransference for remaining in my own psychic sphere was a sense of insignificance and loneliness. It was not difficult to see that this had been my patient's experience in the past and in his present working life, where he felt that he functioned on the rim of the world.

As a child, Mr B had found a hideaway where he could be unknown to his family. His dreams made clear how significant this secret space was; it became the forerunner of other private spaces, culminating in the creation of the study where he worked. Here, he created in his writing his own versions of himself and placed these replicas in a variety of contexts of his own choosing, which accurately mirrored his internal world. And a bleak and lonely place it usually was. I was to get inside knowledge of this forlorn terrain because it was where he placed me in the analysis. We met there, eventually, in a shared, moorland-like mental landscape that to me felt reminiscent of the place where Wordsworth (1904) met the leech gatherer when driven to despair by Coleridge's "Ode to Dejection". My impression was that the patient benefited from his analysis, and certainly he prospered; I would have liked to think that our encounters may have had a therapeutic effect on him similar to that which Wordsworth ascribed to the leech gatherer: ". . . to find / In that decrepit Man so firm a mind" (p. 157).

What I think we learned in the analysis was the reason for Mr B's self-exclusion. It protected him from being misperceived, or, in Bion's (1959, 1962a,b) terms, from being the contained that would be moulded into the container's definition of a self. On the edge, the patient could define himself as the outsider, as the man who would not fit in. The cost of this identity was exclusion. The passport to inclusion was to be defined by the other's presuppositions and preconceptions; the price for entry into the mind of the other was to be misperceived. The sacrifice to be made to secure a place indoors was to be caged within the limiting framework of the other's comprehension.

Hypersubjectivity and narcissistic adherence

What clinically characterizes this group of cases is their difficulty. These patients find life with others difficult; they find tolerating themselves difficult; they find being in analysis difficult; and, in a characteristic way, their analysts find working with them difficult. When analysts bring such cases for consultation, they almost always begin by saying, "I want to talk about my difficult patient," or "I seem to have particular difficulty with this case." It is often accompanied by a sense of shame in the analyst, who feels that he or she has either let the patient down, or has become involved in a collusive analysis in a way that is hard to acknowledge to colleagues.

Of course, many patients pose considerable technical and countertransference problems, but the characteristic problem that leads analysts to use the word difficult with such emphasis is of a particular kind. It is the way that the analytic method itself is felt by the patient to be a threat, by virtue of its structure, method, and boundaries. The corollary of that in the analyst is a feeling of inability to properly establish an analytic setting. This impasse has been used by some analysts to promote as a superior analytic method an alternative strategy, which, in reality, was dictated by the patient as a necessary condition. This, I think, corresponds to the patient's belief, secret or not, that his or her atypical method of growing up was a more authentic way, and that those who were ordinary children (and who become more tractable analytic patients) are either victims of oppression or are collaborators.

While working empathically with the patient and validating his or her subjective experience in a way that the patient finds helpful, the analyst may begin to feel like a mother who does not really exist in her own right. The patient becomes reliant on this function and on the analyst as this receptive figure, but the analyst fears a loss of his or her own analytic identity. If, however, the analyst asserts him- or herself and produces objectively based interpretations, the patient will feel persecuted, leading either to masochistic submission or an explosion. The patient will then, one way or another, eliminate what the analyst says or eradicate those elements of difference in it. The patient may feel the need to remove his or her mind from the analyst's presence by psychic withdrawal, and some patients even find it necessary to remove their bodies in order to remove their minds, thus breaking off the analysis. Such individuals are inclined to leave one analyst or to stay in an impasse with another; the risks are of analytic abortion or interminable analysis. Subjective and objective realities are believed to be more than simply incompatible—in fact, to be mutually destructive.

Objectivity appears to be associated with visual gaze. There is a fear of being seen, just as there is a fear of being described. A child with such problems in psychoanalytic psychotherapy serves well as an example because of the directness of the exchange with the psychotherapist. In a case I supervised, a seven-year-old girl was clearly very persecuted simply by being in the therapist's room, screaming whenever he tried to speak. Eventually, with the therapist's help, she managed to make it clear to him that if she blindfolded and gagged him so that he could not see or speak, but could only listen, then she would talk to him. When he was able to say to her that she believed his words would spoil and mess up her thoughts, she burst out, "They will, they will! So shut up!"

Such situations in their adult versions can evoke existential anxieties in the analyst because empathic identification with the patient seems incompatible with the analyst's objective clinical view of the situation and belief about what is necessary. Therefore, the analyst feels cut off from the theories that link him or her to colleagues and that bestow a professional identity. This problem also manifests in the analyst's difficulty in using general experience or general ideas, since such use appears to intrude on the singularity of the encounter with this particular patient and the uniqueness of the patient's psychology. Particularity seems to be at war with generality in much the same way that subjectivity is with objectivity. In terms of the figures of the Oedipal triangle, one might say that, when the analyst is able to follow and enhance the patient's emergent thoughts, he or she is identified as an understanding maternal object; but when introducing thoughts of his or her own, derived from general experience and analytic theories, the analyst is identified as a father who is either intruding into the patient's innermost self, or pulling the patient out of a unique, subjective psychic context into one of the analyst's own.

So, we have a defensively organized Oedipal situation, with the fantasy of a totally empathic, passively understanding, maternal object, juxtaposed to an aggressive, paternal figure who is objectivity personified, seeking to impose meaning. While this defensive organization of the Oedipal triangle is maintained, it guarantees that reintegration will never take place between the understanding object and the misunderstanding object—which would result, it is believed, in the annihilation of understanding.

In this hypersubjective mode, the positive transference expresses its energy not by penetration but by extrapolation. Its intensity is conveyed by extension. It encompasses the object and invests everything it covers with heightened significance. The physical person of the analyst—and, by extension, the contextual details of the analysis—are given great importance, including the minutiae of sessions, the analytic office and its contents, and so on. Patients may collect and retain physical remnants of the analysis, such as bills or paper tissues, which serve a function similar to that of religious relics.

The negative transference is equated with a penetrating third object, while feeling understood is attributed to the primary object. Both positive and negative transferences are at play: one craved and sought after, and the other dreaded and evaded. The desired transference is skin-deep and enveloping. Its epistemological mode

is empathy, its physical expression is touch, and its emotional qualities are erotic or aesthetic. What is dreaded most is the conjunction
of the encompassing transference with the penetrating transference—that is, of subjectivity with objectivity.

Malignant misunderstanding and the need for agreement

In Chapter Four of *Belief and Imagination* (Britton, 1998), I explored
the mental catastrophe that is anticipated as following the integration of two different points of view. From the transference, it seems
that the basic fear is of malignant misunderstanding. By this, I
mean an experience of being so misunderstood, in such a fundamental and powerful way, that one's experience of oneself would
be eliminated, and correspondingly, the possibility of the self's
establishment of meaning would be annihilated.

This represents, I think, the fear of a return to primordial chaos,
which corresponds to Bion's (1959, 1962b) notion of nameless
dread, which he posits as following a failure of containment. Bion
gives two accounts of the production of nameless dread from a failure of maternal containment in infancy. In both of these, the uncom-
prehended becomes the incomprehensible. One could say that there
is a dread of the namelessness of everything. If this failure of understanding is experienced in early infancy as an attack rather than as
a deficiency, a force is believed to exist that destroys understanding
and eliminates meaning. One sees this repeated in the transference,
when the failure of the analyst to precisely understand the patient
is experienced by the patient not simply as a deficiency of the
analyst, but as an attack on the patient's psychic integrity.

When there is a desire for understanding coupled with a dread
of misunderstanding, there is also an insistent, desperate need for
agreement in the analysis and the annihilation of disagreement. I
have come to believe that a general rule arises from anxiety about
misunderstanding, which applies in all analyses: it is that the need
for agreement is inversely proportional to the expectation of understanding. When expectation of understanding is high, a difference
of opinion is tolerable; when expectation of understanding is fairly
high, difference is fairly tolerable; and when there is no expectation
of understanding, the need for agreement is absolute.

Conclusion

Psychic atopia

I have asked myself these questions: Is there something in the temperament of some individuals that predisposes them to this particular development or response to trauma? Is there anything in the endowment of these persons that might encourage them to believe that an independently existing object will destructively misunderstand them? Is there an innate factor in the infant that increases the risk of a failure of maternal containment, and, if so, what might it be?

In reply to these questions, I suggest that there may be an allergy to the products of other minds, analogous to the body's immune system—a kind of psychic atopia. The immune system is central to our physiological integrity and functioning; we cannot survive without it, and yet it is often the source of pathology. Is the same true of our psychic functioning? It certainly appears to be so in our social functioning, where the annihilation of the perceived alien is commonplace. The not-me or not-like-me recognition and response might fulfil a psychic function similar to that in the somatic. And just as the immune system sometimes makes for physiological trouble between mothers and babies, as in the familiar rhesus incompatibility problem, so, perhaps, might there be troublesome psychic immunity responses. Are there psychic allergies and is there sometimes a kind of psychic autoimmunity?

In the realm of ideas and understanding, we do seem to behave as though we have a psychic immune system. We are fearful about our ability to maintain the integrity of our existing belief systems, and whenever we encounter foreign psychic material, a xenocidal impulse is stimulated. Psychoanalysis made possible by the establishment of a shared mental space both exposes these difficulties and provides an opportunity to explore them.

Notes

1. This passage is from a paper read at a conference on "The Oedipus Complex Today" at University College London, in September 1987.

References

Abraham, K. (1919). A particular form of neurotic resistance against the psycho-analytic method. In: D. Bryan & A. Strachey (Eds.), *Selected Papers of Karl Abraham* (pp. 303–311). London: Hogarth, 1973.

Bion, W. R. (1959). Attacks on linking. In: *Second Thoughts* (pp. 93–109). New York: Aronson, 1967.

Bion, W. R. (1962a). A theory of thinking. In: *Second Thoughts* (pp. 110–119). New York: Aronson, 1967.

Bion, W. R. (1962b). *Learning from Experience*. London: Karnac, 1984.

Britton, R. (1989). The missing link: parental sexuality in the Oedipus complex. In: J. Steiner (Ed.), *The Oedipus Complex Today* (pp. 83–101). London: Karnac.

Britton, R. (1998). *Belief and Imagination*. London: Routledge.

Chasseguet-Smirgel, J. (1984). *Creativity and Perversion*. New York: Norton.

Cohn, N. (1993). *Cosmos, Chaos and the World to Come*. New Haven, CT: Yale University Press.

Green, A. (1997). Chiasmus: prospective—borderlines viewed after hysteria; retrospective—hysteria viewed after borderlines. *Psychoanalysis in Europe, Bulletin 48*(Spring): 39–42.

Klein, M. (1928). Early stages of the Oedipus conflict. *International Journal of Psychoanalysis*, 9: 167–180.

McDougall, J. (1971). Primal scene and sexual perversion. *International Journal of Psychoanalysis*, 53: 371–384.

Rey, H. (1979). Schizoid phenomena in the borderline. In: E. Spillius (Ed.), *Melanie Klein Today, Vol. 1* (pp. 197–223). London: Routledge, 1988.

Rosenfeld, H. A. (1987). *Impasse and Interpretation*. London: Routledge.

Searle, J. R. (1995). The mystery of consciousness: Part II. In: *The New York Review of Books*, 42(18): 4–61, 16 November.

Wordsworth, W. (1904). *Wordsworth Poetical Works*. Oxford: Oxford University Press, 1969.

PART II
TRIANGULATION IN THE TEMPORAL DIMENSION

Introduction

This part of the book brings together two papers by the author which are concerned with looking at how triangulation as a concept can help us be more generalized about thinking about a patient's experience and about the means by which we can observe this experience. The first paper looks at the use of standardized psychometric questionnaires, which were used to establish an audit of a primary care service. This audit was essentially about effectiveness of treatment. Could it be shown that reliable and lasting change had been brought about in a treatment? To do this, measures were set in train to collect the views of the patient, their psychotherapist, and someone who was known and trusted by the patient. Thus, three data points were established and information collected from each simultaneously over the period of the treatment.

The second paper looks at the psychoanalytical treatment from the point of view of it being an iterative learning system. Its iterative quality means that various mathematical analyses can be made of it to show that this iterative quality has the potential to bring about disturbances to the system under consideration and to create disturbances that must somehow be contained by the treatment. It proposes that any psychotherapeutic treatment must have the potential to both disturb and contain.

Using the iterative quality of the psychoanalytical learning system brings in triangulation, but this time not in a solely spatial sense, but in a temporal sense as well. It also sets the stage for thinking about the qualities of the system in which there is input from the analytic exchange and output reflecting learning in both the psychoanalyst and the analysand. In addition, there is the quality of presence and absence of party from the other which forms an essential feature contributing to the power of iteration.

CHAPTER FIVE

Consultation or assessment: engagement and treatment decisions in psychotherapy with young people in a community-based setting*

James S. Rose

Introduction

I am going to address in this paper an apparent dichotomy, antinomy, or paradox in how we think about the first encounter between a patient and a psychotherapist in the primary care setting. This dichotomy concerns our priority: to what extent are we assessing and to what extent are we offering a consultation. We have to find a balance, in the time available, between making a diagnostic decision with all the associated resource implications and helping the individual understand whatever it was that brought them to see us. To do this, we have to find a way of blending the nomothetic with the idiographic (Meehl, 1954). By the nomothetic is meant the search for general laws or propositions governing individuals within a particular category or class. The idiographic refers to the description of the individual case or

---

* Paper read to the City University Counselling Service Conferene entitled "Therapeutic consultations with students", 3 July 1998.

experience. In seeking to understand the variance among data sources, there is usually some residual variance written off as error by the nomothetic endeavour. To the idiographic endeavour, on the other hand, this so-called error is what makes the individual an individual. The consequence is that finding a blend of the two can seem like mixing chalk and cheese or comparing apples with an orange.

I am going to focus on the first point of contact between someone seeking help and a psychotherapist offering help. The actual situation in the process of contact and engagement is complex, as described by Wilson (1991) and Baruch (1997). However, in part it may be contended that, in such a situation, there are usually three players. This trio comprises the patient, the provider of help and the provider of the resources that enable the first two to meet. This situation potentially entails a tension between the patient, who has only themselves to be concerned about, the provider of help, who is going to have to keep both the patient and other patients in mind, and the provider of resources, who will be concerned with the delivery of services to all actual and potential patients. This tension will inevitably create an antinomy. The question is whether this is essentially irresolvable. This situation marks a profound difference with private practice in that, because the seeker of help and the provider of resources are usually, but of course not always, identical, the discourse between the seeker and the provider becomes potentially timeless.

It seems to me that the words consultation and assessment preclude the notion of a timeless encounter. Assessment relies essentially on observation. Consultation goes beyond that to a time of understanding on the part of both patient and professional and potentially a moment of conclusion. It can be thought that the existence of the trio identified above somehow "degrades" the quality of the encounter between the patient and the professional. However, it will be argued in this paper that the recognition of the trio offers an open system whereas the duo runs the risk of being timeless, endless and closed.

Essentially, the point I will be seeking to make in this paper is that the linking of the processes of assessment and consultation in a community-based setting provides a means of monitoring the extent of closure and openness in a patient's psycho-pathology which is of practical, theoretical, and clinical significance. How do these ideas find any practical expression in the settings in which we work?

Background

This paper focuses on the engagement and maintenance of troubled young people in psychotherapy and will use clinical experience gained and data obtained from the audit of the psychotherapy service at the Brandon Centre (formerly the London Youth Advisory Centre) in Kentish Town in London. The audit was introduced by the present director, Dr G. Baruch; the details of its introduction, the audit procedure, and some preliminary findings are presented in Baruch (1995). A considerable amount of further information is contained in Baruch, Fearon, and Gerber (1998), which discusses findings from the evaluation of mental health outcome.

The Centre is a charitable organization that has existed for over thirty years. It was started as a contraceptive service for young women aged twelve to twenty-five years during the 1960s. The founder, Dr Faith Spicer, recognized that young women needed to have access to a service that allowed them time to talk through emotional issues that accompanied requests for contraception. Shortly after the founding of the contraceptive service, an information service and a psychotherapy service were initiated for young women and young men due to the scale of the emotional needs of young people in the local community, which reached beyond the psychosexual. These services were made accessible by allowing self-referral and confidentiality, by providing comfortable, welcoming, and "non-institutional premises" in the heart of the local community, and by receptionists being friendly without being intrusive. The contraceptive service quickly gained a reputation for working effectively with young women from dysfunctional backgrounds that put them at risk of unwanted pregnancy and sexually transmitted diseases. The Brandon Centre now offers a community-based referral and self-referral individual psychodynamic psychotherapy service for young people aged between twelve and twenty-five years. The Centre also acquired a reputation for imaginatively applying psychotherapeutic principles in devising innovative services for young people, especially high priority groups of young people, and in combining service delivery with audit and research, including the rigorous evaluation of mental health outcome.

I describe first something of the Brandon Centre, as an example of a community-based organization, in terms of

- the kinds of people who come to us;
- the kinds of difficulties that they bring;
- how we assess their difficulties;
- some results from comparing initial assessment with follow-up data as a means of tracking change.

I then look at three cases individually to demonstrate possible clinical uses of this information to inform assessment and treatment that form part of the discourse between patient and professional and lend meaning to the consultation.

The nature of the patient population

In terms of demographic details of the population that come to the Centre, a full description is given in Baruch (1995) and Baruch, Fearon, and Gerber (1998), which describes the approach adopted by the Centre to the issue of evaluating the outcome of the psychoanalytic psychotherapy service that is offered. In summary, Table 5.1 shows some basic characteristics of the population.

Table 5.2 shows the characteristics of young people who seek help at the Centre in terms of the assessment of their functioning; the kinds of chronic or immediate stresses they face and the diagnoses of their psychopathology in the assessment period. *Functioning* is assessed using the global assessment of functioning scale (GAF). The therapist rates the adolescent's level of functioning on scale from 1 to 100. *Stresses* (*chronic and immediate*) are assessed using the severity of social stressors scale (SPS). *Diagnoses of psychopathology* are made according to ICD-10. Fuller details are given in Baruch (1995).

The point to be made by these tables is to show that the population coming to the Brandon Centre can be called clinically significant in so far as patients bring what are accepted generally as patterns of psychopathology needing treatment. This picture is

Table 5.1. Some demographic characteristics of young people at intake (*n* = 106).

Mean age, years	18.7 (3.2)
(standard deviation)	
12–16 years	29.2
17–21 years	44.5
22–25 years	26.3
Female	73.8
Male	26.2
Ethnic minorities	22.0
Living arrangement	
With single parent	36.8
With both parents	15.1
Alone	15.1
Co-habiting	9.4
Sharing	8.5
Hostel	7.5
Other	7.6
Occupation	
School	34.9
College/university and training	24.5
Employed	19.8
Unemployed	15.1
Other	5.7

confirmed by the young people themselves, both in the consultations with them and from the results of the standardized questionnaires which they complete.

Outcome measures

Also described in Baruch (1995) and Baruch, Fearon, and Gerber (1998) are the various diagnostic tools and outcome measures that are used.

All new patients who come to the Brandon centre are administered two modified versions of the Child Behaviour Checklist (CBCL) developed by Achenbach and Edelbrock (1986, 1987). The Youth Self Report Form (YSR) was designed for adolescents

Table 5.2.   Some clinical characteristics of young people at intake ($n = 106$).

Severity of psychosocial stressors scale (SPS):	%
1. No acute events or enduring circumstances	2.8
2. Mild events or enduring circumstances	7.5
3. Moderate events or enduring circumstances	20.8
4. Severe events or enduring circumstances	41.5
5. Extreme events or enduring circumstances	25.5
6. Catastrophic events or enduring circumstances	1.9

Global assessment of functioning scale (GAF)	%
10–19	2.8
20–29	1.9
30–39	7.3
40–49	20.2
50–59	38.7
60–69	24.4
70– (normal range)	4.7

ICD-10 diagnostic categories (frequencies)	
1. Neurotic, stress-related or somatoform disorder	66.0
2. Other mood disorder (depression or hypomania— single episode or persistent)	84.0
3. Hyperkinetic or conduct disorder	17.9
4. Specific developmental disorder	6.6
5. Other disorder with childhood onset (e.g., tics, mutism)	2.8
6. Substance abuse	33.9
7. Psychosis, organic syndrome, pervasive developmental disorder or mental handicap	8.4
8. Syndromes with physiological symptoms (eating, sleeping and sexual dysfunction)	48.2
9. (Adolescents or adults) personality disorder, disorder of gender identity or sexual orientation, habit/impulse disorder	42.4

Principal *ICD-10* diagnosis	
1. Neurotic, stress-related or somatoform disorder	21.7
2. Other mood disorder (depression or hypomania - single-episode or persistent)	37.8
3. Hyperkinetic or conduct disorder	11.3
4. Specific developmental disorder	—
5. Other disorder with childhood onset (e.g., tics, mutism)	—
6. Substance abuse	2.8

between eleven and eighteen years old. We have modified the form slightly to make it easier to fill out for young people who are not used to "American" English, and also to make it more appropriate for older adolescents. For instance, reference to "kids" was changed to "young people". The YSR presents the adolescent with 118 statements, which are rated according to whether the statement is not true, sometimes true, or very true/often true.

The Teacher's Report Form (TRF) was developed by Achenbach and Edelbrock, because teachers, next to parents, are usually the most important adults in children's lives, and also because school is a significant setting in which children exhibit normal and problem behaviours. We have modified this form, and called it the Significant Other Form (SOF). The SOF is filled out by a significant other: for instance a friend, parent, sibling, GP, or teacher chosen by the young person.

The great strength of these measures is the way they allow a wide range of adolescent disorders to be assessed. Eight syndrome scales have been empirically identified, each of which is associated with a cluster of items on the questionnaire and reflect a common theme such as anxiety/depression, aggression, etc. Norms for each syndrome scale, which take account of age and gender, have been calculated by Achenbach and Edelbrock from a carefully chosen sample designed to reflect a cross-section of the population of the USA. Using these norms, it is possible to assign a T-score to the raw scores of each scale, which indicates whether the young person is within the normal or the clinical range on a given syndrome scale. For the scales, a T-score of sixty-seven (the ninety-fifth percentile) is normally considered to mark the cut-off point between the normal and the clinical ranges.

The syndromes have also been banded together so that scores exist for the total of the internalizing scales (including withdrawn, somatic complaints and anxiety/ depression), the total of the externalizing scales (including aggressive behaviour and delinquent behaviour), and the total of all the scales. Norms have been calculated for these scales and the cut-off between the non-clinical and clinical populations is sixty. Figure 5.1 shows how these scores are presented graphically in the form of a chart showing a profile over the eight scales in relation to the cut-off between the clinical and non-clinical range.

Figure 5.1.   Graphical presentation of YSR profile scores on eight dimensions.

	Internalizing			YSR Profile — Boys 11–18			Externalizing		T Score
			31				21	37	
	17		30	15		17		36	
					13		20	35	95
	13	16	28	14			19	34	
		15	27			16		33	
				12			18		90
	12	14	26	13			17	31	
					15			30	
		13	24	12	11		16		85
			23			14	15	29	
		12	22	11				27	
					10		14		80
		11	20	10		13	13	26	
	10	10	19					25	
					9		12	24	75
%ILE		9	18	9		12	11	23	
			17					22	
98	9	8	16	8	8			21	70
	7		13		7	10	8	18	
93		6	12				7	17	65
	7		11	6		9		16	
	6	5	10	5			6	14	
84			9			8			60
			8		4	7	5	13	
	5	3	7	4					
69				3		7	4	11	55
	4		6	3		6		10	
		2	5			5	3	9	
50	0–3	0–1	0–4	0–2	0–2	0–4	0–2	0–8	50
	I	II	III	IV	V	VI	VII	VIII	
	WITHDRAWN	SOMATIC COMPLAINTS	ANXIOUS/ DEPRESSED	SOCIAL PROBLEMS	THOUGHT PROBLEMS	ATTENTION PROBLEMS	DELINQUENT BEHAVIOUR	AGGRESSIVE BEHAVIOUR	

One-week test–retest reliabilities have been calculated for the YSR syndromes and their totals. The correlation for the internalizing, externalizing, and total problems scales was very high ($r = 0.91$) (Achenbach, 1991a). The TRF fifteen-day test–retest reliabilities for these scales were also high, respectively, $r = 0.91$, $r = 0.92$, $r = 0.95$ (Achenbach, 1991b).

The CBCL has been widely praised in the literature as a highly reliable and valid means for assessing child and adolescent psychopathology, and is relatively easy to administer. Many researchers stress the difficulties, particularly in child and adolescent disorders, of assessing behaviours that are deviant only when seen in combination and when compared in severity with norms for their age and gender (King & Noshpitz, 1991). The CBCL solves this problem by basing its entire set of results on comparisons with appropriately matched norms. Verhulst and colleagues (1989) also point to the usefulness of the CBCL questionnaire in eliciting descriptions of behaviour from adolescents that they might not reveal in clinical interviews. The YSR is the only self-report questionnaire for adolescents that looks at a broad and meaningful range of disturbing behaviours and feelings, and organizes them into relevant disorders.

Our experience certainly bears out the views found in the literature. After looking at several self-report measures, and considering the possibility of finding an alternative to the YSR for older adolescents (19–25 year olds), we rejected the idea because we felt that the items were sufficiently close to the experiences of these young people, and, on the whole, would be meaningful to them. Generally, this has proved to be the case. There is now, however, a set of questionnaires appropriate for late adolescents and young adults. These are called the Young Adult Self Report Form (YASR) and the Young Adult Behaviour Checklist (YABCL).

The YSR is administered by the patient's therapist, who also gives the young person the SOF to be filled out by a significant other. The forms are administered to all new patients at the beginning of treatment (no later than the second appointment) with follow-ups after three months, six months, a year, and thereafter annually. If the young person has finished, or dropped out of, treatment, the forms are sent to her/him for completion. The therapist also fills out an SOF after three appointments; then, if the young person is in treatment, completes one after three months, six months, etc. This was introduced nine months after the study had started because we were worried about the rate of attrition of SOFs (Baruch, 1995).

We have now made several statistical analyses of data gathered because we have been doing this form of assessment for some years. The most significant finding is that significant and reliable change, or improvement in the clinical picture (in the statistical sense) is to be found for all three data collection sources. Furthermore, there is a correspondence between the patient's, the significant other's and the therapist's assessment, but the therapist tends to be more cautious than the other two. See Baruch, Fearon, and Gerber (1998) for a more detailed analysis of data based on a one-year follow-up after a young person first came for treatment.

The fact that the significant other observes reliable change means that the patient improvement is not purely illusory or a flight away from therapy into health (although this undoubtedly happens in some cases, as we will see). The fact that the psychotherapist is more cautious in his/her assessment of the situation *suggests* that in some cases *they may think* that such a flight is occurring, or (1) that in some cases the patient manages unconsciously to create an impression of greater disturbance than they themselves feel because they do not wish to leave the therapeutic situation; (2) that the therapeutic situation is managing to contain the patient's disturbance, which permits more balanced living outside the consulting room.

There is evidence that suggests that the follow-up questionnaires form part of the therapeutic dialogue so that the results *can* mean that where there is little evidence of any change, then it means that the patient does not wish to terminate the treatment and is apprehensive that the psychotherapist so wishes. *Thus, the questionnaire, when repeated, becomes part of the discourse between patient and psychotherapist.*

This means that the questionnaire becomes a means for the patient to express themselves to their therapist and, in so doing, make transference statements.

It could be objected that the implication of this is that the instruments lose their reliability and validity if scores on repeated testing are influenced in these circumstances by the relationship between therapist and patient. There are many possible hypotheses for the particular results for an individual patient. Very dependent patients seem to change very slowly, sometimes if at all. Very disturbed patients sometimes seem to hide their disturbance from themselves and their psychotherapists and change very suddenly and dramatically but, apparently, spuriously. There is variation in how these questionnaires are used in individual cases and this provides an invaluable backdrop for therapeutic work in the consulting room. However, in our view, this does not render the instrument scores statistically invalid. There is too much reliability and consistency within and between individual scores for this to be a criticism capable of questioning the validity of the statistical conclusions on outcome.

One of the most intriguing features of the Achenbach tests is that, while the test is both a statistically reliable and valid test when used to make comparative judgements with others, it seems to have the capacity to be used and interpreted clinically at the level of the individual. This feature is not, of course, unique, but it does offer a way of finding a bridge between the nomothetic and the idiographic modes referred to earlier.

I look now at three cases.

- A young woman suffering from anxiety and depressive reaction following the suicide of her mother. *Purpose*: to demonstrate change after a comparatively short intervention.
- A university student finding it hard to leave home after the death of her mother. *Purpose*: to demonstrate suppression of symptoms because of mourning difficulties.
- A young man treated over a period of years. *Purpose*: to demonstrate a very gradual and then clear quantitative and qualitative change reflecting both changes in external circumstances and the therapeutic work in the consulting room.

Patient 1: a young woman suffering from anxiety and depressive reaction following the suicide of her mother

A young woman in her early twenties, who was referred by her GP because she had become extremely anxious and depressed following the death of her mother by suicide in violent circumstances. My patient had become extremely anxious that she would become like her mother, who had suffered from manic–depressive illness throughout most of the patient's life. Shortly after her mother's death, she had been so disturbed that she asked the GP to admit her to the same hospital that had cared for her mother and was a cause of considerable concern to her GP, family, and husband. She was married with two children and the marital relationship was reportedly secure. She had a sister who acted as the significant other. About a year or so before her mother's death, she suffered the loss of a child through a cot death, about which she was extremely guilty, and this compounded her depression and anxiety over the loss of her mother.

Her attendance for therapy lasted about a year, and she attended punctually and apparently took some trouble over her appearance. She was, at the outset, very anxious that I would accuse her of being neglectful, and it took some months for her to allow herself to be in touch with her angry feelings towards her mother. Despite her mother's illness, her father had stuck by his wife, who had been reportedly provocative and promiscuous but, of course, the true extent of this was difficult to assess.

The questionnaires show the progressive improvement of this patient reflected both in her reports and those of her sister. She successfully terminated, and informal contact with the GP suggests that she now leads a normal and stable life.

Figure 5.2. This shows graphically the improvement this young woman made in the six months' treatment. (See upper profile scored at intake and after six months (lower).)

	Internalizing		YASR Profile — Females			Externalizing		T Score
		31				21	37	
	17		15				36	
		30			17	20	35	95
	13	29	14	13		19	34	
	16	28				18	33	
					16		32	90
		27				17	31	
	15	26				16	30	
	12		12		15		29	85
	14	25				15	28	
		24	11	11			27	
					14		26	80
	11	13	23	10		13	25	
		22		10		12	24	
		21				11		75
%ILE		12	9				22	
		20				10	21	
98	10	11	19	8	9	12	9	20	70
	9	9	16	7	7	10	7	17	
	8							16	
93		8	15	6				15	65
			14		6	9	6	14	
	7		12	5	5	8	5	13	
84									60
	6	6				7	4	12	
		5	10					11	
69		4	9		3	6	3	10	55
		3	7	3				9	
	4		6		2	5		8	
50	0–3	0–2		0–2		0–4	0–2	0–7	50

I	II	III	IV	V	VI	VII	VIII
WITHDRAWN	SOMATIC COMPLAINTS	ANXIOUS/ DEPRESSED	SOCIAL PROBLEMS	THOUGHT PROBLEMS	ATTENTION PROBLEMS	DELINQUENT BEHAVIOUR	AGGRESSIVE BEHAVIOUR

Patient 2: a young woman suffering from anxiety and depressive reaction following the death of her mother

This patient came when she was in her late teens, following leaving university in another part of England. She had left after one year because she had found the particular university town too violent. The fact was that she lived in a part of London very similar to the town in question, so the "reason" for leaving did not seem to add up. After several interviews, it was revealed that this patient's mother had died rather suddenly in the year before departure, and what was very mysterious was that her doctors were unable to determine the cause of the death. The patient was now attending a university outside London, but remained living at home and seemed to have achieved equilibrium. She had, however, gone to the university counselling service, who had suggested that she come to see us. She came to us in the summer term of her first year of her second university course.

Figure 5.3 (see p. 122) shows her YSR results at intake and that of her therapist. Her form reveals her reluctance to think about these difficulties, perhaps because of a fear that if she did she, too, would die of unknown causes. The therapist form shows her as being assessed as a much more disturbed person than she saw herself as being. Unfortunately, she did not continue in the consultations. It was agreed that we would meet once the new university term had started but, on being invited, she did not reply.

It was clear that she had found great difficulty in mourning her mother's death and that this mourning was arrested. It was also clear that she was very reluctant to think at any depth about the effect of her loss and was seeking to "get on with it" in the hope that she could get on in the university town. It was, it seemed, perceived to be similar in some ways to the first, which suggested that her aggressive feelings were being projected on to the "university town", leaving her feeling paranoid and unprotected.

Patient 3: a young man treated over a period of years

This was a young man who was treated for several years, who came in his late teens at the recommendation of the counsellor of the

Figure 5.3. Profile scored by therapist (upper) and patient (lower).

	Internalizing		YABCL Profile – Females			Externalizing		T Score
	28		18	14	22	16	34	22	
			17	13	21	15	32		
	26							20	95
	25		16	12	20	14	30	19	
			15	11			29	18	
	24	10			19				90
	23		14				28	17	
					18		27	16	
	22	9	13	9		12	26		85
	21				17		25	15	
				8		11	24	14	
	20	8			16				80
	19		11	7		10	22	13	
			10	6	15		21	12	
	18	7						11	75
%ILE			9	5	14		20		
							19	10	
98	16		8		13	8	18	9	70
		5	7	3	10	7	15		
							14	5	
93	12		6			6	13	4	65
	10	4		2	8	5		3	
	9		5		7	4	9	2	
84	8		4		6		8		60
	7				5		6		
	6	2	3		4	3	5	1	
69	5						4		55
	4		2		3	2	3		
	3	1			2				
50	0–2	0	0–1		0–1	0–1	0–2	0	50
	I	II	III	IV	V	VI	VII	VIII	
	ANXIOUS/ DEPRESSED	WITHDRAWN	SOMATIC COMPLAINTS	THOUGHT PROBLEMS	ATTENTION PROBLEMS	INTRUSIVE	AGGRESSIVE BEHAVIOUR	DELINQUENT BEHAVIOUR	

College he had been attending. He said that he was lacking in confidence and felt very anxious in the presence of other people. He had been living with his maternal grandmother for the past five years. The significant facts of his family history were that his mother had suddenly left the family home when he was eight. He and his brother had lived with his father for a while. Their father then met and married his stepmother, and they all tried to live together until the situation broke down and he moved to his grandmother's flat when he was thirteen. This was experienced as very difficult, and consciously he had little but contempt for his stepfamily. It was this contempt, of course, that he saw in others towards him. The dominant features of the therapy were the extreme sensitivity he felt about the ends of sessions and holiday breaks and his yearning for male figure with good authority.

When this young man arrived he was unemployed, but obtained work as a delivery man for an manufacturing company and, in the first year of therapy, he re-established contact with his father, from whom he had been estranged for five or more years. Then he moved from delivery to a more creative job in the company employing him and this was accompanied by a quantum shift in his perception of himself. He had, he thought, a chance of becoming normal and adult. One of the most significant features of this period was that he claimed to give up smoking marijuana, to which he had been apparently quite habituated.

This paved the way for him to find and visit his mother again, whom he discovered not to be the violent heartless bully of his fantasies, but actually depressed herself. This was a shock to him because it upset all the fantasies he had built up to rationalize what had happened to him. This new mother did not fit the violent mother who had left him and whom he felt hated him. It put in question his fear of women, and then it began to be revealed that he often watched pornographic cable TV. He could now see that his fear of women arose from his hatred of women, and in particular his mother. What was especially interesting was the belief that developed in him that he needed to stay in contact with his mother to enable him to have a relationship with a woman. The relationship with his mother went through many vicissitudes; not least of which when he recommended to his mother that she get some therapy herself. Perhaps unsurprisingly, this angered her and her reaction angered him. In any event, the gradual repair of this relationship indeed enabled him to think instead about having a relationship with a girl, which he successfully achieved. At the conclusion of our work, this was established, as was his continued occupational success.

When followed up some time later, he sent back a form that suggested that everything had broken down. I offered to see him, and he returned to show that things had not broken down, but that he received the forms on a day when he had been accused by his family of cheating another family member. This had induced a degree of depressive anxiety, reflected in his form, but may well, in addition, have been a way of communicating a desire to see me again. Figure 5.4 shows his YSR results at the outset and at two years, when there seemed to be a very marked improvement following a long period

Figure 5.4.   Profiles at intake (upper) and at two years (lower).

Internalizing			YABCL Profile — Males			Externalizing		T Score
		31				21	37	
	17	30	15		17		36	
				13		20	35	95
13	16	28	14			19	34	
	15	27			16		33	
				12		18		90
12	14	26	13			17	31	
					15		30	
	13	24	12	11		16		85
		23			14	15	29	
	12	22	11				27	
					10	14		80
	11	20	10		13	13	26	
10	10	19					25	
					9	12	24	75
%ILE	9	18	9		12	11	23	
		17					22	
98	8	16	8	8			21	70
	7				7	10	18	
93	6	12					17	65
	7	11	6		9	7	16	
	6	10	5	5		6	14	
84	5	9			8			60
		8	4			5	13	
	5	7			7			
69	3		4	3		4	11	55
	4	6			6		10	
	2	5			5	3	9	
50	0–3	0–1	0–4	0–2	0–2	0–4	0–2	0–8	50

I	II	III	IV	V	VI	VII	VIII
WITHDRAWN	SOMATIC COMPLAINTS	ANXIOUS/ DEPRESSED	SOCIAL PROBLEMS	THOUGHT PROBLEMS	ATTENTION PROBLEMS	DELINQUENT BEHAVIOUR	AGGRESSIVE BEHAVIOUR

when little change could be seen either in the therapy or the questionnaire results. This shift coincided with the move into more creative work, substantially reducing his intake of drugs, and taking the decision to contact his mother. There was also a very noticeable change in him in that he seemed to make the move from adolescence into young adulthood.

Conclusions

I draw three, perhaps provocative, conclusions from these studies for discussion.

1.   That it is ethically, professionally, and politically sound to embark on audit exercises of this kind. They become part of the setting and protect the patient from the professional's

omnipotence and enable the professional maintain the resourcing of the provision.

2. Although the most obvious use of the audit is the pooling and analysis of data from all patients, significant others, and professionals, there is a clear indication of the potential use of these data in the individual case, especially during assessment. The fact that such data can be used in the assessment and subsequent treatment phases means that such data can be used meaningfully with the patient. This is because they differ from the *diagnostic indices* derived from *DSM-III*. They are descriptions by the patient of the patient's own experience to the therapist, and, therefore, will become part of the many transference communications within the treatment setting when they are repeated. They need not be used directly, but can be used to inform the therapist during the assessment phase and, by that means, meaningful consultation with the patient can begin to converge with assessment.

3. The YSR and related questionnaires have obvious reliability and validity, when used at the outset of contact with the young person, that is largely unaffected by the transference phenomena mentioned in point 2, above. What does seem very difficult to assess is the length of time that an individual will need before a meaningful change begins to appear. In the cases described above, change appeared much more rapidly in case one compared to case three, even though at the outset the psychopathology in case one would have been judged as more severe. This feature means that while there can be a conversion of assessment with consultation, there can never be an overlap, coincidence, or equation of the two. Thus, the nomothetic can penetrate and inform the idiographic, but it cannot substitute for it because the consultation/therapeutic endeavour is a learning system in itself, but not closed off so that it becomes a thing in itself.

References

Achenbach, T. M. (1991a). *Manual for the Youth Self-Report and 1991 Profile*. Burlington, VT: Department of Psychiatry, University of Vermont.

Achenbach, T. M. (1991b). *Manual for the Teacher's Report and 1991 Profile*. Burlington, VT: Department of Psychiatry, University of Vermont.

Achenbach, T. M., & Edelbrock, C. (1986). *Manual for the Teacher's Report Form and Teacher Version of the Child Behaviour Profile*. Burlington, VT: Department of Psychiatry, University of Vermont.

Achenbach, T. M., & Edelbrock, C. (1987). *Manual for the Youth Self Report and Profile*. Burlington, VT: Department of Psychiatry, University of Vermont.

Baruch, G. (1995). Evaluating the outcome of a community based psychoanalytic psychotherapy service for young people between 12 and 25 years old: work in progress. *Psychoanalytic Psychotherapy*, 9(3): 246–267.

Baruch, G. (1997). The process of engaging young people with severe developmental disturbance in psychoanalytic psychotherapy: patterns of practice. *Bulletin of the Menninger Clinic*, 61(3): 335–353.

Baruch, G., Fearon, P., & Gerber, A. (1998). Evaluating the outcome of a community based psychoanalytic psychotherapy service for young people: one year repeated follow-up. In: R. Davenhill & M. Patrick (Eds.), *Rethinking Clinical Audit (The Case of Psychotherapy Services in the NHS)*. London: Routledge.

King, R. A., & Noshpitz, J. D. (1991). *Pathways to Growth: Essentials of Child Psychiatry, Vol.2: Psychopathology*. New York: Wiley.

Meehl, P. (1954). *Clinical Versus Statistical Prediction: A Theoretical Analysis and a Review of the Evidence*. Minneapolis: University of Minnesota Press.

Verhulst, F. C., Prince, J., Vervuurt-Poot, C., & de Jong, J. (1989). Mental health in Dutch adolescents: self-reported competencies and problems for ages 11–18. *Acta Psychiatrica Scandinavica Supplementum*, 356(80): 1–48.

Wilson, P. (1991). Psychotherapy with adolescents. In: J. Holmes (Ed.), *Textbook of Psychotherapy in Psychiatric Practice* (pp. 443–467). London: Churchill Livingstone.

CHAPTER SIX

Is twice a week enough? Thinking about the number of sessions per week as a determinant of the intensity of psychoanalytic psychotherapy

James S. Rose

Introduction

This chapter is based on a paper I gave some years ago to the Guild of Psychotherapists. The topic under discussion was the rationale for defining a particular number of sessions per week as the requirement for a psychoanalysis of someone being trained as a psychoanalytic psychotherapist. The Guild had set two sessions per week as their minimum requirement when they had first established themselves, because their founders felt that to require a greater frequency precluded many from being able to embark upon a training and, thus, hampered the opportunity of patients in the world to have the opportunity for psychoanalytical treatment.

This paper is an effort to address the question of how frequency can be related to intensity. In other words, why does increasing the number of times a patient is seen per week increase the intensity of the treatment? The impact of a psychotherapeutic experience seemed to me to need separating into disturbance and containment. But it was the realization that the psychoanalytical endeavour rested on the creation of an iterative learning system that led to the ideas about chaos theory and its implications for understanding complex systems. The fact of iteration could also be said to have two consequences. First, it created the disturbance and the containment necessary to address the task and the rigours of changing. Second, it meant that the impact of the treatment could not be confined to the time when the patient and psychotherapist were in each other's presence. What happened in their absence would also be of great significance.

In reproducing the paper, I have decided to keep it in the same tense in which it was read. This places the reader into the position of a listener as if to a paper at a conference. You will notice that, at certain points, the understood difference of opinion between presenter (me) and the listeners (the Guild of Psychotherapists) is easier to see, giving rise to a sense of difference. I retain this feature as a device to approach more closely the experience of psychoanalytical psychotherapy, in which one treads a path that embraces empathy for one's patient while at the same time recognizing the essential difference of perspective that respect for individual human experience entails.

In addressing the question "Is twice a week enough?", it is obvious that it is a part question because of the implied "for what?" Every psychoanalytical psychotherapist will know that we are talking about the number of times a week a patient visits his or her therapist. That is the behaviour we are talking about; the question is to do with the rationale for different frequencies ranging in number from one to five. At least that is the conventional range of option but not necessarily the full range.

When we ask the "for what" question, the first issue that we might consider is whether twice a week is enough to *establish and maintain a psychoanalytic process*. The question, of course, turns on the definition of such a process. For the sake of the argument, let us use Molnos's (1995) statement about the essence of psychoanalytic psychotherapy:

> In order to do psycho-analytic psychotherapy, one has to create a special place in which the past can re-appear in the here-and-now, a place in which past emotional conflicts are re-lived and understood with clarity, and in which new solutions to old problems are found.

Although we might vigorously debate some aspects of this statement, it will serve to act as some kind of defining statement with which to begin. Now, many have taken the view that the actual frequency of sessions has little to do with the creation of a psychoanalytic process, and certainly it is my experience that something like such a process as described above will be able to be discerned at all frequencies of working from once to five sessions per week. One is led inexorably to the conclusion that the actual number of times may be only part of the picture, and that other variables have a function. Usually, the two main candidates for the other variables are the patient and the psychotherapist themselves.

The next "for what" we might consider is the question: "enough for training psychotherapists?" As I understand it, the Guild of Psychotherapists sets twice a week as a minimum and lets each individual set their own frequency of training therapy at the level they desire, at or more than that, at their own discretion. As is well known, there is a range of frequencies set by the psychotherapy organizations. This situation seems to have led to various conceptual by-products, two of which are: (1) an idealization of five times per week and its associated denigration revealed in institutional splits; (2) a belief that a psychotherapist should not treat at a frequency above that experienced in their own therapy.

One effect of the first is that conceptual advance is arrested by the necessity to maintain the political position of one's home organization.

The second of these has the implication that a situation may come about in which a therapist sets a minimum of twice a week in their practice that colludes with a patient's desire to reduce the impact of their psychotherapy for fear of the upset to their internal equilibrium. The point I wish to make is that institutional definitions of what is required have helped very little but have, I think, created a situation in which political priority has superseded the scientific.

As a result of all this, I have found myself left with the question of how to make sense of the fact that while I practise at all frequencies from once to five times per week, the experience of each regime is different. I personally find that three times plus per week has significantly more impact, and that this increases as the number of sessions increases. Now, of course, I can be accused of simply seeing what I wish to see and that my deference to greater frequency simply arises out of cognitive dissonance: that is, because I trained in a regime of five times per week, I cannot bear to recognize that lower levels of frequency are just as effective, if not more so in some cases. So, I think I must be careful to say what I mean by effectiveness. In essence, effectiveness arises out of the kind of psychic contact achieved between a patient and their therapist.

If we say that all patients seek therapy because they are in some kind of pain, I do not think we will disagree. Patients, however, vary greatly in their desire for change, and this is reflected in the formulation of the reasons for their pain that they bring with them. Thus, some patients are in pain but do not want to change because this might mean taking back into themselves something that they would rather delegate in some way to somebody else. Other patients are so fragile that any level of disturbance will bring the threat of catastrophe, for example, a suicidal attempt reflecting a negative therapeutic reaction. My point, in brief, is that any effective therapy must have *the capacity to disturb and also to contain*.

Thinking of Molnos's view, above, we can see that a psychotherapeutic encounter needs to be capable of arousing the painful experience but in such a way that it can be thought about and a new perspective on it can be developed. To change involves experiencing *disturbance*, while feeling *contained* makes it safe enough to discard old defences and develop new ones. One responsibility of the psychoanalytic psychotherapist is to gauge the dose. I suggest that the effectiveness of contact arises from the appropriateness of the balance of disturbance and containment relative to the difficulties that the patient brings. It might also be taken as axiomatic in psychoanalytic psychotherapy that the difficulties that bring the patient for treatment will be experienced by both psychotherapist and patient in the transference as the treatment progresses. It is this feature that necessitates the need for disturbance and containment. Without disturbance, the treatment is therapeutically inert; without containment, the anxieties created by the disturbance may prevent the possibility of change.

Of these two aspects, I think that containment is much better understood than disturbance. When we think of disturbance, we are led to ideas about the challenge of defence or resistance or confrontation, but all of these will bring with them ideas to do with the desire of the therapist to have an impact actively upon the patient's psychic structure. This has little directly to do with frequency. The question is whether *frequency of itself* creates something that has an impact on the outcome. Within the psychoanalytic literature, I have found that there is a remarkable silence on this matter, which has led to a situation in which preference (to be followed) or perception of another person's dogma (to be reacted against vigorously) are the means by which such matters are settled by individual psychotherapists. This highly unsatisfactory situation has bothered me a great deal, but then I ran across chaos theory.

There are three concepts taken from chaos theory that I would like to consider, which, I have found, have some bearing on the issue we are discussing. These are (1) the notion of iteration; (2) the concept of the strange attractor; (3) scaling.

Iteration

Chaos theory developed recently in the natural sciences in an attempt to understand what happens when dynamic systems become unpredictable and turbulent. It also reflected a realization that the model for understanding systems based on dividing a system into its component parts and then adding them together to understand the workings of the whole was flawed. In other words, the idea that the whole is more than the sum of the parts gripped the natural sciences as they endeavoured to grasp "real" problems rather than the abstraction of the problems imposed by accepted methods of analysis. This was forced upon scientific investigators when they began to study complex systems where the relationship between variables was not linear. These complex systems could not be seen as units in themselves, but had to be viewed as being in some kind of dynamic relationship with their environments. Thus, the study of population growth and decline of a particular species in a particular environment meant not just consideration of the fecundity of the species and the abundance of food supply, but also the prevalence of disease and any other feature affecting the survival of individual members of the species.

What assisted the emergence of these ideas was the computer, which enabled the study of the various mathematical concepts, used to build models of dynamic systems, in a new way. The differential equation became a focus of special attention because it was possible, using computers, to see how these equations, which have been the most successful yet to model complex systems, behave when used iteratively. What this means is that starting from a particular point, the equations are solved and the output of the solution becomes the input to next process of solution, and so on. It is this repetitive procedure that is referred to by *iteration*, but there is more to iteration than simply repetition. It has been found in recent years that it is possible to predict the onset of turbulent conditions in a complex system. Furthermore, it has been shown that the onset of turbulence is predicted by contextual variables that remain remarkably constant across models of different complex systems. What we mean by turbulence here is the *breakdown of linear relationships between variables*.

Let us take a concrete example to illustrate this. It can be shown that the apparently random annual fluctuations in the populations of birds or insects can be predicted through the use of an algorithm known as the *logistic difference equation*; it is possible to show why what seems random or chaotic is predictable. It can be shown to be, in fact, predictable by using the logistic difference equation to compute population growth or decline by taking account of the reproductive efficiency of the species and relating this to the food supply and those factors that affect the probability of the survival of an individual member of the population in question. This enables examining the growth (or decline) of a population over a period of years in which $N1$ (the population in year 1) is used to calculate the population in year 2, given that reproductive efficiency and the factors affecting survival are known (for example, food supply, disease) and quantifiable. By iterating these calculations over a period of years, such that Nn for any one year is used to calculate $Nn+1$ for the following year, we can see that for certain conditions of reproductive efficiency and survival rate, N becomes apparently random or unpredictable linearly.

Now, if we regard an aspect of the psychoanalytical procedure as being one in which whatever it is that is produced in any one session, learnt, or otherwise results, is fed back in some way into the psychoanalytic experience of the next session, then I think we can start to regard the psychoanalytic process as an iterative one. I think it is a matter of daily observation that a psychotherapist cannot readily predict what is going to happen in any one session from what has happened in the previous one. However, I think it is also a matter of readily observable experience that as the number of sessions per week increases, the very frequency of meeting permits a sense of deeper emotional contact and gradually accumulating understanding or learning about the patient. Hence, to regard the psychoanalytical procedure as an iterative learning system helps us to think about the relationship between frequency and intensity, because we can see how frequency can predict and, indeed, produce the breakdown of linear relationships within the mind and, hence, the disturbance necessary to enable change to first, be possible and then, to occur.

There are a number of other features of complex non-linear systems that have been identified and are relevant to thinking about the psychoanalytic process.

The strange attractor

On first encounter, the notion of the strange attractor might seem a romantic one, for example,

> "You can't know how happy
> I am that we met,
> I'm strangely attracted to you"
> (Cole Porter, "It's All Right with Me")

However, it is also a term that gets nearer to putting the idea of an internal object or an unconscious phantasy into mathematical terms than anything else I have encountered. What I am seeking to get at here is that in psychoanalytic work one can find oneself pulled in all sorts of directions and into different situations. Of course, this is reflected in the conscious psychic content of the material, but what strikes one, often in the countertransference, is the insistent presence of a something that lurks on the edge of conscious experience. It is insistent in the sense that it seems to be highly influential and draws attention to itself, but it is very reluctant to allow itself to be contemplated in reflective consciousness. Clinically, it will be a phenomenon often observed in the treatment of depressed patients suffering from unconscious guilt. Another example is the description of the clinical picture offered by Fairbairn in "The repression and return of bad objects" (1952).

It is easier to begin to think about the strange attractor by thinking about simple attractors in the mechanical, not the psychic, sense. An example is a pendulum which is initially disturbed by displacement and which returns to a resting point as a result of friction in its pivot. Plotted graphically, the oscillations will gradually dampen until the resting point is achieved. A pendulum is a simple *one-dimensional* system in which the energy of the initial disturbance is dissipated by friction. It returns to a resting point and provided the pivot does not move, or the pendulum lengthen, the resting point will be the same. Conceptually, this resting point is a simple attractor, which emerges when the response to disturbance is *linear*.

Imagine now a multi-dimensional system in which the response to a disturbance is *non-linear*. This has given rise to the notion of the non-linear system, which sounds very new-agey. More accurately, the term refers to those systems whose behaviour is describable only by considering the interaction of the components within the system and between the system and the environment in which is situated, and not simply by the summation of the system's functions.

Next, imagine the outputs of the equations defining the system being input into these defining equations in the *iterative* manner, described above, over and over again. To get an idea of what might be being modelled by such a system, we could think of turbulent fluid flow or, for that matter, the mind. *At any one point in time*, it is possible to define the state of the system by a point with a number of co-ordinates defined by the number of dimensions of the multi-dimensional system. The multi-dimensional space thus implied we can call *phase space*.

When the functioning of complex or non-linear systems is modelled in this way, it is commonly found that the point referred to just now, representing the state of the system, settles down into a restricted area of phase space, when these points are plotted through successive points in time. While it may be found to be jumping around chaotically and unpredictably within this space, the system is drawn over time into this restricted area in the same way as our pendulum returned to a discernible point. But the single point of rest of the pendulum is replaced by this restricted area, otherwise known as the *strange attractor*. In essence, my argument is that the possibility of the discovery and identification of strange attractors in psychic reality arises out of the continued iteration of the encounter between patient and their psychotherapist.

This way of describing attractors suggests a restricted area of the phase space within which there is nothing but chaos, rather like a "bag" of unpredictability. In fact, when such strange attractors are studied, they are often found to be exquisitely structured. Any section of such an attractor, when magnified, reveals itself to be just as detailed as the larger part from which it was taken. In other words, there is an infinite regress of detail, a never-ending nesting of pattern within pattern, these patterns being isomorphic with one another. This phenomenon is known as *scaling*.

In order to show the relevance of these ideas for the practice of psychoanalysis, this idea of scaling was recently used by Galatzer-Levy (1995) to show the isomorphism of the structure of a single psychoanalytic session, the pattern of several weeks' work, and the structure of a patient's life. This and another paper by Moran (1992) show in greater detail the relevance of some of these concepts to psychoanalysis. I also recommend a paper by Hofstadter (1981), which is a good introduction to some of these ideas.

My thesis, therefore, may be summarized as follows. In order to discern the strange attractors that govern and structure a patient's psychic reality, we need to be able to engage with the patient's psychic reality in an iterative way so that the structure of these strange attractors can reveal themselves. To me, it does not much matter, for my purposes today, whether they are called internal objects or unconscious phantasies, because the concepts are descriptive of similar structuring phenomena, even if they have different theoretical foundations. What I propose is that it is partly this *iterative process in itself* that provides the disturbance necessary. It does not, therefore, solely rely on the disturbance that the patient brings or the active intervention of the psychotherapist to produce this disturbance, as suggested by those who advocate brief focal psychotherapy, for example, Davenloo. It has the advantage of creating a disturbance through which the structure of a patient's experience emerges and is not, therefore, an imposition of the psychotherapist's reality upon that of the patient's.

Further, it seems that the more frequent the sessions, then the more readily will the patterns emerge because the effect of the previous sessions will be more readily available to consciousness and recall. We should also consider *nachtraglichkeit* or the "après-coup" effects which play their part in the input to the following session and are the essential driver of the iterative psychoanalytical process. In terms of what Charles Hanly called "The Third" (see above), it seems to me that the notion of *nachtraglichkeit* entails a reflection on immediate past experience. It is, thus, an expression of an experience of the Third. If *nachtraglichkeit* is thought of as some kind of reflection on immediate experience, it follows that psychotherapeutic effects cannot simply be confined simply to what happens when the patient and psychotherapist are in each other's presence. What happens in their absence from one another may also have a powerful significance. This will be especially true in a discipline whose theory places an emphasis on the psychological impact of separation and loss.

A question that remains is whether the logic of the argument is such that it leads to a position of saying simply that the more frequent the sessions, the better. Again, it depends on the purpose of the treatment. When it concerns the psychotherapeutic treatment of patients, in my view, the answer must be "not necessarily", because some patients bring with them so much internal disturbance that the main issue is containment. For example, in the psychotherapeutic treatment of adolescents, there can be so much going on internally that, while there may some cases where frequent treatment is desirable, many do not need frequent treatment to produce the disturbance necessary for change and it may overwhelm them.

However, when the issue concerns the training of psychoanalytical psychotherapists, it seems to me that the logic of the argument above must point towards recommending that trainee psychotherapists need to have experienced the disturbing effects of the iterative psychoanalytic process to the full. They are being trained to create and use an iterative learning system with their future patients. To leave it up to them is perhaps to leave them alone with their resistances and may mean that some trainees cannot become familiar with the full potential of the technique they are using.

References

Fairbairn, W. D. (1952). The repression and return of bad objects (with special reference to the war neuroses). In: *Psychoanalytic Studies of the Personality* (Chapter 3, pp. 59–81). London: Tavistock Publications.

Galatzer-Levy, R. M. (1995). Psycho-analysis and chaos theory. *Journal of the American Psychoanalytic Association, 43*(4): 1085–1113.

Hofstadter, D. R. (1981). Metamagical themas. Strange attractors: mathematical patterns delicately poised between order and chaos. *Scientific American, 245*(5): 22–43.

Molnos, A. (1995). *A Question of Time*. London: Karnac.

Moran, M. G. (1991). Chaos theory and psychoanalysis: the fluidic nature of the mind. *International Review of Psycho-analysis, 18*: 211–222.

PART III

TRIANGULATION IN THE PSYCHOANALYTIC SETTING

Introduction

This part of the book brings together four clinical papers, each of which illustrates some aspect of the use of the concept of triangulation. The first paper looks at the temporal dimension in so far as it considers distortions of time in the transference. Patients' distortions of time can be frequently and readily observed in clinical psychoanalysis, reflecting both their psychopathology and their reactions to the temporal and iterative aspects of the psychoanalytic setting. This paper, therefore, develops the idea of the impact of the iterative aspect of the psychoanalytical learning system. Patients' distortions of time are considered to examine the assumptions that can be implicitly made about the nature of space and time in object relations theory. Two case histories are given to exemplify these clinical phenomena, the first being an example of a fixation and the second one of a psychic retreat.

The second paper looks at symbolization as a triangulating process. Change inevitably creates anxiety because of loss and the confrontation with the unknown. It is proposed that one function of symbols is to manage the anxiety of change. They do this by creating a means by which anxieties can be presented to the subject and then communicated to another mind. These creations are called symbolic because, it is proposed, their purpose is communicative as well as simply incorporating internal anxieties and desires with external exigencies, which might be termed symptoms. Viewing them in this way enables the analyst to put symbolic phenomena as they emerge in an analysis into an intersubjective perspective. The author suggests that thinking of symbols as purely intrasubjective phenomena limits our perspective. It is more technically useful to look at the communicative aspects of symbols as they present themselves to the symbolizing subject, and, subsequently, to the analyst in the dialogue within the psychoanalytic setting, because, thereby, the objective and temporal dimension of the setting can be included. In this way, the triangulating features of the psychoanalytic encounter are harnessed as a means of exploring a patient's psychic reality. Two clinical examples of symbols are discussed. The first was brought for analysis, and a second developed in the course of an analysis. One is given as an example of resistance to change, whereas the other revealed an unconscious drive for change.

The third chapter looks at the experience of absence in the transference and, in particular, at a paradox in which a patient declares that the psychoanalyst cannot help him, but he keeps coming to tell the analyst that this is the case. The purpose is to look at the clinical phenomenon of decathexis and the paradoxical clinical situations which can be created. It is easy to confuse these situations with a patient's destructiveness, which has the danger, if thus interpreted, of driving them deeper into despair.

The final paper makes a proposal that in the course of psychoanalytical work, those clinical moments of identification and those of differentiation triangulate with the alternating presence and absence of psychoanalyst and analysand with, and from, each other. This paper develops and uses the ideas put forward in the earlier paper on the use of concepts derived from chaos theory to understand the disturbing and containing aspects of the iterative process implied by the psychoanalytical learning system.

CHAPTER SEVEN

Distortions of time in the transference: some clinical and theoretical implications*

James S. Rose

Summary

P atients' distortions of time can be frequently and readily observed in clinical psychoanalysis; reflecting both their psychopathology and their reactions to the temporal aspects of the psychoanalytic setting. These phenomena are considered to examine the assumptions that can be implicitly made about the nature of space and time in object relations theory. Two case histories are given to exemplify these clinical phenomena, the first being an example of a fixation and the second one of a psychic retreat. These cases are compared to demonstrate the unconscious processes underlying the particular time distortions being considered, their impact on the patient's lives, and their manifestation in the clinical setting. From these studies, it is suggested that the asymmetry of the "arrow of time" cannot be assumed in the structure of psychic reality. The clinical evidence suggests that that psychic

---

* First published in 1997 in *International Journal of Psychoanalysis, 78*: 453–468.

reality has to be seen as discontinuous and the structure of the discontinuities will be revealed by the impact on the patient of the temporal aspects of the psychoanalytic setting.

Introduction

In this paper, I wish to consider the distortions of time that can be observed in clinical psychoanalysis. As we all know, when a patient begins an analysis which involves meeting the analyst at predetermined points in time and for fixed periods of time, there is an impact on his external life and upon his internal world. It emphasizes something finitely limiting that may threaten various internal structures that are built upon a denial of time. Hence, from the outset, we are in a position to observe a patient's reaction to the structure of the setting that serves to organize and structure experience. The analyst's experience of the impact of the limits and boundaries on the patient come in many ways. As the transference "gathers", the patient can express this impact in verbal form; in enactments and/or in somatic experience. Indeed, my interest in time began with the everyday observation of how patients seemed to create a characteristic sense of time and space in the transference. This occurs from the beginning, but does become more focused and structured as the analysis proceeds and becomes particularly apparent when termination becomes a matter for consideration, for whatever reason. But I think there are reasons for being interested in time other than the practical use of the denial or distortions of time as they reflect a patient's psychopathology.

In order to examine some of the implicit theoretical assumptions made about time and space in psychoanalytic theory, I have found it helpful to set some of our more familiar theory in comparison with other thinkers on time and space taken from the natural sciences.

For example, Einstein (1920) felt that concepts of space and time emerged through the linking of direct experiences with material objects; in particular, with the experience of their movement or dynamics. He felt that the concept of a material object must precede the development of notions of time and space and he was certainly *not* discussing here a theory of the development of these notions in children. His ideas enable us, as explorers of the internal universe, to wonder whether we assume particular notions of time and space when we think about the dynamics of *psychic* objects. These assumptions may also somehow bind us if we do not examine them. *From here, we might ask whether looking for the distortions of time and space in the transference would help us understand a patient's psychic reality because it implies thinking about the movements of his objects in psychic space.*

The Greeks distinguished two senses of time: *chronos* and *kairos*. While chronos refers to clock time, kairos refers to a sense of a special time that is significant and meaningful. I think it is more accurate, following the concepts due to Einstein, to think here of a space–time. Mander (1995) recently used this distinction when discussing the significance of once weekly psychotherapy sessions in a patient's life. Thus, she saw the session as a time in the week set aside from all other existence—sacred as against the profane— in which past, present, and future can come together. The obvious religious associations implied by this division of course imply that the separation is benign, which must remain an open question when it comes to psychotherapy.

Nevertheless, the concept of *kairos* gives us the ability to wonder whether a patient may seek to create a space–time of *kairos* as a defence against the insistence of *chronos*. In other words, what we may be observing when see distortions of time in the consulting room is evidence of different space–times in the patient's psychic reality.

It is quite easy to think of how the passage of time and its denial is of significance in clinical psychoanalysis. Denying the passage of time is intrinsic to resistance to change, to mourning, and, ultimately, death. It is also intrinsic to the denial of bodily and psychic development. Many forms of psychopathology carry with them implicit statements or theories about reality which can be thought of as "wrong". Money-Kyrle's paper on cognitive development which developed Bion's neo-platonic theory (as Money-Kyrle thought of it) of "innate preconceptions" saw psychopathology as reflecting a patient's denial of "facts of life", among which was the passage of time. But he went further than that in that he suggested that "a baby has not only to form a number of basic concepts in terms of which he can recognise these 'facts of life' but also to arrange their members in a time-space system" (1968, p. 697).

He saw that the individual had to develop two of these main systems. One, to represent the outer world in which we have to orientate ourselves; the other, originally an internalization this, develops into an unconscious system of religion and morality. Essential to the sense of orientation in either system is that it has a base, the O of co-ordinate geometry; in other words, the point of origin of the equivalent of the ordinate and the abscissa in a two-dimensional system. What is of some interest here is that the space–time system was being thought of in terms of Cartesian co-ordinate geometry. To my mind, this is a hypothesis that deserves thought and some testing. This is because it offers a perspective on the structure of the internal world that is different from that implied by the *chronos–kairos* categories offered by the Greeks. In short, the question turns on whether a continuous time–space frame can be said to exist in the mind. What Money-Kyrle proposed was the "possible development of a kind of psycho-analytic geometry and physics with which to represent a patient's changing true and false beliefs about his relation to objects and their nature in his inner and outer worlds" (*ibid.*, p. 697). What is implicit to this notion of innate preconceptions is a model based on what we know of human development. On the face of it, it seems to be quite acceptable that it is a "fact of life" that the prime source of all goodness for an infant is the breast, but then to assume that there is an innate preconception in the infant for this may be carrying the conclusions of empirical observation a little too far. The danger is that our conceptions become a kind of anthropomorphism, so that the innate preconception becomes simply a reflection of our conception. Despite this, Money-Kyrle makes a theoretical challenge that deserves taking up.

At a practical level, what I want to examine in this paper is the idea that the understanding of resistance to movement and development can be advanced by taking particular note of a patient's concepts of time as they are manifest in their psychic reality and, by extension, how they are expressed in the transference. To do this, I shall consider two patients where clinical issues to do with time were particularly apparent. I do not wish to imply that the only way of understanding the clinical material of the patients I will now present comes from addressing the questions arising from the patient's concepts of time. Clearly, the ideas will link with other theoretical concepts. However, in these cases I found it helpful to think of their implicit experiences of time and, indeed, more particularly their use of it. Consequently, to grasp the sense of these patients' psychic reality was aided, it seems to me, by a consideration of the sense of time they created.

Clinical material

The first of my two cases was one in which the patient seemed to be developmentally stuck in the psychological sense in early adolescence. In other words, there seemed to be a developmental fixation. I shall seek to contrast this patient with another, who did not show a fixation so much as a development of a psychic retreat (Steiner, 1993). I think the differences between the cases lie in the sense of the first patient coming to analysis essentially feeling frustrated, but with a desire for change, even if it was not clear what change was desired. The second patient sought to recreate and reinforce his retreat so that he could feel safe. At some level, becoming a patient was part of the retreat because he used his illness as a retreat.

Patient 1. Miss Z: a neurotic young woman

My first patient came to London to have an analysis. This move had been precipitated by a near breakdown following the ending of a love affair. The relationship had never been a sexual one. Indeed, when this patient began her analysis, she was still a virgin, but well into adulthood.

A tall, rather gangling woman; she was a middle child from a small family. Her mother was described as someone who lived for her husband and found motherhood difficult and draining. Mother was also described as someone who avoided her feelings or the existence of her psychic life, although she was felt by my patient to be capable of great depth if only she would permit it. Her father was a self-made businessman who had achieved great financial success. At the outset, he was seen as an exciting man of action, intolerant of the complexities of psychic life. However, he was also seen as someone who had regarded my patient as his "favourite", which was seen as intrusive, controlling, but, one sensed, secretly gratifying.

From the beginning of her analysis, time entered her thoughts because she was absolutely determined to have an analysis that would last, she thought, five years. But in regard to other aspects of her life, her capacity to procrastinate was very marked. This feature was extant on many fronts. In her professional and academic work, it was constantly there and was displayed by her inability to meet deadlines. This, I think, contained the idea of wanting to know if she was someone special to the person capable of granting a variation of the time limit. Her sense of the time limits on her capacity to bear children were to become increasingly conscious. To balance against this was her desire for an analysis, but with the knowledge that it could not be timeless. Some day, she would have to decide to return to her country of origin. The final year of the five years was conducted against the clock that in this case was not imposed by the setting, but by the patient and her plans for the future, which developed in the course of the analysis.

I would like to offer some clinical material, which mainly centres around a dream that was reported before a weekend. She had found that she was going to miss the last day of that week because of a planned trip abroad with a female friend. She had thought to ask for an earlier time on the Friday but somehow had felt embarrassed to raise the matter and felt that she was not explaining sufficiently what was going on. *This material, therefore, gives the chance to see some of the anxieties and fantasies stirred by a request for a change of time, or, in other words, whether she was someone special.* On the day before the Friday, she began the session with this dream.

> Last night I had this dream about you. We were in my flat and it was late at night. You thought it was about 12.30 but I knew it was 2.30 or 3.30 in the morning. It was time to go to sleep and you lay down in the alcove where my books are. The alcove was bigger in the dream than it really is and there is more room. Where you lay was separated from my bed by this trellis that my landlady has put up. Then some friends came into the room.

She didn't say anything immediately in relation to the dream, but began with the difficulties that she was experiencing in talking about the problem in coming to the session the following day. She didn't want to go abroad, but felt that she had to, and also noted how hard it was to say to her friend that she wanted to go to analysis. I replied by saying that from the predominant feeling of the dream and from what she had just said, it seemed that she regarded her analysis as a guilty or shameful secret. She said both guilty and shameful. She went on to say that she had often felt that she wanted to get up off the couch and move around and look into my eyes, but that to do so would be unwelcome to me. After some further thoughts on the theme of guilt and shame, I commented on how hard it seemed to be for her to think of coming to analysis as an act of maturity with the aim of working something out. She seemed to see it as something in which she was impossibly immature. She agreed with this, but felt that there was something about the idea of looking into my eyes that would be too daunting. I said that she was afraid of seeing rejection in my eyes. She responded by talking about a friend of hers at university who had had the ability to use her when the friend got into difficulties. The friend had been quite lacking in self-consciousness and indeed unaware of the impact of her demands. She wished she could be the same.

The dominant affect displayed in this dream arose from the patient's self consciousness. In consciousness, it seemed to arise from the difficulty in telling a female friend about her being in analysis. However, we can, I think, surmise that she was also ashamed of telling me what she wanted because of the associations concerned with looking into my eyes. Furthermore, there is a primal scene quality to the dream that came from my lying down next to her bed, with the friends eventually entering the room contributing a conscious sense of being watched. We can, therefore, surmise that the reason that she found difficulty in telling the friend (i.e., the analyst) why she wanted to come to analysis was because the wish to come contained a sexual wish.

At this stage in the analysis, one of the most important features concerned her struggle to separate from her mother. Often, the analysis was used to put her mother in the dock, and she often demanded reconstructive interpretations because they carried the promise of yet more evidence for the prosecution. Thus, it often happened that after some analysis of the transference situation between us, she would then say "what does this mean?" It usually carried the implication that whatever we had been talking about should be thought of in terms of her history. It became fortunately more and more obvious to her that the quest was really to reinforce her grudges and grievances that she bore towards her mother. These timeless and unending grudges, of course, bound her ever more tightly to her mother and reinforced the developmental arrest which sought to deny the reality of her mature, sexual body.

Following this period, she began a relationship with a young man of her age who was decidedly quite different from the counterpart of the sickly self image with which she had arrived. It was a sexual relationship, but with a sense of dissatisfaction with the absence of real orgasm. She became far less prone to procrastination, and her professional life became much more successful. She had her five years of analysis and, despite all sorts of twists and turns to avoid the pain of mourning, the analysis did reach an end. It was clear that the sexual difficulties she encountered had a great deal to do with sexual feelings aroused by a paternal figure, which became increasingly conscious in the transference. This seemed to me to provide fairly conclusive evidence that the developmental arrest had held in place a phantasy of a relationship with her father before the arrival of her adolescent sexual body, which she had been very reluctant to relinquish.

Discussion

We can, with justification, hypothesize that the compulsion to procrastinate was the reflection of a incestuous wish that had led her to become developmentally stuck at a pre-pubertal stage because of the fears of the consequences of having the sexual body of a woman. The fear of the acquisition of a sexual body was reflected in her history by her developing an eating disorder in early adolescence of sub-clinical severity and in the unrequited love affair in which she sought essentially a narcissistic relationship in which she gained the contents of her object and took flight from her sexual self into a pre-pubertal body from which she could in phantasy remain in safety the deadly rival of her mother for her father's favours. This was also reflected in her desire to be brilliantly successful, which meant that she found it very difficult to give something up when it had been finished. It could not be given up because it was never "good enough" and, therefore, to give it up was to accept mediocrity. In the analysis, this was reflected in her opinion that any interpretation of mine about her fear and loathing of being mediocre was, in fact, a contemptuous recommendation on my part that she accept that she was ordinary. This led her to be furious because I was seen as seeking to thwart her ambitions to identify with the all-powerful object that existed in her mind.

Looking now at her experience of seeking variations in time boundaries, we can see how the picture in the transference was to seek a relationship with a powerful and impressive male figure from whom she would get undivided and special attention. Breaks and weekends generated strong reactions at the outset, as might be expected. If we look at the dream, I think we can see on the one hand a desire for the all-powerful figure betrayed in the guilty feelings about analysis. There was also a resistance to the structure imposed by the session time and a desire for it to be changed so that she could consciously feel special and, at the same time, unconsciously triumph over the structuring but containing maternal object of the analytic setting. Her unconscious awareness of this was, I think, reflected by the daunting prospect of looking into my eyes, or, in other words, looking at herself in the mirror of the transference. Set against this fear was the desire to be free of self-consciousness, as expressed by her unself-conscious friend who could ask for help, which meant acknowledging a wish to be in touch with her desires without the need to hide or feel ashamed of them. Thus, I propose that we can see the session and its sequence echoing some aspects of the temporal sequence of her analysis and the sequence of her life. *By this, I mean a developmental thrust towards an "I" in a mature sexual body, but with elements of the preceding immature phases of this sequence in close proximity.* This is revealed in the dream and the associations to it, but in consciousness in the session the patient remains in a state of self-consciousness and seeking the approval of the analyst, perhaps envious of the perceived internal structure of the analytic setting and seeking to destroy it. However, it suggests that it is possible that in the patient's internal world there can be different time spaces that coexist. This, I think, must mean that any psychic geometry will not be a simple Euclidean one and, hence, need not have single points of origin in the Cartesian sense hypothesized by Money-Kyrle, but many of them, coexisting with each other. It also means that the implicit sense of time here is different from the *chronos* of developmental time.

I think it is appropriate and useful to think of this first patient in terms of fixation. The overwhelming picture was one of frustration. We might hypothesize that the compulsion to procrastinate was the reflection of a wish that had led her to become developmentally stuck at a pre-pubertal stage because of the fears of the consequences of having the sexual body of a woman. Thus, the picture in the transference was to seek a relationship with a powerful and impressive male figure from whom she would get undivided and special attention. These dynamics became acted out in professional life but, when interpreted, enabled her to have the relationships more appropriate to her age. We need to remember that however unconsciously gratifying these dynamics were, they were fundamentally unsatisfying, and this realization ultimately led her into analysis. *It is for this reason that we need to distinguish her from my next patient who sought the gratifications of the retreat in a much more intractable way.*

Patient 2: a patient diagnosed as obsessional

This patient, diagnosed as obsessional, was treated in the London Clinic of Psychoanalysis. The particular form that his obsessions took was to experience episodic states of mind during which he ruminated about violent fantasies that filled him with anxiety and led him to isolate himself from other people.

When we first met, he presented to me as a cheerful, personable character who was breezily good humoured. I was complimented on being an analyst "who had a sense of humour", which seemed significant at the time in that it was his parting shot at the end of the initial consultation. It seemed to carry the implication that I would be a good chap who would not disturb or upset him.

An experience that he often regaled was of being rejected by an adolescent sweetheart, with whom he had had his early sexual experiences but which stopped short of intercourse. In particular, he recalled his fearful and enthralled fascination at the prospect of touching her pubic hair. She then rejected him in favour of another after about six months, when he was fourteen. He recalled seeing them together in the school yard as he looked down from a classroom and feeling full of humiliation and a sense of bursting rage.

For the first two years, my patient attended as would be expected of a patient who was anxious to please. He appeared to be fearful of disturbing me and related in his customary cheerful but, I increasingly felt, false way. He had various ruminatory onsets and we noted that these were usually ended in response to a sense of contact with me, but then this was got rid of so quickly that insight was not maintained.

In order to resist his sense of dependency on me, he acquired new ills with which I could not help but which had a symbolic relevance to his relationship with me. Very often, these took bodily form: problems with his teeth, his stomach, or his prostate. He became obsessed with the house to the rear of his own, which was reported as disturbing, enraging, and frightening him, and he became very preoccupied with his own house and anxious that it was falling to bits. Thus, the situation in the transference was transformed into bodily reality or external reality. All this was interpreted in the transference, but the impact was slight, so far as could be observed.

Gradually, he lost his obsessional punctiliousness in attendance and payment, such that a constant enactment of his desire to get rid of me and treat what I had to offer with contempt was suggested. There were long periods when analysis seemed to be quite irrelevant to him, but I had a sense that he kept a very careful eye on me to see how I reacted. I do not think he was conscious of this, but it resided in him as a constant state of tension and watchfulness. I also got the impression that many of his excuses for lateness and non-attendance were rather far-fetched, as if I was being tested to see if I believed them.

What this seemed to be amounting to was that the analysis was turning into one that was *endless and timeless*. However, when patients are treated in the London Clinic, there is an initial limit of three years, which can be extended in certain cases. I had obtained two extensions, but it was agreed that this was enough. Hence, we began a new analytic year in the knowledge that, so far as the Clinic was concerned, there was a known termination date. This did not necessarily mean the analysis would end, if he and I chose not to end it. I made this clear to him as we began in September. Despite this, he reacted as if he was determined not to think about it and continued on in his timeless way, apparently in a state of sublime denial. This continued until the approach of the last Easter break. Then, there were signs that the prospect of a real ending was starting to become conscious. There came a day when he asked what would happen in the Autumn after analysis had ended. This session gradually ushered in a powerful onset of the ruminations. I will describe a session during this period.

The session I wish to describe began by the patient saying that it was as if no time had elapsed between when he had left and when he had arrived that day. His ruminations had been going full blast. Being mindful of how he seemed to attack the sense of time, I took this up with him, which met with an irritated response as if to say why wasn't I interested in his illness. Despite these protestations, I persisted with my concern about time and he replied he was always like that. He wiped things out when he left, but he added that suffering the ruminations seemed to pull people towards him. I said that his mind was full of ruminations to pull me towards him and to make sure that I would not send him away at the end of the session without having something about which to feel guilty. This led him to observe that he could always fall ill to get out of things and when he thought people were angry with him. I chose to intervene into his discursive review of his past by wondering what it was that had been going on between us that he got out of by being ill. After some skirmishing, he expressed his view that I saw him as a "little fuck" who couldn't do without analysis and he hated me for that. This enabled us to explore his feelings and reactions at the end of a session when I said it was time. He acknowledged that his rage vanished into ruminations, which hid his anger with me and his fear of me which resulted from the anger in a single cut. Once in the ruminations, he was ill, and immune from the painful feeling arising from separation.

The anxiety that underlay the ruminations eventually began to recede as a result of his gaining some insight into a part of himself that was forever perverting ordinary affectionate feeling for men into a homosexual conception, which he began to recognize as being very deprivingly self-destructive. Initially, this was felt as a burst of anger from within his bodily self against somebody who represented this aspect of him. When he saw that this person represented a part of himself, he became capable of a deeply felt depression that seemed to be considering what could be done about how he had wasted his life. The reparative quality of this seemed in contrast to the paranoid feel of the anxieties underlying his ruminations, and had a new kind of feel to it.

Discussion

I think it can be concluded from the clinical material that the obsessional symptoms of this patient were concerned with the experience of, reaction to, and defences against separation and ending. One way of formulating this is to say that the experience of ending evoked such powerful anxiety that the entire conscious experience of ending had to be obliterated and the sense of time had to go with it. This suggests that the anxiety we are dealing with here is extremely persecutory and primitive.

I have found it useful to think about the meaning of this patient's ruminatory symptoms as representing the creation of a psychic retreat (Steiner, 1993) into which he could escape from the adult anxieties of life and, in phantasy, merge with his object. The situation inside this retreat seemed to be one in which the passage of time would not be experienced in the same way as outside it. Inside, there seemed to be a timeless immobility, as represented by a dream of a candle shining against a featureless background which he reported early in the analysis. The implication is that he reacted to separation by making a cutting severance.

Fixation and retreat

With this second patient, the position was more complicated than in the first, because the illness itself represented a retreat. Indeed, the very treatment could be subverted to that end. I think it may be possible to hypothesize that the fixation of my female patient for a while took the form of a retreat formed of grudges against her mother. It seems likely that this broke down in the face of recognition that she wanted children and a sexual relationship as a woman. Time, therefore, imposed an imperative upon her. There was no such imperative for my male patient, but as time has gone on he has acquired an increasing impatience with his failure to use his talents.

In their discussion of fixation, Laplanche and Pontalis (1973) say that

> fixation is repeatedly encountered as a way of accounting for a clear empirical fact i.e. the neurotic—or any human subject—is marked by childhood experiences and retains an attachment to archaic modes of satisfaction, types of object and relationship. [p. 162]

It is a concept that Freud used at every stage of development of his theory. For example, fixation at the anal stage is said to be at the root of obsessional neurosis and of a certain character type. At the same time, fixation prepares the points to which regression will occur in all types of patient. Laplanche and Pontalis reached the conclusion that, incontestable as fixation is as a *descriptive* term, it contains within itself no principle of explanation. Indeed, without other theoretical structures, a degree of circularity is inevitable. Perhaps it is this attitude to the concept of fixation that can lead one to overlook some more exciting aspects of the ideas. Fixation has to be fitted at least into the topographical model to acquire any explanatory power. In their discussion of regression, Heimann and Isaacs (1970) suggest that fixation can be thought of from the progressive as well from the pathological point of view. They draw on Freud's suggestion in the Schreber case that

> The delusion formation which we take as a pathological product is in reality an attempt at recovery. . . . The symptoms of the illness are but a sign of the process of recovery which then "forces itself so noisily upon our attention". [Freud, 1911c, p. 182]

Perhaps it is this impression of noise that marks the difference between the fixation and the psychic retreat. The psychic retreat is more noted for its silence and stability than its noise until the analysis starts to threaten it in some way. The notion of a psychic retreat can seem more complex because of the implication that it represents an organized response to something. It is a patient's creation. Indeed, we might say that whereas the fixation presents a problem for the patient, the retreat represents a solution. Steiner (1993), to whom we owe the term, saw a psychic retreat providing a patient with "an area of relative peace and protection from strain when meaningful contact with the analyst is experienced as threatening". I do not propose to summarize here Steiner's linking of the psychic retreat to the concept of pathological organization or the "borderline" position. What I would like to introduce here are some ideas concerning time. They derive from the observation that in both the fixation and the retreat, there is an area of the patient's personality that might be described as a space that is, to varying degrees, sealed off from the remainder. Within this space, there is a different sense of time. This sense, however, shows itself in the overall presentation of the patient such that the patient with the fixation brings a sense of urgency and demand, while the patient in the retreat seems to bring a request for help but without the dreaded pain involved in change.

Time inside the psychic retreat

It will be recalled that in the discussion of the male patient above, it was suggested that all separation left him feeling little and powerless in a small and helpless body. It could be observed that he reacted to this by violently and sadistically severing from his object. At the same time, he projected his sadism such that he could have an idea of being a helpless victim. It is proposed that, by a kind of twisting manoeuvre, he managed to be a sadist and a masochist at the same time, enabling him to have the gratifications of being the aggressor and the victim simultaneously.

It seemed to me that there was a coexistence of two processes that functioned in countervailing ways. Something was disavowed and projected into the object (in this case, aggressive impulses). Something else was gained, at the same time, from the object (in this case, the gratification of being a victim, either of the object or the illness). From the point of view of technique, interpretation of one process was stymied by the functioning of the countervailing process. It presented a formidable defence based on the determination to maintain the retreat as a closed system. *It was not surprising that within a structure designed to prevent change, the predominant sense of time within it was akin to that in Narnia under the rule of the White witch—time had stopped: such that* chronos *became a sterile* kairos. In the transference, this could be experienced as a desire for an analysis that was endless and which sought no change. The only hope of any change began to emerge when the spuriousness of these gratifications began to dawn on him.

The general conclusion we may reach from these two clinical examples is that the patients' conscious experience of, and reaction to, the time boundaries of the setting reflected very powerful wishes that could not be allowed into consciousness. These wishes not only were expressed in their reactions to the time boundaries of the setting, but were strongly reflected in the pattern of these patients' lives.

Some theoretical and clinical implications

These clinical studies have certain clinical and theoretical implications that deserve discussion. Let me begin by suggesting that any theory of object relations implies the concepts of time and space. When we talk about the dynamics of physical objects, using Newtonian mechanics, we are talking about their movement in space, implying speed and acceleration that, in turn, imply the notion of time. In this viewpoint, time and space provide a frame within which movement occurs. Furthermore, they are givens, and are continuous in nature. This assumption was later questioned by Einstein (1920), who showed that time and space could be neither givens nor continuous. He was discussing this in terms of the dynamics of physical objects, but, it seems to me, it is also particularly true of the dynamics of psychic objects.

Freud (1933a) made the interesting observation that, in dreams, time may be referred to in spatial terms. Thus, a dream involving small figures might be a statement about events long ago, as though looking at objects from afar. He (1925a) also took the view that there was no sense of time in the Unconscious. He advanced the hypothesis that the origin of the sense of time came from the discontinuous method of functioning of the Perceptual conscious. He says, "It is as though the unconscious stretches out feelers, through the medium of the system Pcpt.-Cs towards the external world and hastily withdraws them as soon as they have sampled the excitations coming from it" (p. 457). Thus, we see a sense of time coming from the iterative sampling of the external world. I think we may surmise that here Freud is talking about time solely in its chronological or clock time sense. Within these ideas of Freud, we have two lines to follow. The first suggests that there is a link between time and space such that they are not independent of one another. The second is that there can be senses of time other than the chronological.

Marie Bonaparte (1940) summarized this work by Freud in a fascinating survey of scientific, philosophical, and psychoanalytic thinking about time up to that point. The first aspect that she discussed was the various means available to adults to mount an assault on the fact of chronological time. In so doing, she brought into focus the endless struggle between the pleasure and reality principles. In discussing the philosophical approaches, she drew attention to a remark attributed to Janet, who said,

> Generally speaking, it (i.e. time) inspires little enough affection in men's hearts, but philosophers regard it with particular loathing: they have done their very best to suppress it altogether . . . We are not surprised to find that even today [*sic*] there are patients who have a horror of time. The philosophers have felt the same. [p. 454]

Why should time have engendered such horror in the philosophers? It seems to arise from the fact that time, among all concepts, can be thought of in ways that challenge the idealist and the materialist. In any event, our clinical observation forces us to recognize that there is a phenomenal experience of a sense of time and that this is separate from chronological time.

Chronological time has been linked to the notion of the "Arrow of time" derived from the assymmetry of past and future, which is akin to the Greek idea of *chronos* mentioned earlier. It is suggested by Davies (1995) that the notion of the "arrow of time" stems from the second law of thermodynamics, which rests on the observation that almost all physical processes are irreversible. Imagine, for example, trying to reverse the breaking of an egg or the mixing of milk in tea. In contrast to Newtonian mechanics, in which time becomes part of the stage of events as a result of the potential reversibility of mechanics, the irreversibility of physical processes gives rise to an asymmetry symbolized by the passage of time from past to future. From this we derive the "arrow of time" which is operationalized by chronological time.

The second law of thermodynamics, which, broadly speaking, states that heat cannot flow from cold to hot bodies, can be made more precise by introducing the concept of entropy. In a simple system, such as a closed flask of water or air, if the temperature is uniform then nothing happens and the system remains in a state of thermodynamic equilibrium. The flask will contain energy but nothing can be done with it. If heat is concentrated in a particular place then things will happen by convection, but will reach equilibrium and a uniform temperature. This means that the second law of thermodynamics can be reformulated into: *in a closed system, entropy never decreases*. The restriction to a closed system is important, because if heat or other forms of energy can be exchanged between the system and its environment, then entropy can be decreased. This is what happens in a refrigerator, where heat is extracted from warm bodies and delivered to the environment, but where there is a price to pay, which is the expenditure of energy.

These ideas about the openness and closedness of systems enable us to think about psychic reality comprising fields or systems that are open or closed. In closed fields, we might find equilibrium but a lack of dynamic, and where the "arrow of time" does not seem to apply. Perhaps the whole point of their existence is to create the illusion of the invalidity of the "arrow of time". In more familiar words the "arrow of time" suggests the reality of death and an interminable analysis is sought. Hence, any closed fields might be thought of as containing illusions that deaden or defend against anxieties arising from the sense of castration, the associated feeling of lack, and the connotation of death. It seems to me that this provides a link with the idea of the psychic retreat. As we have seen in the second patient described above, his psychic retreat was a closed system created to defend against the anxieties aroused by the threat of change. It follows that to seek to open up, by therapeutic action, these closed psychic systems will arouse intense anxiety, which is often empirically observed. The nature of the anxiety could be seen in the second case described above, when we consider the nature of the projective processes and the implicit gratifications which created the retreat. In the broadest of summary, these entailed the gratifications of appearing to be the victim in passive submission to the aggressor, combined with the secret pleasure of being full of aggression, as revealed by the violence of the ruminations.

The clinical implications arising from this formulation are significant. Fink's paper (1993) on the treatment of an obsessional patient who showed a sense of timelessness suggested that, by careful attention to the distortion of time in the transference, significant therapeutic advances could be made. Using the theoretical terminology due to Matte-Blanco, he showed that his patient began to develop a sense of assymmetric or chronological time, which enabled him thereby to have a sense of a past, a future, as well as a present. Fink noted that his patient even appeared to age physiologically. Fink suggested that since one of the functions of transference interpretations is to help a patient to distinguish psychic reality from external reality, it is this that enables the analyst to help such patients to develop a sense of chronological time. With such a sense of time comes a separate sense of themselves in the now, and in the past, and the future. One has only to consider that one of the important consequences of failing to do this is to be unable to situate oneself in intergenerational history, such that the passage through the Oedipal process to psychic complexity is obstructed (Bollas, 1993). Given this, we can see that consideration and interpretation of distortions of time can give significant entries into severe psychopathological processes.

Two implications of a more theoretical nature flow from these clinical studies. These concern the understanding of the psychoanalytic setting and the nature of time and space in psychic reality.

In his paper on the temporal dimension of the psychoanalytic space, Sabbadini (1989) suggested that

> The timeless quality of the content of analysis is determined by and in constant interaction with such formal time arrangements, set by the analyst and altered only by exceptional circumstances. It is this contrast of temporalities that shapes the analytic encounter, modulating its rhythm and punctuating its discourse. Each of these temporalities is unthinkable without the other. [p. 305]

Following this, I think it is possible to conceive the psychoanalytic setting as structuring and containing the patient's multitudinous fields of desire, with the patient's fields in collision with the analyst's and with the psychoanalytic setting. A visual image of such could be said to exist on many mosques in Islam: that is, the Arabesque contained by the Geodesic.

As I think is amply demonstrated in the clinical studies above, the collision of the patient's desires with the temporal boundaries of the setting permitted the observation of the first patient's desires to be treated as someone special and the second patient's desire for an interminable analysis. These essentially sexual demands are thus made apparent in the transference by the temporal structure. Analysis of the demands could then easily proceed because they are shown in an unambiguous way, which is enormously helpful to the analyst and, by extension, to the patient. We can see that, in many ways, in order to be able to observe this collision of the setting with patient's desires, we have to treat the temporal aspect of the setting as an absolute and this necessity may bring its own problems. I think the problems of technique often stem from the difficulty of allowing the time necessary to permit the manifestation of these processes in an unambiguous way. Premature, and, therefore, experienced by the patient as critical, interpretation of the patient's distortions of time (otherwise known sometimes as attacks on the setting, which, of course, they undoubtedly are) may lead to a zealous compliance by the patient with the psychoanalyst's perceived demands, and the essential data yielded then vanishes into this form of enactment. However, if these processes are allowed to develop, the temporal structure of the setting allows the different temporalities of the patient's internal world to be become conscious and apparent to the patient and the psychoanalyst alike and, therefore, capable of articulation.

Several contributors to this field of investigation have suggested that a sense of time is created in the patient as a result of the session's time boundaries, which operate as a superego. It is not difficult to see that the end of a session can be experienced as an injunction "thou shalt not . . . continue". Immediately, this injunction creates a sense of the future and, by implication, a present and a past. Kurtz's (1988) paper shows how psychoanalysts of different theoretical persuasions would treat a patient's desire to extend a session in completely different ways. By contrasting the ego-psychologist, the self-psychologist, and the Lacanian views of the significance of fixed session time, he suggests that each psycho-analytical theoretical system is embedded in a metaphysics that profoundly affects the direction of treatment. Thus, the ego-psychologist attempts to strengthen a patient's capacity to distinguish and negotiate a commonsense (as he called it) reality. The framework of treatment is thought of as "real", so that the patient's distorting attitudes or efforts towards the temporal structure are necessarily "unrealistic" and, therefore, constitute evidence of ego failure. A self-psychologist, by contrast, might take the view that much distorting attitude reflects current ego needs and should be met by departure from commonsense reality behaviour. Thus, the analyst may allow himself and the situation to be manipulated according to the patient's needs. Kurtz saw the Lacanian system being radically different from these two in its very conception of reality. To the Lacanian, thinks Kurtz, the analyst is not present as an emblem of commonsense reality, nor does he offer himself as a self object—an illusion deemed by the self-psychologist as necessary for development. The analyst remains the impossible Other, challenging the me-connaisance of the patient's ego. Thus, we see a rationale for Lacan's short sessions being derived from these ideas and in particular for obsessional patients because of their tendency to transform the treatment into a psychic retreat. They do this by settling into a comfortable position in their analysis, where they say just enough to keep the analysis going but not enough to discover anything new. In this way, the obsessional controls the analysis and can use the analyst as the ideal Other who verifies what the subject thinks and believes. In this structure, the analyst is reduced to being a mirror that simply reflects the subject's own narcissistic image of itself. There is no dynamic, and, hence, there is no sense of time.

Turning now to the nature of time and space in psychic reality, I referred above to Einstein's thoughts on the notions of time and space. It may be thought by some that such views are irrelevant to psychoanalysis, but I think we should take seriously Kurtz's view that each psychoanalytic theoretical system is embedded in an implicit metaphysics. For this reason, some consideration of views from other disciplines throws our own theoretical assumptions into sharper relief.

The revolutionary consequence of Einstein's theory of relativity for the concepts of space and time was that a space–time was seen as no longer resolvable into space and time as separate co-ordinates. It is noteworthy that this echoes with Freud's view that space and time are interchangeable in the unconscious. In the view of Abraham (1976), Freud made a possibly unwitting contribution to the Einsteinian revolution in the form of advocating that time and space are relative and variable. From the above discussion on open and closed systems, we can see that a model of the creation of the discontinuity of psychic space–time is the establishment of closed systems as a defence against movement and change

One of the problems we may experience in recognizing these phenomena may arise from the difficulty in accepting the relativity of time. It is doubtless true that we gain a notion of time and space in a commonsense way as we grow up. No matter how much we seek to understand Einstein's theory of relativity, I think it is hard to avoid treating time and space as constants and independent of one another, as did Newton. We need to remember that whereas

Newton, for his purposes, was quite justified in these assumptions, if we do this then this may affect unwittingly our conception of psychic reality and, as a result, make it hard to enter and understand another's. One consequence would be to limit the view we might take of a patient's desire to "attack the setting". Our conscious minds, being rooted in the age of reason, may find it very hard to follow Freud's insight into the interchangeability of the representation of time and space in the unconscious. The fact that psychoanalysts of different theoretical persuasions take radically different positions in their interpretation of similar phenomena as seen in behaviour confirms this worrying possibility.

Being objective about internal reality involves something similar to the process of development of scientific thought as envisaged by Einstein. But, in our case, it may be more accurate to say that the observation of distortions of space and time in the transference can precede our becoming aware of the existence and nature of internal objects in the psychic reality of our patients. I think we can see some of the different senses of time in the psychic reality of the patients I have discussed and how this was displayed in their interactions with me. The importance of these effects was that they betrayed structures that had a profound influence on their lives.

Another important feature is that neither space nor time seemed to act as a continuous stage, but indicated that their minds could be conceived as comprising different coexisting fields in which different conditions prevailed. Empirically, this has been frequently observed upon: for example, Rosenfeld's concept of psychotic islands. What these islands are, of course, are islands of experience which are capable of linking, to a greater or lesser extent, with other experiences—sometimes not at all. The clinical studies above showed how the temporal structure of two different patients' psychic realities became apparent in the collision with the *chronos* of the setting. For this reason, the *chronos–kairos* distinction should be seen not as a dichotomous split, but as two elements, struggling for dynamic equilibrium, of a dialectic in which each assumes and implies the other.

And yet, it is, I think, true that there is another, third, sense of time besides that of the chronological or asymmetric time distinct from the atemporality of the unconscious. To distinguish the two cases I have described above, we can bring the notion of a developmental time implied by the maturation of the body and, ultimately, death. The impact of the reality of the limits on the reproductive life of my female patient was readily apparent in the undoing of her neurotic structures, which was not so observable in my male patient. In his case, there could be glimpses of a desire for children, but this could be easily swamped by the fears evoked by the prospect of emergence from his retreat.

My reason for adding this, at the conclusion, is that it is easy to arrive at the idea that the concept of time is purely a creation of the mind; that it derives not from an actuality of experience, but from an ordering of experience. Time is, therefore, to this point of view, purely a cultural creation like language.

At the conclusion of the paper referred to earlier, Bonaparte asked whether it was conceivable that time could be nothing but a form of her perception. She could not bring herself to believe it, and brought in support of her view the psychoanalytic finding that a sense of reality and a sense of time appear simultaneously in the system of the perceptual consciousness alone. If this was the case, she argued, surely there was some link between them. What she sought to tie together here was time and reality, not in the reality principle sense, but as arising from an external reality. The aversion of men to the notion of time pointed in the same direction. Time did not arise from the pleasure principle; indeed, that principle took every favourable opportunity to help us forget it. Yet, did the perception of reality arise from *a priori* in the mind, as envisioned by Kant? In a conversation after he had read her paper, Freud told Bonaparte that his views were potentially in agreement with those of Kant. The sense we have of the passing of time, he thought, originated in our inner perception of the passing of our own life. With the awakening of consciousness comes the perception of this flow, which we then project on to the outside world. We are led, therefore, to a notion of a developmental time, which is rooted in both the internal and external worlds.

The observation of the existence of a developmental time complicates the picture in some ways, but does offer a means of setting the struggle between the reality and pleasure principles in some context. This context seems, on the face of it, very similar to Money-Kyrle's facts of life. May I finish by saying that it is, I submit, more useful to think of the *chronos–kairos* dialectic as being in dialectic itself with the arrow of time implied by the body and its maturation and the pressure that this places on psychic life, conscious or unconscious. The "facts of life" provide the geodesic within which, and against which, the arabesque swirl of conscious and unconscious life is contained and struggles. The relationship between the psychoanalytic setting and the life of an analysis is analogous, if not the same.

Summary

In summary, where I have found these observations and ideas about time and its distortion in the consulting room of clinical psychoanalysis useful in my thinking is in the following.

1. It seems to me that we can learn much about a patient's psychic reality and its structure if we observe its impacts upon us and that important clues to this will be found in the distortions of the space and time of the psychic field between us and the form that these distortions take. I think that our awareness of these distortions comes in a great variety of forms and may be felt predominantly in the countertransference, very often initially in a non-verbal manner, and will take time to develop.
2. Looking at the analytic setting from the point of view of creating a time–space that contains and challenges the patient does offer a means of refining our understanding of the reasons for creating a particular setting. As an example, the reasons for treating someone five times a week as opposed to less frequently. Thus, we have a link between an understanding of the setting and the impact it will have on patients' internal psychic structures.
3. Looking at the temporal aspects of the clinical material of these two patients enabled me to grasp some important aspects of these patients' experience. I think I could get a direct insight into their use of the analytic setting and relate this fairly directly to significant issues in their lives that were not conscious to them. As I think we start in psychoanalysis by seeking to understand, by observation, a patient's experience and their use of the analysis, then the more articulated and

related these conceptual frameworks are, the more we will see and the more organized will be our perceptions.

References

Abraham, G. (1976). The sense and concept of time in psychoanalysis. *International Review of Psycho-Analysis*, 3: 461–472.

Bollas, C. (1993). Why Oedipus? In: *Being a Character*. London: Routledge.

Bonaparte, M. (1940). Time and the unconscious. *International Journal of Psychoanalysis*, 21: 427–468.

Davies, P. (1995). *The Cosmic Blueprint*. London: Penguin.

Einstein, A. (1920). *Relativity: The Special and The General Theory*. London: Methuen.

Fink, K. (1993). The bi-logical perception of time. *International Journal of Psychoanalysis*, 74: 1–10.

Freud, S. (1911c). Psycho-analytical notes upon an Autobiographical account of a case of Paranoia (Dementia Paranoides). *S.E., 12*: 1–80.

Freud, S. (1925a). A note upon the 'mystic writing pad'. *S.E., 19*: 227–234. London: Hogarth.

Freud, S. (1933a). *New Introductory Lectures on Psycho-analysis* (Revision of the theory of dreams). *S.E., 22*: 7–30. London: Hogarth.

Heimann, P., & Isaacs, S. (1970). Regression. In: M. Klein, P. Heimann, S. Isaacs & J. Riviere (Eds.), *Developments in Psychoanalysis*. London: Hogarth.

Kurtz, S. A. (1988). The psychoanalysis of time. *Journal of the American Psychoanalytic Association*, 36(4): 985–1004.

Laplanche, J., & Pontalis, J.-B. (1973). *The Language of Psycho-analysis*. London: Hogarth.

Mander, G. (1995). In praise of once weekly work: making a virtue of necessity or treatment of choice. *British Journal of Psycho-therapy*, 12(1): 3.

Money-Kyrle, R. (1968). Cognitive development. *International Journal of Psycho-analysis*, 49: 691–698.

Sabbadini, A. (1989). Boundaries of timelessness. Some thoughts about the temporal dimension of the psycho-analytic space. *International Journal of Psycho-analysis*, 70: 305.

Steiner, J. (1993). *Psychic Retreats*. London: Routledge.

CHAPTER EIGHT

Symbols and their function in managing the anxiety of change: an intersubjective approach*

James S. Rose

Summary

C hange inevitably creates anxiety because of loss and the confrontation with the unknown. It is proposed that one function of symbols is to manage the anxiety of change. They do this by creating a means by which anxieties can be presented to the subject and then communicated to another mind. These creations are called symbolic because, it is proposed, their purpose is communicative as well as simply incorporating internal anxieties and desires with external exigencies, which might be termed symptoms. Viewing them in this way enables the analyst to put symbolic phenomena as they emerge in an analysis into an intersubjective perspective. I suggest that thinking of symbols as purely intrasubjective phenomena limits our perspective. It is more technically useful to look at the communicative aspects of symbols as they present themselves to the symbolizing subject, and, subse-

* First published in 2000 in *International Journal of Psychoanalysis, 81*: 453–470.

quently, to the analyst in the dialogue within the psychoanalytic setting because the objective and temporal dimension of the setting can be included thereby. Two clinical examples of symbols are discussed. The first, which was brought for analysis, and a second, which developed in the course of an analysis. One is given as an example of resistance to change, whereas the other revealed an unconscious drive for change.

Introduction

I will begin with the idea that the symbolic functioning available to an individual determines the way he or she anticipates and experiences change. I have indicated in my title that I shall take an intersubjective approach to thinking about symbols, so I would like to set out my reasons for bringing in this perspective. The current debate about subjectivity in psychoanalysis begins with the recognition that the encounter in the consulting room is a meeting of two minds. It seems to me that this fact has to be incorporated somehow into an understanding of the process by which a psychoanalyst helps a patient come to know their own mind. Goldberg (1998) has suggested that a plethora of different attempts to take on board this fact of the psychoanalytic endeavour have led to an agreement that

> the fluidity of the exchange of information in messages between patient and therapist does not allow one to isolate either the one or the other as a fixed point in order to gain access to some reliable set of mental contents. [p. 215]

When taken into thinking about the psychoanalytic encounter, there is, thus, a theoretical conundrum created by the acceptance of an analyst's subjectivity. If an analyst's perception of reality is open to doubt as a result of the analyst's subjectivity, does psychoanalysis become an impossible profession?

Much of the heat in the current debate on subjectivity seems to derive from the implicit assumption by some that subjectivity implies nothing more than a lack of objectivity. For others, for example, Renik (1998), subjectivity means more than simply not being objective. He argues that to be truly objective, we are forced to accept the fact of the analyst's *irreducible* subjectivity. This looks at first sight to be incorporating an indisputable fact, but it has many logical consequences. For example, we have to ask about the patient's countertransference to the analyst's transference (Atwood & Stolorow, 1984, p. 47). Indeed, distinguishing whether the analyst's countertransference, an indisputable experiential phenomenon, arises from his lack of objectivity or is the result of a creation within his mind of an aspect of the patient's experience captures precisely the theoretical predicament. It could be one or the other, or, maybe, both. Theoretically speaking, they could be sequential or contemporaneous.

In this debate, objectivity becomes as much a problem as subjectivity, to the point where it is almost equated with it. The result is that the protagonists in the debate seem to accuse each other, on the one hand, of being "wild", or, on the other, unreal and positivistic. Ogden's (1986) theory of the "analytic third", arising from the interaction of patient and analyst, tries to find a way through the conundrum but possibly does so by altering the sense of what we mean by a subject. His sense seems more akin to the notion of "becoming a subject" Cahn (1998) or, indeed, Lacan's sense of the entry into the Symbolic order as defined in his (1945) theory of logical time. In this formulation, we have a theoretical structure that has links with the recognition of dyadic states of consciousness recently postulated by some infant researchers, for example, Tronick and Weinberg (1997). What makes this possible is that these formulations about what happens between two minds takes into account that the interaction is about something other than those two minds themselves.

Cavell (1998), coming at this problem from the stance of a philosopher, has taken the view that, in order to know our own minds, we require an interaction with another mind in relation to what could be termed objective reality. Without the inclusion of objective reality in a process of what she terms progressive triangulation, she argues that a so-called intersubjective approach collapses into another subjective one. It is this collapse, perhaps, that led Goldberg (1998) to conclude that the new ideas developed by the "inter-subjectivists" were a family of related concepts but with no unifying theory.

In Cavell's analysis of the problem of how we can come to know our own minds, she argues that an implicitly Cartesian notion of

subjectivity underpins much psychoanalytic theoretical conceptualization. The sense of this Cartesian notion is that our knowledge of
our minds is not connected in any presumable and essential way
with the external world, and knowledge of other minds is either
impossible or mysterious. If this is how subjectivity is to be defined,
it opens it to the kind of attack recently mounted by the intersubjectivists. This is because, in order to avoid the embrace of solipsism, an "objectivity" must be introduced which can be accused of
being a positivistic illusion unless it is anchored to something. But
the intersubjectivists, she feels, will find themselves in the same
position, taking the same risks but with greater risk of the accusation of "suggestion" if they ignore objective reality.

Renik (1998), as mentioned above, has suggested a "pragmatic"
solution to this problem such that the test of the effectiveness of
a particular action taken by an analyst is whether it works: that
is, whether it serves to reduce the unhappiness of the patient in
the long term. The difficulty with such a pragmatic posture is to
determine who decides what is therapeutic; in particular, when
such a decision can be made and whether the pragmatic analyst can
avoid being in the position of Solomon. I am in agreement with
Cavell's position, but the question then is how to work in accor-
dance with it. An answer, it seems to me, may be found in the observation of the patient's use of the setting as it occurs over time and
in the changes of this use. What I seek to do in this chapter is to
examine how the essentially subjective (in Cavell's terms) concept
of the symbol can be used in an intersubjective way by carefully
observing its use, development, and change in the psychoanalytic
setting.

The title of this paper embraces such a broad field of thought
that, in order to begin, I need to be specific. There can be few more
dramatic changes in one's life than bereavement. The immediately
bereaved can feel "in" a state of mind experienced as endless and
timeless, whereas an observer, no matter how identified with the
bereaved, will be separated from the experience because they will
link it with the loss of someone external to the bereaved. The link
is not always available to the bereaved, because the loss is experienced as a loss of part of the self as well as the loss of someone
external. This internal aspect of the experience pervades the self
and is bound up with the process of mourning. I have used

bereavement as an example of change; in thinking about change, I would like to reiterate the notion that all change will involve loss of some kind and, hence, mourning.

It is easy, in considering change in this way, to become caught in the notion of it somehow implying that, in all cases, there is an ejection from a Garden of Eden. However, a frog is not a tadpole in mourning. We know that change arising from bereavement is likely to be painful, but the arrival of a first child also brings a profound change. Not only has one a child, but also one is a parent, and there is a new relationship which influences all other relationships. One's life is instantly more complicated and restructuring and adjustment is necessary. However, we cannot stop there and say simply that some changes are painful whereas others are pleasurable. I think we have to acknowledge the situation as being more complex. This is because, from conception, we may be thought of as systems in dynamic equilibrium with our environment.

This concept we owe to Claude Bernard; that is, that the organism's prime task is to maintain the integrity of its internal milieu. The infant researchers Tronick and Weinberg (1997) have suggested that Bernard did not appreciate that a critical feature of the homeostatic regulatory process was a dyadic collaborative process (as they put it), which echoes the point made by Cavell. In plainer words, in order to maintain our inner milieu, we deal with other minds. Hence, change presents a challenging duality in that it will threaten a status quo, but will need to do so as growth occurs and maturation unfolds. The problem remains whether the anxiety stirred by change mainly concerns loss of the familiar. Laplanche (1997) has suggested that the Copernican-like assault on human narcissism wrought by psychoanalysis is an assault that must be continually mounted because of the persistent temptation to return to the self-centred Ptolemaic outlook. This is brought about by the fact that our body is our outlook, and, thus, point of view, on the world (so the sun does indeed appear to revolve around us). But, he goes further than that by suggesting that change brings with it the threat of the alien unknown. It is this sense of the alien which comes from the awareness of others' minds that we only partially know and the part of our own minds that we do not know: our unconscious. Laplanche, therefore, puts forward the view that we find this alien other both in the internal and the external world and they support each other. Thus, the unknown other alien mind resonates with and supports the alien-ness of the unconscious.

This means that the two can be potentially blurred and confused and the choice open to the subject is whether to manage the anxiety of change via the spurious safety of egocentricity or to sacrifice this at the risk of experiencing helplessness, with the association of impotence. In the face of these twin dreads, the temptation to return to a self-centred view can be readily understood. To the anxiety stirred by the unknown other alien mind and our own unconscious mind must, of course, be added a third influence: the future, which we can never know in full. The sacrifice of egocentricity permits, of course, the opening of a dialogue with an other mind. We must conclude that the anxiety stirred by change must result from the confrontation with the unknowable as well as loss.

Having offered some very general thoughts about change and its complexities, I will introduce some clinical material. I would like to discuss a patient who came into analysis because he experienced states of mind in which he said he could not stop thinking about headless bodies and a desire to stab. He found these experiences impossible to understand, because he felt no affect other than the terror stemming from having such a thought. All concealed spaces, that is, what he could not know, contained headless bodies, which he was about to see. Consciously, he experienced no anger or aggression, but felt himself tormented by what he termed the "ruminations". We might pause here and ask what we mean by "think". It would be truer to the spirit of his description of his state of mind to conceive of his mind being occupied by some things that we could call thoughts. When he experienced these states of mind, he could do little else than be in them and try not to be in them. This presented him with the impossible dilemma of trying not to think about something he was thinking about, which is an impossible task. To try not to think about something is, of course, to think about it, and round and round he went in an obsessive nightmare.

It is clear that, in terms of symptoms, this patient could be diagnosed as an obsessional neurotic, but, it seems to me, the observable phenomena can be thought about in broader terms than diagnosis. The question to my mind is whether these symptoms can be thought of as the subject communicating something to the other. It could be said, as part of the initial assessment, that the symptoms created a countertransference pull towards the patient because it was hard not to be become intrigued by these headless bodies and feel drawn towards understanding and interpreting them. Hence, something is projected in the transference which creates a complementary projective counter-identification in the manner described by Grinberg (1962). The question might then be whether the symptomatic thoughts represent something; in other words, have some symbolic significance. However, the emotional appeal experienced in the countertransference represents the analyst's subjectivity. The question is whether the patient's and the analyst's subjectivities will meet through the link partially provided by the symptomatic symbol.

The symbolic content of symptoms was referred to by Freud (1916c) when he suggested that while the hat had been sufficiently well established in the analysis of dreams to be a symbol of the male genital organ, it was not, he thought, an "intelligible one". In order to understand the meaning of the symbol, he suggested that one must find a link between the symbol and the anxiety to which it is related. He referred, in the case of hats, to the tortures that some obsessional patients inflicted upon themselves when they compared the manner in which their friends might doff their hats to them in greeting. From this, they might then impute all kinds of neurotic meanings as to whether a friend might perceive himself as being more important than they, depending on how he doffed his hat. Thus, the anxiety in these instances was castration anxiety; the symptom was in the intertwining of castration anxiety with ordinary social conventions and the communication was in the manner of hat doffing. The hat provided the medium for the expression of the anxiety and, thus, in a sense, managed it by enabling it to be expressed in a symbolic form. With this in mind, we are taken immediately to the theory of symbols and their formation and functioning.

Theories of symbols

Laplanche and Pontalis (1973) suggest that, in psychoanalytic thinking, broadly speaking, symbolism refers to any mode of figurative or indirect representation of an unconscious idea. However, there is, they further suggest, a more restricted sense where it is suggested that there is a constancy of the relationship between the symbol and that which is symbolized. This constancy is found not only within an individual, but also between them, and, to a certain extent, in the mostly widely separated cultures.

Such an assertion of a constancy of relationship is rather unique because, in linguistics, there need be no logical or intrinsic connection between the signifier and the signified. However, the link between the notion of a symbol and language has not been given equal weight by all psychoanalytic theorists. Indeed, I shall argue that psychoanalytic conceptualization of the symbol has tended to concentrate on the symbol as an intrapsychic phenomenon. The effect of this has been that the symbol as an interpsychic medium has been less thought about, with the exception, of course, of Lacan. When I come later to discuss the work of Cavell, I shall follow, as I understand it, her concept of the difference between the subjective (or the intrapsychic) and the intersubjective.

Psychoanalytic theories of the nature of symbols, and their formation and function, often differ because the phenomena of symbolism are taken as evidence in support of other psychoanalytic concepts. Indeed, it could be said that psychoanalytical understanding of the symbol is largely epiphenomenal. When a proponent of one outlook criticizes another from another, one gets the impression that the criticism arises from a failure to understand the profound, but unstated, philosophical differences between the proponents, which are separate and distinct from the psychoanalytic differences. In the literature about symbolism and symbolic functioning in psychoanalysis there is, therefore, something of a tower of Babel. However, each theoretical strand offers much and it is for this reason that I am going to take some space and time to set out my understanding of a number of different approaches. I will refer, initially, to three main strands of conceptualization in psychoanalytic theory developed by British thinkers.

First, we may consider the early work of Freud, which was used by Ernest Jones in his 1916 paper "The theory of symbolism". The paper is a combative one directed at the post-Freudian ex-colleagues of Jones who he regarded as revisionists or separatists backing away from Freud's radical views of the human mind. The paper is a virtuoso performance that sets out a psychoanalytic view of the nature of a symbol and the process of symbolization, which it is necessary to keep conceptually separate in our minds. His main thesis was that it was possible to distinguish one fundamental type of indirect representation of one idea by another from other more or less closely allied ones. Consideration of the points of distinction throws light on the nature of indirect figurative representation in general and Jones' view in particular of "true" symbolism.

To distinguish what Jones called "true" symbolism from all other types, he first drew attention to what he saw as the difficulty that is indicated by all forms of symbolism, which concerned the adequate apprehension of affects. In the very broadest sense of the term "symbolism" (which could include metaphor), he felt that it betokened a relative incapacity for either apprehension or communication. This incapacity could be thought of as intellectual or affective in origin, the second of which was much the more important. Further, the mind tends to notice especially those features that interest it because of their resemblance to previous experiences of interest. The appreciation of resemblance facilitates the assimilation of new experience by referring the unknown to the previously known.

In the briefest of summary of his ideas, I quote the following from his paper:

> All psycho-analytic experience goes to show that the primary ideas of life, the only ones that can be symbolised—those, namely concerning the bodily self, the relation to the family, birth, love and death—retain in the unconscious throughout life their original importance and that from them is derived a very large part of the more secondary interests of the conscious mind. As energy flows from and never to them and as they constitute the most repressed parts of the mind, it is comprehensible that symbolism takes place in one way only. Only what is repressed is symbolised (in the true sense): only what is repressed needs to be symbolised. This conclusion is the touchstone of the psycho-analytic theory of symbolism. [p. 116]

Here, we see Jones drawing directly on the topographical model of the mind developed by Freud arising from his work on dreams and their interpretation. It will be recalled that Freud saw dreams as the expression of unconscious wishes that had to be disguised in order to preserve sleep because the wishes would disturb sleep if they were allowed into consciousness. In 1915, he wrote about repression, saying that "The essence of repression lies simply in turning something away and keeping it at a distance from consciousness" (1915d, p. 146). The distinction he later made between thing presentation and word presentation in "The unconscious" (1915e) anticipates a development away from the repression model of symbolization. Its significance is that it enables us to see that the kinds of symbolization available affect not simply the availability of particular experiences (which have been repressed), but also concern the very possibilities of thought and experience. Thus, he proposed a notion of *agnosia* (implying something which cannot be known) in addition to *aphasia* (that for which there is no word).

Of particular note is Jones' thought that symbolism betokened an incapacity to communicate. Perhaps one of the most irksome ideas is that of the idea of a "true" symbol, which is an epiphenomenon of repression. Precisely because it is taken to be evidence of repression, it means that something is kept from consciousness and yet something about this "unintelligibility" draws attention to itself and, hence, communicates. As we have seen above, the patient's preoccupation with unintelligible headless bodies inevitably draws our attention. It may appear odd that Jones made so little reference to language, particularly as symbolic phenomena are associated with language and it was in linguistics that much conceptualization about symbolic phenomena had been developed. But Jones was concerned with what he considered the "true" symbol in the psychoanalytic sense. Jones' priority, at the time, was to make Freudian psychoanalytic thinking distinct by demonstrating the unconscious, which had political as well as scientific purpose. As a result, it can be concluded that Jones' conception of symbolism was essentially a subjective, rather than an intersubjective, one.

Nevertheless, returning to the man mentioned earlier, with these ideas in mind, we might be led to wonder what repressed ideas the headless bodies represent, why they have to be repressed, and what they prevent from being known. This leads to the relationship between the symbol and the symbolizer. The next theoretical development I wish to consider is that deriving from Klein and its development by Segal (1957) through her distinction between symbolic equation and symbolic representation. Segal illustrated this difference by comparing two male patients. One was a musician who, when asked why he no longer played his violin, replied with indignation whether the inquirer wished him to masturbate in public. In other words, the violin was, in effect, *equated* with the penis, and in an extremely concrete way. The other, also a musician, reported a dream in which he and a young girl were playing a violin duet. He had associations to the dream of fiddling and masturbating, from which it emerged that the violin represented his genital and playing the violin represented a masturbation phantasy of sexual intercourse with the girl. We can see that, in this case, the violin acts as a *representative* and is not *equated* in the same concrete way. The two kinds of symbol are, of course, epiphenomenal of the depressive and the paranoid–schizoid positions, respectively. Thus, Segal (1957) says, "Not only the actual content of the symbol but the very way in which symbols are formed and used seems to reflect precisely the ego's state of development and its ways of dealing with its objects" (p. 392), and, in addition, that

> symbol formation is an activity of the ego attempting to deal with the anxieties stirred by its relation to the object and is generated primarily by the fear of bad objects and the fear of the loss or inaccessibility of good objects. [*ibid.*]

What I wish to emphasize is the difference between the situation in which separateness is difficult, if not impossible, *as is implied by the symbolic equation*, and where it is possible to separate out oneself from others and retain the separateness of different experiences in relation to the same other, *as is implied by the symbolic representation*. Symbolic equation is to be still lost in the immediacy of a moment in a potentially persecutory way. Symbolic representation enables the symbolizer to be separate from the symbol and symbolized. Hence, we can see two different possible ways in which the symbolizer mediates his experience through a symbol, each with their psychic advantages and drawbacks.

There is, however, a difficulty in making fear or loss the essential drivers of symbolism, because it precludes the possibility of symbols representing the creation of something new emerging from unconscious processes in response to demand for change. In essence, my idea is that the complexity created by unknowable nothingness, or an absence of being, stimulates symbolization as much as the threat of the bad or the loss of the good. It is equally true that the representative symbol permits the embrace of complexity, because of the triangulation of symbol, symbolized, and symbolizer. This embrace of complexity the symbolic equation cannot fulfil and seeks to obviate or avoid.

The theory of symbolization in a representational sense is especially useful for understanding mourning and the pathologies of mourning. A capacity for symbolization in a representational sense means that the pleasurable aspects of the lost object can be distinguished from the unpleasurable and internalized into the self, which feels enhanced as a result. When symbolization is on the basis of equation, loss can only be felt as a persecution. The bereaved is stuck with and in their pain and cannot find relief. The difference between these two positions is that the symbolic equation creates a situation in which the symbol is indistinguishable from the self, whereas in the representation, something separate is possible. This means that it is possible to think with the representative in a manner different from the equation. This arises from the difference between the equation and the representation resting on the degree of projective identification utilized by the individual. We might say, for example, that in the symbolic equation described above, there is an equation of the meaning of words because there is a massive projective identification between the musician's penis (as an internal part object) and his violin. So far as this musician is concerned, there is, therefore, apparently no difference in reality between playing his violin and masturbating in public.

However, as listeners to the account, we might wonder whether the questioner is having his leg pulled or whether he is being seen by the musician as someone who is asking the musician to humiliate himself. In other words, the meaning of the musician's reply depends on its context. This idea of context relates to the notion of *triangulation* of symbol, symbolized, and symbolizer. In essence, this enables the possibility of assessing the relationship between two elements relative to the context created by a third. The link with the notion of progressive triangulation introduced earlier seems obvious, and the triangular space suggested by the symbolic representation offers a model of the embrace of complexity by allowing increasing elaboration of this triangular space over time. At any one point of time, it means that a relationship can be placed in a context that, in turn, means that the meaning of this relationship can be assessed in a way that is impossible without any kind of contextual referent.

In principle, there is no contextual referent in a pure symbolic equation; hence, the equation seems quite "real" and subjectively indisputable. In the symbolic representation, the presence of the context dissolves this concrete equation. The result is that meaning, and its elaboration, becomes a possibility. It must be said, however, that probably the symbolic equation hardly ever exists in pure form. There is always a context, even though it may be that, in an analysis, it is the analyst's task to provide and then identify a context so that what are meaningless symbolic equations to an analysand can become symbolic representations. Hence, the analyst provides the means of triangulation, where necessary. Indeed, this may be a major function of interpretation and creates the space to think.

The symbol of the headless body

Returning to the man who could not easily shake the ideas of headless bodies out of his mind, two features stood out from the beginning in the pattern of his feelings and ideation. First, it seemed there was some kind of representation here, but what was represented remained unconscious. The patient had no conscious means of interpreting the meaning of his ideas, but felt enveloped in them. Indeed, at times, he lived in them and was unable to escape these characteristics of a symbolic equation.

Second, whereas I could feel a strong temptation to try and interpret these ideas, I noted a strong resistance on his part to any efforts of this kind, even though he kept talking about his thoughts. This interesting feature brings forward two aspects of the word "symbol" in its derivation from Greek. In one sense, as pointed out by Wright (1991), it means a throwing together of things (*Symballein*), but it also derives from the Greek *symbolon*. This denotes the division into two of a recognizable something that was used as a means of recognition by members of forbidden religious groups; by the means of joining the fragments together, Wright brought this etymology to attention as a means of showing how the symbol (or fragment) betrayed the separation of symbol from symbolized. This he linked to Freud's theory of repression concerning the separation of thing presentations from word presentations. It illustrates an interesting duality about symbols in that they can both represent and also hide, and that can be part of their intention. There was the possibility that, however much my patient felt persecuted by these ideas, he seemed, paradoxically, not to wish to be separated from them.

Therefore, this man wanted not to think these ideas but he could not stop. The compulsion suggested that there was something very powerful or painful associated with, and hidden by, these ideas, and this was the only way they could be mentally accommodated. If we combine the theoretical views we have so far, we can say that something is being repressed and that, whatever this is, our patient is extremely reluctant to give up something about it. Furthermore, this seemed to be a very active process. It seemed that I must accept that there would be a lot of resistance towards me if I were seen as desiring to bring these somethings, whatever they were, to consciousness. This takes us to the nature of the relationships in which this man found himself, or, in other words, the context of the symbol.

In treating this man, I noticed the following.

First, he experienced onsets of these thoughts intermittently. They seemed to start when there was a sense of loss or disillusionment with someone important to him, but they seemed to recede and, indeed, disappear after there had been some emotional contact with me. When I made an interpretative link between their onset and his loss of contact with me, it met initially with steadfast denial. On the other hand, the interpretation of their disappearance in relation to emotional contact with me did not meet the same fate.

Second, the thoughts were experienced as coming from outside him.

Third, there seemed to be an experience of me as someone who was a detective, who was seeking to discover something for which he should feel guilty and should be condemned.

Fourth, the thoughts became very powerful when there was a conscious realization of approaching separation and permanent loss.

As a general observation of him, it seemed that here were three typical reactions to the prospect of separation. The first was to deny its importance: that is, to seek to obliterate any sense of the importance of the loss and any emotional reactions to it or, indeed, any sense of pain. The second was to cut himself off from the experience as if to deny that it ever happened. The third was to suffer powerful onsets of the thoughts that represented a need to fall ill. It was clear that, despite the denial, the prospect of separation at some level provoked terrible anxiety. There was a fear of being destroyed and the response was in part to destroy that which has created such anxiety. In addition, there seemed to be a possibility that, in the process of falling ill, there was a phantasy of regaining what had been lost. Once the "unintelligible" symptomatic symbol of the headless body was linked to the experience of separation, it seemed to me that the symbol began to acquire some meaning. Separation provided a context in which what the symbol represented could emerge. We may, therefore, hypothesize that a symbol hides when the context is removed, ignored, or denied.

Separation and the headless body

To substantiate my hypothesis that that his symptomatic symbol had been unconsciously created as a refuge into which he could withdraw when faced with the prospect of separation, I offer the following clinical material after some years of his analysis. This patient was treated in the London Clinic of Psychoanalysis. For patients treated in the London Clinic under its subsidized scheme, there was at the time an initial limit of three years, which could be extended in certain cases. I obtained an extension of one year. At the beginning of this fourth year, we had begun in the knowledge that, so far as the Clinic was concerned, there was a known termination date. This did not necessarily mean the analysis would end, if he and I chose not to end it, but it would no longer be under the auspices of the London Clinic. I made this clear to him as we began in September.

He reacted as if he was determined not to think about it and continued on in his timeless way until the approach of the Easter break. Then, when he returned, there were signs that the prospect of a real ending was starting to become conscious. There came a day when he asked what would happen in the Autumn after the analysis had ended. In other words, he was assuming, despite what I had said, that I would end his analysis. This session gradually ushered in a powerful onset of the ruminations. I will describe a session during this period.

This session took place on a Tuesday. On the day before, he had reported a dream, which was not that common for him to do. In the dream, he was lying on the couch in the consulting room but he was facing the opposite way round. I was behind him and moved my leg and it rubbed against his. He was embarrassed in telling me this dream because of what he considered was the homosexual content; that is, he felt that he was telling me that he thought I was homosexual. Being conscious that this was a dream told on a Monday, that there were signs of reversal in the dream, and that the prospect of ending hung over us like the sword of Damocles, I had the impression that this dream contained an anxiety even more fearful for him than telling me I was "queer", as he put it. I interpreted that what was consciously felt in the dream as my approach to him was a means of reversing a situation in which he felt I abandoned him, leaving him feeling as helpless as he felt in the dream.

He replied to this by telling me that he always wore brown shoes, in contrast to his father, who always wore black ones. This brought to my mind an oft-repeated memory of his father coming to his bedroom and touching him on the bedclothes, resting his hand "on top of my dick". In telling this story, he had often left me with the question in my mind of whether he was talking about an abuse, or whether he resisted his own affectionate feelings of love towards his father by transforming them into a homosexual approach. By telling about the colour of his shoes, I felt I was his father in the transference and that somewhere he feared a sexual approach. However, his embarrassment, rather than anxiety, at telling the dream suggested to me that it was not all like that. I thought he might be embarrassed at his affectionate feelings towards me and I told him so. In addition, I said that he found analysis sometimes very dangerous because it could be that I held up a mirror to him and showed him something horrifying which was derived from the strength of his needs for what he experienced me as being. This was followed the next day by this session.

The session began by the patient saying that it was as if no time had elapsed between when he had left and when he had arrived that day. His ruminations had been going full blast. Being mindful of how he seemed to have attacked the sense of separation by replacing it with the ruminations, I took this up with him by wondering why it was no time seemed to have elapsed when, of course, it had. This met with an irritated response, as if to say why wasn't I interested in his illness. Despite these protestations, I persisted in taking this up because I knew from work in previous sessions that there was something about separation that he found very disturbing. He replied that he was always like that. He wiped things out when he left, but he added that suffering the ruminations seemed to pull people towards him. I said that perhaps his mind was full of ruminations to pull me towards him and to make sure that I would not send him away at the end of the session without having something about which to feel guilty. This led him to observe at some length that he could always fall ill to get out of things and when he thought people were angry with him.

I chose to intervene into his discursive review of his past by wondering aloud what it was that had been going on between us that he got out of by being ill. I did this because I was wondering whether separation, at the unconscious level, initially produced anger at being displaced, but was experienced, at the conscious level, as anxiety at the prospect of being seen as angry. By interpreting the possibility of displacement of immediate anxieties into the past, I felt we might get closer to angrier feelings that his review of the past seemed designed to avoid.

After some skirmishing, he expressed his view that I saw him as a "little fuck" who could not do without analysis and he hated me for regarding him as contemptibly dependent. This seemed to be nearer to the anger that I had suspected, but which he seemed to be so afraid to express because of his fear of the consequences. This enabled us to explore his feelings and reactions at the end of a session when I said it was time. He acknowledged that his rage vanished into ruminations, which hid his anger with me and his fear of me, which resulted from the anger, in a single destructive cut. Once in the ruminations, he was ill and immune from the painful feeling arising from separation. However, the violence of the severance meant that the experience in the *après coup* was void.

Symbols as creations

What I now wish to examine is the link between the experience of change arising from the experience of separation and the various ways in which the symbol of the headless body seems to manage the anxiety associated with these changes. To pursue this, I will turn to a third strand of psychoanalytic theory: Winnicott's theory of transitional objects and transitional spaces, because of its intersubjective conception of the genesis and development of a symbol, which includes a temporal dimension.

At the heart of Winnicott's theory (1945) about the infant's experience in the early months of life is the notion of illusion. He envisaged the newborn infant as being like an organism without a skin to separate and protect it from the physical environment. In the early months, Winnicott said that the mother must enable the baby to maintain a sense of what he called omnipotence. Winnicott's use of the word in this context refers to the infant's system of thought being based entirely on wish fulfilment, or primary process thinking, for example, "I want it to be so and it is so". He is not referring to a defence.

At the beginning, the infant's mother has to act as a skin for it. The mother, by an almost total adaptation to the infant's needs, affords the infant the opportunity for the illusion that her breast is part of the infant. It is, as it were, under the baby's magical control. As Winnicott put it

> omnipotence is nearly a fact of experience. In another language, the breast is created by the infant over and over again out of the infant's capacity for love or (one can say) out of need. A subjective phenomenon develops in the baby which we call the mother's breast. The mother places the actual breast just where the infant is ready to create and at the right moment. [p. 238]

Winnicott believed that the mother's eventual task is gradually to disillusion the infant, but that she had no hope of success unless at first she had been able to give sufficient opportunity for illusion. If the mother failed in this task, a premature shattering of the omnipotence may occur, meaning that the baby had to turn its attention to external objects prematurely and conform to them, thereby creating a compliant false self. If things proceeded well enough, the infant would be able to tolerate increasing degrees of separation from mother. Thus, in his view, a *space* develops between mother and infant. The nature of this space and its perception and use is of central interest to us.

Winnicott (1951) took the view that, while psychoanalysis had established beyond doubt the need to distinguish between internal and external reality, there was a need to define what he called "the third part of the life of a human being". This was:

> an intermediate area of experiencing, to which inner reality and external life both contribute. It is an area that is not challenged because no claim is made on its behalf except that it shall exist as a resting place for the individual engaged in the perpetual human task of keeping inner and outer reality separate yet interrelated. [p. 230]

It will be clear that, within the infant's omnipotence, all objects will be perceived as part of the infant. There is no such thing, therefore, as a "not-me" object. Gradual separation from the mother and the accompanying process of disillusionment introduces the idea of objects outside omnipotence; while these objects are experienced within the intermediate space of experience described above, they will be experienced as "not me" objects, but it will not be clear whether they are outside omnipotent control or not. It is common to observe that infants latch on to a something that is clearly evaluated by the infant more highly than others. What will be clear to the infant's parents will be the special relationship that their infant has to this object—otherwise known as a transitional object. The transitional object may be called by we adults the teddy bear, or a bit of blanket, but to so regard this object as such with the adult mind is to risk missing the point.

If we defined the transitional object as the infant's teddy bear and put it away in our mental toy cupboard, we will lose sight of the importance of the area of experiencing, or the developing transitional space, in which the transitional object is situated. For the infant, the development of this space and the manipulation of objects within it permits the experience of becoming aware of the difference between inner and outer reality and the limits on omnipotence. Where we find, in an adult, evidence of a means by which this distinction is blurred or obviated, then we may hypothesize that for some reason the subject has sought to retain omnipotent control over something against all the evidence.

Transitional phenomena and the management of anxiety

In the case described above, it seemed that the anxiety that the patient sought to manage was separation anxiety. However, consciously acknowledging separation anxiety turned him, in his own mind, into a dependent "little fuck", which was a crippling narcissistic wound. He told me that a customary response to difficult situations at school had been to go to the sick room, but this had been at considerable cost to his self-esteem. When he grew into an adult in an adult body, a new "sick room" or refuge had to be created, and the headless body ideas emerged during adolescence. In the work of analysis, it became possible to identify a number of themes condensed into the idea of the headless body.

The first of these was that they contained a sense of himself cut off from his object. All separation was experienced by him as a cut. Second, his retaliatory response of cutting himself off from those who left him and obliterating any trace of their effects could also be detected. This was revealed in the analysis by his reaction at the end of a session, in which he could wipe it from his mind. Third, the sense of murderousness implied by this obliteration not only destroyed what it was that caused him psychic pain, but also gave him a powerful sense of his violent strength. This had to be kept quite secret for fear of retaliation by others if they found out the "truth" about him. This led directly to the sense of his analyst being experienced as a detective. Finally, the ideas would easily provide a sense for himself and others that he was ill (which, of course, he indeed was).

Presented like this, it is easy to wonder why this man came into analysis at all, because the secondary gains from his symptoms were as great as they were. But, somewhere, he was aware of how crippled he was because he deprived himself of the rewards of relationships in order to seek an unending relationship in which separation from his object of desire never occurred. With this patient, insight came only when, after long and careful attention to his reactions to separations, there was a realization that the violence contained by his symptomatic symbol stemmed from the violence of his reaction to loss. He had, therefore, created a symbol to deal with the intolerable experience of loss—intolerable because of the desire for total control—but had then become lost in it. He lived almost symbiotically in his symbol and could only separate from it and look at it through analysis. When he saw the headless body as his own creation as a response to the prospect of change, which eventually he did, he began to separate from it and see why he had created it. He could then see that, for all its gratifying illusions, it actually was self-defeating. The effectiveness of this analysis was revealed by the fact that when, some years later, he went through a tumultuous series of changes in his life which he partly initiated, but to which he also had to respond, there was no return of the obsessive ruminatory thoughts, which astonished him.

When asking whether these headless bodies are symbols, I think it is important to consider how this patient used these ideas in a communicative way with others and, therefore, in the transference. The question, therefore, is not whether they are symbols, but *how they can become symbolic*. With his ruminations in his mind, he was ill and could not be expected to do anything. He compared them, at the outset of his analysis, to spectacles or glasses, that is, "you don't hit a man with glasses on". Because the ruminations had been experienced as coming from outside him, they rendered him in his consciousness of himself as mild and inoffensive. Paradoxically, they were revealed to him by analysis to be full of aggressive intent, but this could only happen when the symptom was seen in the context of separation. This betrays the subject's unconscious desire to the other and provides the means of undoing the riddle of the repression, which, by its nature, will not give up its secret willingly. This is particularly the case where the symbol is expressive of a desire for a retreat from change and, thus, may be thought of as antagonistic to change.

Winnicott's work tries to capture the significance of symbols in the creation of experience. In relating the transitional object to symbolism, Winnicott said that whereas we could understand the nature of transitional objects while not fully understanding the nature of symbolism, symbolism could only be properly studied in the process of the growth of the individual. What is reflected by these thoughts is Winnicott's concern with the use and function of the transitional object. This gives us a model that enables us to think about how the individual uses a symbol and why this active and creative process functions in the way it seems. A symbol, as a transitional phenomenon, therefore, can be thought of as a creation linking psychic reality with external reality and unconsciously using it in the discourse with the other. We can, therefore, observe the progressive triangulation, postulated by Cavell, through the link between the use of the symbol and its entwining with external, material reality. This permits a symptom to become symbolic and, thereby, communicative, because seeing the symptom in the context of setting enables it to become a symbol.

The question remains as to why it is created, to which the answer could be that the only alternative is to remain in egocentric subjective isolation. The crucial point is the entry of external reality and its use in response to the thoughts or actions of (m)other's mind. This separates Winnicott's transitional object from Jones' and Segal's conceptualizations of the symbol. The second feature that distinguishes these ideas is that the transitional object develops over time, which brings in the dimension of historicity. We can see a comparable analysis by Lacan in his thoughts about the "fort da" game, which brought together the notions of temporality and the development of the symbolic order.

It is with respect to this *temporal* aspect that I wish to contrast the patient discussed above with my next patient, who did not bring a symptom expressed in a symbol, but who developed one in the course of an analysis. When this was analysed, it revealed a possibility that this was not evidence of something which had been repressed, but something which was being de-repressed. My evidence for this contention is that it was hard to see how the particular development of this analysis could be much other than the recommencement of a normal process of development that had been arrested during latency. Therefore, it seemed to be evidence of a fixation which was opened up by the creation of a symbol that provided the communication to the analyst of showing the way the analysis would develop and also the anxieties which would be aroused. It is because it developed in the course of the analysis that I regard this case as an example showing the *temporal* aspect, because it demonstrably developed and changed.

A symbol as a creative response

When my second patient came into analysis, there were two features about her history and presentation that stood out from the beginning. *First, she had been abandoned at about the age of five by her mother, who left her husband (my patient's father) to care for their three daughters, of whom my patient was the eldest. The second feature was that despite being in a stable relationship and having a determination for a baby, she had very little idea of the impact that becoming a mother would have on her life.*

From the outset, this patient was very concerned about the boundaries of the setting. She always arrived precisely on time and was intolerant of even the slightest overrun by a minute of the session. She paid punctiliously on time, and yet she refused to use the couch. It was clear that she could envisage herself on the couch but could not bring herself to lie on it. This reflected the quality of the analysis in this period, which was not one character-ized by an easy ability to free associate. The refusal to use the couch could not but arouse a curiosity in me, because here was a woman who wished to have an analysis but acted in such a way as to impede substantially its efficacy. In view of her history, it seemed to me that, despite my curiosity, it was important to wait until the meaning became clear. At that point, I hypothesized that the apparent phobia was a reaction to being alone in the consulting room with a male analyst, which clearly might well have something to do with being left with her father on her mother's departure.

She became pregnant and gave birth to a daughter, to whom she was devoted. For the next year, she attended her analysis with her daughter, and the analysis turned in many ways on her anxieties of being able to be a good mother. She was extremely reluctant to leave her daughter in the care of someone else when she came to analysis, which, on the face of it, seemed to be a refusal to be the rejecting and abandoning mother that she had in her mind. When she began to attend on her own once more, she became more deter-mined to use the couch. But she would sit on it, sit on the floor with it at her back, and feel very self-conscious. It soon became apparent that to enable her to actually lie on it required an interpretation of the anxieties giving rise to her self-consciousness. After a short period, during which she became progressively less phobic of the couch, there developed an intensely erotic transference. It was as though she was finally able to be a woman in the room and let the analysis penetrate her mind.

I bring this case because it seems that the phobia of the couch and the analysis represented both her conscious fear of her male analyst, and, more particularly, her unconscious desires and her fear of her analyst's reaction. She was, as it were, reliving her experience of being left with her father by her mother, but this time through the medium of being in possession of a fully mature, female sexual body. While this did have a psychotic quality in that it was experienced so concretely, despite the obvious hostile possibilities, it seemed to me that it concerned more her final acquisition of her woman's sexual body for herself. In this case, it seemed to be clear that the erotization of the transference was not a resistance to the analysis and that it would have been incorrect to interpret it as such.

There are two aspects that deserve emphasis. The first is that the phobia represented the repression of sexual desires. However, the choice of the focus of the phobia (the couch) and her deliberate seeking of a male analyst (i.e., with a couch) represented an unconscious drive to realize her sexual self as a woman. *In her process of selecting me, she had seen two men and, at the outset of the analysis, told me that she had rejected the other because he had looked at her breasts in an unwelcome way. After some years, however, she stated that the truth was that she hadn't found him sexually attractive. I doubt that this "truth" had been available to her at the time.* Hence, we see a pre-conscious creative drive for change in the presence of the defence against the original difficulty. The refusal to use the couch provides the cue to activate the analyst's subjectivity in the countertransference. The couch, which was the focus of the phobia in consciousness, was also the unconscious goal, which was to realize her sexual self in union with the male analyst. Hence, what was initially "I couldn't lie on the couch" became "I want to lie on the couch with you" as her psychic centre of gravity moved from her self-consciousness to her drives and, hence, from preoccupation with the other mind (i.e., the analyst) to thinking about her own mind.

Symbols and change

My purpose in recounting some aspects of these analyses has been to point to some links between the inevitable anxiety of change and symbols which have been brought to, or are created in the course of, an analysis as a response to it. These, then, bring a meaning to the change and eventually reveal, through their examination in the context of the analytic dialogue over time, the manner in which the patient, in the first case, developed a psychic retreat and, in the case of the second, sought to undo a fixation which had created a developmental arrest. When I used the word "meaning", above, I am emphasizing the possibilities for the analyst to use the emergence of a symbol *as a means of helping the patient triangulate and, thereby, separate the conscious content of the symbol from its unconscious meaning, which can then be communicated.* This means listening for what the patient is unconsciously saying to the analyst, which can be done if we allow the psychoanalytic process to create a context for the symptom as it presents itself. The first patient says to his analyst that he cannot bear to be separated from his analyst; the second says that she wishes her mind to be penetrated by her analyst and/ but she cannot distinguish her mind from her body.

A useful criterion, therefore, for thinking about these different types of meaning concerns the opportunities offered by a symbol for the symbolizer to stand outside the situation they are in and understand what is happening to them. We could call this *the opportunities for triangulation* offered by a symbol. The symbol described in the first case above did not allow this, and, indeed, this was its very purpose. The symbol in the second case can more accurately be said to have developed in response to the setting. It provided the means to stand outside the situation because it provoked the self-consciousness that it did. Hence, it is perhaps more helpful to consider the opportunities for triangulation offered by symbols than to try to identify and systematically interrelate different kinds of symbols.

Does a symbol represent or present?

In an analysis, there is a development of a language between patient and analyst about the patient's inner world, for which, before the analysis, there were no words, or a kind of *aphasia*. We can see in the case of both, but particularly my second patient, that this was preceded by a phase of *agnosia*, during which something was not be allowed to be known. This suggests that preconscious activity is an essential component of symbol formation and functioning.

To begin to think about this issue, I have found it helpful to use Langer's (1942) concepts of *presentational* and *discursive* symbolism. In short, she considered that *presentational symbols* developed in artistic reaction expressed as a mode of symbolic activity with its own rules and rigour, as has verbal language, but with a different purpose. The purpose of presentational symbols was to present the patterns of our emotional and experiential life in an evocative and sensual way. Their purpose was not primarily to present ideas as propositions, which was the role of language, but to show the nature of the patterns in which we live and the experiences we have. In other words, they are the means by which we can come to know something before we are sure we know it, and precede a communicative capability. The *discursive symbolism* of language, on the other hand, conveyed relations and discriminations in the world of objects through an agreed set of conventional symbols, which merely referred to, but did not iconically or imagistically present, that which they symbolized.

At this point, we have arrived at the idea that a symbol that develops in the course of an analysis or is brought for analysis must be seen as part, and in the context, of the discourse between patient and analyst. The symbols used or developed in the discourse will inevitably have discursive and presentational aspects. At the outset, the presentational aspects will inevitably be far more in evidence. Although it may not be immediately apparent to either analyst or analysand what the meaning of a symbol is, it can become more discursive given time and effort. This takes us to the work of Lacan, because he is concerned with the development of subjectivity over time.

Lacan's significance in psychoanalytical thinking is growing, partly as a result of the increasing interest in intersubjectivity in psychoanalysis. Part of the difficulty that the Anglo-Saxon world has had in understanding him stems from his determination to look at Freud from a different philosophical standpoint, which, at its heart, challenges the notion of the conscious ego being the subject. This exalts the concept of the ego, which was, in his view, simply a phenomenon of the (in his terms) Imaginary order. In essence, this conception of the subject was, in Lacan's view (1954), the legacy of Descartes. It is debatable whether the consequences of this implicit assumption has bedevilled the development of psychoanalytic theory since the dominant language of psychoanalysis ceased to be German and became English.

In her paper referred to above, Cavell (1998), without making reference to Lacan but, I think, essentially agreeing with him, also disputed the Cartesian view that our knowledge of our minds is not connected in any essential way with the external world, and that knowledge of other minds is either impossible or mysterious. Although it could be said, she thinks, that with Descartes, subjectivity in its modern sense is born and has much commonsense appeal, it does now seem that there are insuperable problems created by such a limited view. Cavell points out that Freud unquestioningly accepted the Cartesian ocular view of self-knowledge. For example, he says about psychical reality that it "is as much unknown to us as the reality of the external world, and is as incompletely presented by the data of consciousness as is the external world by the communication of our sense organs"(1900a, p. 613).

One of the principal difficulties with the Cartesian subject is that it does not make room for historicity. We, Cavell says, are now inclined to think that knowledge is never certain and it grows not by transcending partiality, but through a dialogue over time. This idea of dialogue immediately implies that intersubjectivity is what is important to consider in the development of a theory of mind and, by implication, a theory of symbolism once the communicative or discursive aspects of symbols are given their proper place.

As I have said earlier, the significance of her dispute of the Cartesian view for psychoanalysts lies in the test to which some of psychoanalytical theoretical assumptions are put by implication. In essence, Cavell's viewpoint is that subjectivity goes hand in hand with intersubjectivity. As discussed above, an intersubjectivity that separates itself from considerations of objectivity and intersubjectively verifiable truth is no intersubjectivity at all, but collapses into a subjectivity. As we have seen, the objective features of the psychoanalytical setting can provide the cues and hooks for the subjectivities of the patient and the analyst to find one another. In the first case, it was the nature of symptomatic symbol that aroused the analyst's attention, and in the second it was the refusal to use the couch. But such a search takes time, which is a crucial feature of the objectivity of the psychoanalytic setting. Given time, the original cue takes on a meaning in the context of the objective setting.

A crucial aspect of the psychoanalytical process, which links it with the objective world, is its temporality, which links with the idea of historicity mentioned above. This is, of course, central to the understanding of Lacan's theory of the Symbolic order and why he regarded the central importance of Freud's paper *Beyond the Pleasure Principle* (1920g) to be its introduction of the notion of temporality. I think that the objectivity of time is what also provides an essential point of triangulation in the model proposed by Cavell, and so there begins to be a convergence of her views with those of Lacan. Not least in this convergence is the idea that subjectivity grows out of intersubjectivity and not the other way round.

What we have observed in the two cases described above is a process in which a patient and analyst could come to understand something centrally important to the patient through seeing how an aspect of the objective, and indisputable, psychoanalytic setting was used by the patient to communicate something about the anxieties that brought them to analysis in the first place. In the first case, it was the fact of the end of the session and the ending of an analysis that was the objective feature; in the second, it was the fact of the couch. This objective feature, on the one hand, acted as a means of focusing the expression of the patient's anxiety in the transference situation and, on the other, provided the means of communication from patient to analyst about this anxiety by enabling it to be lived out in the relationship. Now, this perspective, in both cases, was not immediately apparent, but became apparent through a dialogue between patient and analyst over time. Hence, the significance of the symbols moved from the presentational to the communicative to the subjectively meaningful.

To my mind, the psychoanalytic theory of symbolism becomes of especial interest because of Cavell's views on the *progressive triangulation* as a means by which we can come to know our own minds. It enables us to develop a model that will account for the clinical phenomena observed above. This will also, perhaps, enable psychoanalysts to develop their own theory of symbolic phenomena rather than trying to incorporate non-psychoanalytic concepts of symbolism by fitting them into a psychoanalytic theoretical rubric, which inevitably creaks. The great theoretical and technical promise offered by a better understanding of symbolic phenomena in the psychoanalytic setting and discourse may be that it will provide a means of understanding how to open egocentric closed systems.

Conclusion

To conclude and summarize, my objective in this chapter has been to explore the idea that understanding the process of symbolization available to an individual will help us to understand the way in which they experience changes and manage the inevitable anxiety of the pressure for change. The anxiety of change is always with us, and is the consequence of the fact that we only partially know the future, our own minds, or the mind of the other. The choice open to the subject is to retreat into Ptolemaic egocentricity, or to engage with the world and others. In the egocentric position, the mind reacts to an experience of agnosia by finding a means of *presenting* to the subject the nature of their anxiety, but this may not be necessarily intelligible. At this point, a symbol's function can be both to reveal and to hide (*symballein / symbolon*) and may prove difficult to distinguish from a symptom. From this, the symbol can come to equate to, and be, a psychic retreat (Steiner, 1993). Alternatively, the subject can break out of the egocentric position and use this presentation as a means of managing the anxiety more creatively by communicating the anxiety to others *discursively*. To do this, a context for a symbol must be found, and it can then become representative and communicative. It is in the interaction of the subject with others that the symbol can become meaningful, which is the third stage of managing the anxiety of change. The management of anxiety in any system involves relating that system's internal and external worlds, either to connect or divide them. I propose that symbols, in their formation, function in the manner described above to manage the inevitable anxiety of change.

We seem to have arrived at a position of recognizing not only the subjective significance of symbols, but also their, perhaps original, intersubjective significance. Thus, we seem to conclude that symbols are not only about repression or loss, but also about the management of the anxiety of change and the opening or closing of discourse with other minds. Whereas they do reflect the relationship between the individual and his/her objects, above all they reflect an individual's response to the inevitability of the demand for change created simply because we are alive. They also link the demands of psychic reality to the strictures and exigencies of external reality. In the process of change, they will develop and contain the hopes and fears of the central actor in the process, whether trapping them in a retreat or facilitating a creative response. It is my contention that by seeing and responding to symbols in their intersubjective context, rather than thinking of them as purely subjective phenomena, we can make greater progress in understanding our patients and helping them to emerge from their psychic retreats, if they so wish.

References

Atwood, G., & Stolorow, R. D. (1984). *Structures of Subjectivity: Explorations in Psychoanalytic Phenomenology*. Hillsdale, NJ: Analytic Press.

Cahn, R. (1998). The process of becoming a subject in adolescence. In: M. Perret-Catipovic & F. Ladame (Eds.), *Adolescence and Psychoanalysis* (pp. 149–160). London: Karnac.

Cavell, M. (1998). Triangulation, one's own mind and objectivity. *International Journal of Psychoanalysis*, 79: 449–467.

Freud, S. (1900a). *The Interpretation of Dreams. S.E.*, 4–5. London: Hogarth.

Freud, S. (1915d). Repression. *S.E.*, 14: 141–158. London: Hogarth.

Freud, S. (1915e). The unconscious. *S.E.*, 14: 159–204. London: Hogarth.

Freud, S. (1916c). A connection between a symbol and a symptom. *S.E.*, 14: 339–340. London: Hogarth.

Freud, S. (1920g). *Beyond the Pleasure Principle. S.E.*, 18: 1–64. London: Hogarth.

Goldberg, A. (1998). Deconstructing the dialectic. *International Journal of Psychoanalysis*, 79: 215–226.

Grinberg, L. (1962). On a specific aspect of counter-transference due to the patient's projective identification. *International Journal of Psychoanalysis*, 43: 436–440.

Jones, E. (1916). The theory of symbolism. In: *Papers on Psycho-Analysis*. London: Maresfield Reprints.

Lacan, J. (1945). Le temps logique et l'assertion de certitude anticipée. In: *Ecrits*. Paris: Edition de Seuil, 1966.

Lacan, J. (1954). A materialist definition of the phenomenon of consciousness. In: J.-A. Miller (Ed.), S. Tomaselli (Trans.), *The Seminar of Jacques Lacan, Book 2*. Cambridge: Cambridge University Press, 1988.

Langer, S. (1942). *Philosophy in a New Key*. Cambridge, MA: Harvard University Press.

Laplanche, J. (1997). The theory of seduction and the problem of the Other. *International Journal of Psychoanalysis, 78*: 653–666.

Laplanche, J., & Pontalis, J. B. (1973). *The Language of Psycho-analysis*. London: Hogarth Press.

Ogden, T. (1986). *The Matrix of the Mind: Object Relations and the Psychoanalytic Dialogue*. New York: Jason Aronson.

Renik, O. (1998). The analyst's subjectivity and the analyst's objectivity. *International Journal of Psychoanalysis, 79*: 487–497.

Segal, H. (1957). Notes on symbol formation. *International Journal of Psychoanalysis, 38*: 391–397.

Steiner, J. (1993). *Psychic Retreats*. London: Routledge.

Tronick, E. Z., & Weinberg, M. K. (1997). Depressed mothers and infants: failure to form dyadic states of consciousness. In: L. Murray (Ed.), *Post-Partum Depression* (pp. 54–84). London: Guilford Press.

Winnicott, D. W. (1945). Primitive emotional development. *International Journal of Psychoanalysis, 26*: 137–143.

Winnicott, D. W. (1951). Transitional objects and transitional phenomena. In: *From Paediatrics to Psychoanalysis*. London: Hogarth and Institute of Psychoanalysis.

Wright, K. (1991). *Vision and Separation: Between Mother and Baby*. London: Free Association Books.

CHAPTER NINE

The presence of absence in the transference: some clinical, countertransference, and metapsychological implications*

James S. Rose

Introduction

I t is comparatively common that a young person will come to a consultation describing themselves as depressed, suffering from a lack of confidence and feeling devoid of ambition. Their psychic life can appear to be pervaded with an anomie to the point that it seems surprising to the assessor that they have bothered to come to the consultation at all. Often, there is evidence of disrupted family history, early bereavements, and separations. Despite the seemingly traumatic nature of these losses, they are often dismissed as unimportant because they happened "so long ago". In short, the assessor can see many reasons for the young person's depressed state of mind, but there is an apparent gulf between the young person's and the assessor's understanding that seems unbridgeable and leaves the assessor feeling hopeless and impotent. Often, the apparent emptiness in the countertransference can seem the result

---

* Published in 2002 in *Penser les limites: ecrits en honneur d'André Green*. Paris: Delachaux & Niestle.

of a deficit in functioning, and it can appear that this young person will not be easy to help because of their incapacity to symbolize or to reflect upon their experience.

Paradoxically, these unpromising prospects often prove wrong, despite the initial rejection of the interpretations of early loss. But, while the young person concerned becomes eventually engaged with a psychotherapeutic process, change does not occur at a sparkling rate. Rather, progress can be so slow that it appears non-existent, and the apparently stuck quality of their lives becomes replicated in the transference. This can reinforce the impression of early emotional deficit or perverse resistance, as the analyst can wonder whether any resolution of the young person's difficulties can occur.

In contrast to the "don't help me" (Wilson, 1991) position of many adolescents, these young people appear to say, "you can't help me", *and yet they come for help—and keep coming*. Hence, the question is how to conceptualize theoretically this paradoxical pattern, observed in assessment and in treatment, in which the young person persists in coming to tell their psychoanalyst that they cannot help them and in which there is an uncanny presence of an absence in the transference.

The infinite nothingness of absence

When we say that someone is absent, the word "absent" can have a quantitative or a qualitative meaning. We can mean that they are not in a particular place in the physical and temporal sense, or that they are not with us in the psychological sense. Absence is a deceptively complex idea, being equivalent to nothing, or, alternatively, a negative of something, or a quality in itself. One sense of nothing is, therefore, to imply the absence of something. Indeed, Russell (1903) suggests that the zero of magnitude has been defined as the contradictory opposite of each magnitude of its kind, which implies that zero must imply something as well as mean nothing. We assume, therefore, that absence describes something about an object.

As psychoanalysts, we are led to the question of the various ways in which nothing, like our conception of absence, can, in fact, be experienced in the sense of no-thing. But, a curious aspect that should also be noted is the infinite quality of nothing, because, within the class of nothing, the part is the same as the whole. In the terms of Matte-Blanco (1975), nothing is, therefore, an infinite set. This infinite quality leads more precisely to the idea and experience of the nothingness of absence, which stands in contrast to the quantitative nothing.

At this point, it might be asked, what is the point of thinking about the relationship of nothingness to absence because the point of absence is precisely that it is the absence of something. In reply, I would say that those patients who are wrestling with the consequences of an absence often create an experience in the countertransference of helplessness, pointlessness, and emptiness. Absence, as a description of their experience, is, I feel, too pallid (even though it may describe our countertransference). This is because it is too discrete a notion precisely because of its connotation of something. To my mind, nothingness, in all its infinity, works better.

This infinite quality of nothing is, therefore, a link with the notion of nothingness. However, the subjective experience of nothingness is something other than that which is expressed by the mathematical concept of zero. If absence is a complex idea, the conceptual difficulties of nothingness are even greater. From the point of view of the theory of object relations, it seems difficult to see how we relate to nothingness as an object, and yet it seems to me that in some way we do because we relate to absence. Logically, it is hard to grasp how we could be said to relate to nothing, and yet, as I hope to show, relating to nothingness can be observed. Nothingness, therefore, can be said to have being despite the fact that nothingness might be thought to be the negative of being. Because nothingness seems to stand somewhere between intrasubjective illusion and objective, intersubjective reality, it seems that something would be gained from its examination. This, to my mind, makes an enquiry into the experience of nothingness of theoretical interest and, possibly, clinical value.

The concept of nothingness is an idea that has been approached from an ontological point of view. This creates the question of how we are, or become, conscious of its being. One might say that a glass is full of nothingness and essentially mean the same as if we had said that the glass is empty and there is nothing in it. But, the glass's being is such that it implies being full of something, or having something in it, but this, in turn, depends on the context. Hence, the meaning of the emptiness of an empty glass to a thirsty man in a desert is not perhaps the same as the emptiness of the desert and, therefore, has its own being. The logical positivist, in saying that "nothing noths", is perhaps making a materialist mockery of the existentialist contention that nothingness has being. Nothingness, to the existentialist point of view, has an implication for consciousness and, therefore, can be, according to Brentano, as intentional as anything else in consciousness. Sartre's (1943) analysis of nothingness through the description of going to meet Pierre at a café, only to find that he is not there, illustrates that this experience of absence, or nothingness, is intimately bound up with desire, because of the experience of lack.

Nothingness would also seem to be related in some way to the idea of something being negated. Negation, as a psychoanalytic concept, is no more straightforward than nothingness. Implying both *verneinen* and *verleugnen* (negation and denial), Laplanche and Pontalis (1973) suggest that negation "is a way of taking cognisance of what is repressed"; and . . . "with the help of the *symbol of negation*, thinking frees itself from the restrictions of repression" (p. 263). Thus, we get a view of negation as being a means by which the censor is temporarily misled into letting repressed ideas pass into consciousness by the back door. A patient might say, "I wouldn't like you to think that I don't appreciate your efforts to help me". As psychoanalysts, we see the barely unconscious hostility in such a statement, despite (or, perhaps, because of) it being buried in a double negative. Hence, we can see that Freud's concept of negation was intimately bound up with the theory of the unconscious, which is inevitably a psychological, or a psychoanalytical, theory, to be more exact. Negation, then, takes us to the notion of the negative. It is hard to see how any logical or epistemological system can work without a negative. In his discourse on "The work of the negative", Green (1999) identifies four possible meanings of the negative, referring to opposition, symmetry (implying nothing more than inversion), absence, or latency and, finally, nothing (p.16). In regard of absence, Green refers to Sartre, who asks whether consciousness is based on "what is not?" but, recalling the absence of Pierre at the café, we must include desire as well as what is not. Otherwise, we would be likely to be overwhelmed with the "feeling of what happens" (Damasio, 1999). In other words, there is much that happens of which we are not conscious: we are not looking for it because we do not want it at that moment.

The link with the idea of nothingness is in the implication of something existing that is not there. But, when linked with the concept of negation, the notion of the unconscious is invoked, which adds to the complexity of the notion of nothingness. Unconscious "whatever they are", according to Freud's principles (1915e), do not exist in a space–time frame. Hence, we are stretched theoretically to call them objects. We are, therefore, even more pressed theoretically to call nothingness an object. Yet, it seems to me that we experience and relate to it because nothingness has being. If we begin with our experience as a phenomenon to be accounted for in some way, then we may learn something interesting. As we have seen, there is something about nothingness that is elusive, both as a concept and as an experience. I will suggest that when we look at the experience of nothingness, we see desire: either our own or that of the other. This enables us to address something about subjectivity. As Kennedy (1998) points out, Freud (1900a) came up with an optical image of the mental apparatus to address the question of the location of human subjectivity; thus,

> On that basis, psychical locality will correspond to a point inside the apparatus at which one of the preliminary stages of an image comes into being. In the microscope and telescope, as we know, these occur in part at ideal points, regions in which no tangible component of the apparatus is situated. [p. 536]

If nothing else, then, nothingness is an experience. The question, then, is whether, and if so, how, this experience can be communicated. There is something of the uncanny about nothingness, because it seems to be communicated through the presence of an absence. The clinical significance of the question has been discussed before, but not so much from the direct experience in the consulting room of nothingness, but of emptiness. Looking at these problems from a more clinical perspective, Balint's paper "On being empty of oneself" (1963) traced a sense of emptiness to the early maternal–infant relationship. In her discussion of a patient, Sarah, she describes how the patient's mother thought of her daughter as always having been a happy child. Balint found that Sarah had always been in difficulties as a result of her feeling that her maternal object had never been emotionally in touch with her. This apparently adjusted and productive young woman broke down soon after the outset of her analysis, perhaps because of the collapse of the "false self" erected to deal with her mother's difficulty in accepting the fact of her daughter's psychic reality. Without meaning to her inner world, she faced a terrifying void. Balint found it hard to get much of a conceptual handle on the notion of emptiness without considering how her patient's sense of being "empty of herself" was related to the emotional absence of her early mothering.

Clinical problems presented by absence

Young people of the kind described in my introduction above present in a paradoxical manner at the outset and often continue to do so during treatment. The central issue is the situation whereby the young person appears to be making little progress in their lives at a time when the common pattern is one in which there is considerable change accompanied by conflict within the self and with others. All this is occurring within a maturing sexual body, which has created a new psychosomatic matrix within which relationships with others are experienced. These young people seem doubly disadvantaged, in that the ego strengths they need to cope with the changes entailed in progress are being continually undermined by their lack of progress. Demoralization increases, and there seems to be a sense of giving up the struggle as futile. This is readily experienced in the countertransference in the early stages of the consultations.

One way of thinking about this clinical picture is to regard it, in drive theory terms, as the result of a fixation of some kind, which has become incorporated into the personality and profoundly effects the gradual structuring of the instinctual organization (see Freud, 1905d; Laufer & Laufer, 1984, Chapter One). The individual's history can then be scrutinized for any evidence for this hypothesis, which is sometimes confirmed. A difficulty sometimes arises with this approach in that efforts to link the apparent cause of the fixation with the young person's pervasive mental state do not meet with immediate acceptance or success; thus, it can look as though the young person is clinging to their situation in an ego-syntonic, but perverse, way. The theoretical difficulty then is to determine whether that interpretation of the situation creates what we see. Or, is it possible that something of a patient's psychic life can be determined by something that is absent as much as something that is present?

Another way of understanding the situation, from an object relations theory point of view, is to hypothesize a destructive narcissistic organization (Rosenfeld, 1987) in which all efforts to make developmental progress are perversely attacked. Invoking the destructive instincts in this way can seem promising. However, it is sometimes hard to incorporate in this theoretical analysis not only the real sense of frustration experienced by these young people, but also the fact that they come for help at all, when there is no compulsion to do so from external sources.

Furthermore, neither of these theoretical approaches can easily incorporate the fact that, after an uncertain start, these young people often become strongly engaged with their therapy. The early phase can often be thought of as a testing of their psychoanalyst to see if they can be trusted. Once engagement is achieved, they do not markedly act out, but make only very slow progress and appear frustrating. The transference established is not obviously in the early stages a transference neurosis or breakdown (see Laufer & Laufer, 1984) or "disharmoniosis" (Cahn, 1998), but a transference depression in which the likely duration of the therapy seems endless. In these hours, themes can be repetitively worked over to the point that the work can begin to seem without point or object. The common feature of these young people is not one of directed anger towards the self or others, as in a depressed state of mind (Freud, 1917e), but of a kind of futile absence. They can seem to the adult mind to seek an anarchic deconstruction, which is apparently motivated to defeat any structuring efforts. It can be tempting to regard this emptiness as regressive and provocative. In some cases it may be, but to assume it may be a mistake. It is this deconstruction that provides the link with the experience of the nothingness of absence: the subject of this chapter.

To illustrate these general impressions, I shall now turn to some clinical material taken from treatment of some late adolescent patients in which there was a kind of *enactment* in the transference. The transference, which they established, created what I would like to call a "countertransference depression". They did not appear depressed, but, paradoxically, presented with an urgency to do something about their situation. However, there always seemed to be the hint of an intangible inner conviction that there could be no solution. This gave rise in the countertransference to a feeling of wanting to help, but with the uncomfortable feeling that any effort was bound to fail.

Clinical example: Patient 1

This was a young man (aged twenty-one) referred because he was said by the referrer to be depressed. He had recently dropped out of university because he had found himself unable to study or engage in any meaningful way with university life. He seemed demoralized and unable to explain what had felt to him to be a rather sudden onset of depression. However, he did not, of course, call this depression, but more a sense of self-worthlessness and a sense of feeling compelled to do the opposite of what others wished, which could be called perverse. In the sessions, he was both articulate and apparently co-operative, but sometimes he attended his sessions late or missed them altogether. He professed that, at the outset, he thought that the sessions would be rather pointless. "After all," he said, "what is the point of talking", in a manner that was discouraging but which reflected and communicated his demoralization.

In terms of his history, the most significant fact was that his parents' marriage had broken up when he was five and he had been sent off to boarding school when he was eight. Within the structure of boarding schools, he had seemingly thrived, being both academically successful and popular with his peers. Now, accompanying his sense of failure, he saw himself as being a "fat slob". His parents' marriage had dissolved bitterly. His father was, in consciousness, despised by both his mother and his sister, with whom the patient now lived. He had had some contact with his father, who had remarried and had another family. He saw his father as a man of action in quite some contrast to his mother, who wanted him to have therapy to "sort his head out".

In the course of working with him, it was clear that the main focus of the work was becoming the pattern of his attendance. The discouraging message that he apparently could not be bothered to get out of bed was belied by the effort he seemed to put in when he did attend. Most particularly, he would often enquire whether his psychoanalyst thought he was wasting his time with him, and would not prefer to be helping others. This was so persistent that the position the psychoanalyst was placed in reflected this young man's internal predicament. He felt his father had left him because he was a waste of time. The transference situation seemed to be one in which he found it hard, if not impossible, to believe that he was not despised by his psychoanalyst. Therefore, the psychoanalyst was attacked (i.e., you don't really care, do you?) for disliking what it was that the young man felt he had no other option to be (i.e., despicable and beyond assistance). However, this transference message provided the clue to his difficulty and how to work with it. Forthright interpretation of the meaning of his absence or sporadic attendance patterns in terms of his identification with a despicable object was in defiance of his commonsense. But it enabled him to understand the root of his feeling of being despicable, which was the symptom of his unconscious guilt. Eventually, he began to see that the purpose of the identification "with the lost object" could possibly be a defence against his sense of abandonment. He finished his treatment, went off to see his father again, and returned to university.

In the broadest of summary, it seemed that, within the immediate family, this young man had become the "ghost" of his father, attracting the same antagonism as did the absent figure of his father. By losing the structure of his schools, this young man was confronted with the emptiness and lack of structure within himself. It seemed that he mourned his father, but had no one with whom to mourn this loss because of the other family members' antagonism to his father. His response to this was seemingly to identify with his lost father, or, at least, with the version of his father in the current family mythology.

In regard to this case, the central point I wish to make is that this young person's difficulties were effectively communicated by the pattern of his engagement. He attended for eight months or so, and it could be argued that this was too brief for a marked change to be expected. The changes that he did make in his life seemed genuine. However, to engage him it was apparent that I needed to be quite active and to not concentrate on his apparently perverse destructiveness. What is also of note is the sense of his being a "fat slob", which interfered with his capacity to form relationships with girls. In fact, he was not obese, but it was easy to see how he discouraged people with what appeared to be a show of contemptuous arrogance. I shall consider these aspects later, but the most important question seems to me to ask whether this young man was in identification, in some way, with an image that the family with whom he lived (that is, his mother and sister) had of his father. Therefore, he expressed his protest at his father's departure by being the family's idea of the father and his protest at being sent to boarding school by being as objectionable as he could. All this was fairly unconscious, and the expression of pointlessness of the whole counselling enterprise (his words) was, I think, part of the identification with the family image of the father, who was seen as someone "you couldn't talk to" (because, of course, he was absent.)

Some reflections on the clinical material

In the case just described, a young man had experienced the departure and absence of his father. There was a sense in the countertransference of how the patient thought that he would be experienced. He unconsciously expected to be condemned without reprieve. Thus, he presented with a predicament to which he thought there was no solution, and, therefore, it is easy to see how he came implicitly saying "you can't help me". The theoretical difficulty was that, while we can see that this young man would naturally experience a reactive depression to these circumstances, or, indeed, develop a chronic and severe melancholic position, it is not so easy to see what tied him so firmly to his difficulties. The statement "you can't help me" suggested that he was tied to the difficulties indissolubly, but then we have to wonder why did he come at all. Therein lies the practical expression of the paradox I referred to earlier.

Green (1986) has suggested that, in adults, there is a form of pathological mourning, which is a response to what he terms "psychic holes" (*troux psychiques*) in experience. The notion of a "hole in experience" is an interesting one. He terms the response "blank mourning", and this reflects an impression of blankness or emptiness in the patient's consciousness. In vernacular terms, as he puts it, these patients lack colour. He proposes that such a picture results when an individual's mother becomes depressed, or, indeed, preoccupied, in such a way that she is perceived to be distracted or unavailable to the child. Hence, this picture is not necessarily a reaction to an actual bereavement or loss in itself, but to a situation in which the mother becomes chronically unavailable to the child. The mother cares for the child, but "her heart is not in it".

An implication of this is that when the subject experiences this kind of early loss of the maternal primary object, a twofold problem is presented to the subject. On the one hand, there is loss of the alive, responsive, and available maternal object, and, on the other, the distortion to the ego caused by relating to a depressed mother. The dead mother is the mother dead to the child because her mind is taken up by any preoccupation that persistently takes her mind away from the child. It is important to be clear that this pattern is not specific to loss arising from actual death. Any separation or rupture in the relationship between the parents can lead to this pattern. *The important feature is not the actuality of the loss, but the effect on the mother. The result is that the child is plunged prematurely into an Oedipal situation; or, in other words, the triangle created by the mother's preoccupation.*

In Green's view, the blankness results from a major decathexis of the child by the primary maternal object. This decathexis creates a "hole" in psychic space. It is accompanied by an identification with the absent, distracted, or preoccupied mother, which re-emerges in the transference situation, and, of course, in the countertransference, as a picture of blankness and emptiness. He then suggests that the empty space is filled by a *recathected object*, almost a scapegoat, but is, of course, the reflection of how the trauma of the loss of the present mother is absorbed into a child's psychic reality.

This recathected object I propose instead to call a *virtual object*,[1] precisely because *it is being continually being re-created out of the child's omnipotence*, in Winnicott's (1951) sense of the word, and, therefore, reflects the means by which the trauma of loss comes under the child's ego-control and subject to secondary process. I call this object "virtual" because it reflects something within the patient. This is borrowed from optics, in that the reflection of an object in a mirror is called a virtual object. However, the virtual object is created continuously out of the patient's omnipotence and reflects the patient's understanding of the reasons for the object's absence. Because of this continual re-creation, the virtual object has an infinite quality, which, to my mind, is not quite conveyed by recathexis. Further, it is not a projective identification, because there is not necessarily the presence of a phantasy of voiding the ego of a part of itself.

When I use the term omnipotence here, I use it in the sense that Winnicott[2] had when he discussed the meaning of omnipotence as an experience essential in the first experiences of "me" and "not me". The re-cathected *or virtual object* leads to a distortion of the ego, because there is inevitably a narcissistic identification with it, creating a false self. The result is that the subject's impression of a "lack of confidence" is hardly surprising and often reported. This identification transforms the subject's feeling towards the absent figure, as its "shadow falls upon the ego" (Freud, 1917e). Out of the mouth of this *virtual object* may come an endless stream of complaints about the world. It is, of course, equated with the absent mother and is constructed out of the unconscious explanation for the mother's absence. Therefore, it becomes the hated part of the loved object, which forms the basis of the narcissistic identification.

In Green's view, the subject reacts to *what is not there* (caused by the experience of decathexis) by replacing it with a *cruel* (in my terms, *virtual*) *object*, which in turn occludes a desperately intense homosexuality. This, in both girls and boys, is a feminine homosexuality, which seeks a close identification to the passive, absent maternal figure, which is dead to the child. Thus, the Oedipal triangle, referred to above, is re-created, but now in a defensive form, *because it binds the subject to the maternal figure in a potentially timeless manner as a defence against loss.* This attachment, of course, creates a closeness that is inseparable, which becomes a powerful resistance to analysis because of the reluctance to give up the absent dead mother. If she comes alive, the danger is that she will leave. Hence, there is an extreme ambivalence about the dead mother coming back to life. Thus, the patient is locked into their defensive system against loss because they have created something that will never leave them.

This creates a clinical situation with considerable technical difficulties, but may help to explain the problems that some adolescents have in engaging with a psychoanalytic process. In Green's view, which he acknowledges as a metapsychological speculation, one of the central functions of the mother's "good-enough" disillusionment of the infant is to create a frame, or matrix, for experience. He uses the notion of disillusionment from Winnicott. The containing frame might look like Bion's container, but it is not the same because it is not about containing and detoxifying aggressive and/ or deathly projections. *It is about creating a matrix for experiencing.* This matrix will be inevitably identified with the mother because it shelters the negative hallucination of the mother. When formed without flaw, it creates the basis of the maternal presence in her absence. But, when there is a flaw because of maternal decathexis, the negative hallucination of the mother is compromised by a striving to hold the mother's image captive in the struggle against her disappearance implied by her decathexis.

Green is, I think, here using Winnicott's (1963) distinction between the object mother and the environment mother. Such a conception is, I think, especially appropriate for thinking about adolescence, and is confirmed by the importance now placed on the kind of setting that is necessary to be able to engage with adolescents satisfactorily (see Wilson, 1991). In addition to this structuring effect of the mother's mind, the presence of a preoccupying figure in the mother's mind that seems to take her away from the child creates, of course, a primal scene from which the child will feel excluded but about which it is intensely curious. This experience will be recreated in the countertransference by a sense of an empty exclusion that attracts. It will also be recreated in the transference as the psychoanalyst inevitably takes on the mantle of the virtual object.

But, this primal scene differs from the normal one because it is so chronically excluding. In Lacanian terms, there is a "nom du Père" (i.e., mother's desire), but no actual father to express the "non du Père". The mother's preoccupation is what is responsible for expressing this exclusion. Now this, of course, could be said to describe the normal Oedipal state of affairs when the child grasps that he is not the sole object (name) of mother's desire. What makes the difference in the dead mother scenario is the unremitting quality of the mother's decathexis of the child. There are far fewer cathecting moments to counterpoise against this experience. This is particularly the case in situations where the parent is chronically ill, or imagined, as we will see in the next case I wish to present.

To exemplify these matters, in the first case described above, the patient developed an identification of being a "fat slob", which embraced his hatred of himself, his hatred and his family's hatred towards his father, and his desire to regress and avoid development. Thinking about this case in the light of Green's thoughts on the "dead mother", it seems to me that their application and relevance seems to be to do with the effect of father's absence on the remaining family. A family circumstance was created to which this young man was forced to respond. He, being the only remaining male, did so by becoming the "ghost" of the absent father. In a sense, we might wonder whether this was a case in which the family, rather than just the mother, was dead to him as an individual. His identity was distorted when his family saw in him their image of the departed father. He readily absorbed these projections because of his own difficulties in mourning his father's absence. In the transference, he expected to be treated with contempt. He enacted being a contemptible figure, which could be said to be both his absent father and the protest against his father's absence. He became the virtual object in his absence from his analysis and the analyst was left groping at the nothingness of the patient's absence.

Clinical example: Patient 2

I would now like to discuss a second patient (this patient is referred to in Part 2, in the paper concerning consultation and assessment), who initially reported a lack of confidence and a sense that others in his family were false and objects of contempt. In this case, it was his mother who left the family rather than the father. This was a young man who was in treatment for several years. He came in his late teens, at the recommendation of the counsellor at the Sixth Form College he had been attending. He said that he was lacking in confidence and felt very anxious in the presence of other people.

He had been living with his maternal grandmother for the past five years. The significant facts that he reported of his family history were that his mother had suddenly left the family home when he was eight, following which he and his brother had lived with his father for a while. Their father then met and married his stepmother and they all tried to live together, until the situation broke down and he moved to his maternal grandmother's flat when he was thirteen. This was experienced as very difficult and consciously he had little but contempt for his step-family, seeing them as superficial and "corny". It was this contempt, of course, which he saw in others towards him.

The dominant features of the transference situation in the therapy were the extreme sensitivity he felt about the ends of sessions and holiday breaks and his yearning for a male figure with good authority. In terms of content, he was much preoccupied with how he was going to become more confident in his relations with his friends, colleagues at work, his bosses, and girls. This had a despairing quality about it, and readily provided a means for him to feel that this would never improve. The essence of this was that he wanted me to be with him outside the sessions in real life, and it was no good me abandoning him to the harsh realities of life. These issues came to a dramatic head in the impact of the end of the session and what it meant to him. At the end of sessions, he would look at me with an odd combination of fear and hatred and say "see you later" as he left with a slight air of contemptuousness, which increased as his fear of this contempt seen in me, by projection, receded. The combination of these feelings, in the one moment, captured beautifully the primal scene moment he had in his mind of his mother leaving his father, with whom he identified. This, therefore, communicated to me his imagined angry contemptuous mother leaving him in a state of fear and helplessness.

When this young man began treatment, he was unemployed, but shortly afterwards obtained work as a deliveryman for a manufacturing company and, in the first year of therapy, he re-established contact with his father, from whom he had been estranged for five or more years. Then he moved from delivery to a more creative job in the company employing him, and this was accompanied by a quantum shift in his perception of himself. He had, he thought, a chance of becoming normal and adult. One of the most significant features of this period was that he claimed to give up smoking marijuana, to which he had been apparently quite habituated.

This paved the way for him to find and visit his mother again. He discovered her not to be the violent, heartless bully of his fantasies, but actually depressed herself. This was a profound shock to him because it upset all the fantasies he had built up to rationalize what had happened to him. This new mother did not fit the violent mother who had left him and whom he felt hated him. He could now see that his fear of women arose from his hatred of women and, in particular, his mother. Hence, we could create a hypothesis that this unconscious hatred, which was implied by his conscious fear, had then been the stuff out of which the virtual hating mother had been created. His hatred had then to be denied because consciousness of his hate meant him having to assume responsibility for the departure of his loved object.

The net effect was to void him of his aggression, which led in turn to his lack of confidence and the belief that others looked upon him with contempt. However, this lack of confidence was the price exacted for avoiding a sense of his responsibility for his mother's departure. That is, his overriding need to maintain his mother as a good object transformed the hatred of his loved mother into an unconscious belief on his part that his hatred of his mother had driven her away. Hence, he was in consciousness afraid of her, as he was of all women he desired.

Perhaps in confirmation of this hypothesis was the belief that developed in him that he needed to stay in contact with his mother to enable him to have a relationship with a girl. It was this that enabled him to replace the old hating mother with a present alive mother, through whom he could create a relationship with a woman. The relationship with his mother went through many vicissitudes, not least of which was when he recommended to his mother that she get some therapy herself. In any event, the gradual repair of this relationship indeed enabled him to think instead about having a relationship with a girl, which he successfully achieved. At the conclusion of our work, this was established, as was his continued occupational success.

The first turning point in this young man's treatment occurred when he progressed to a job with more responsibility, which followed his re-establishing contact with his father. In this sense, I think he felt recognized by a significant other in authority, which put in question his defence based on the projection of his contempt into others. This kept from consciousness any idea that his anger had been responsible for driving his mother away.

The second turning point in this young man's treatment was when he decided to meet his mother again. It was at this point that the myths and defences that he had created about himself and his family began to fall to the ground and paved the way to take back some of the aggression that had been the stuff out of which the hating mother virtual object had been created. Green suggests that the subject with a dead mother becomes like a keeper of her. The effect is that the child becomes the carer for the mother, but cannot let her come alive for fear of losing her. Perhaps this can become true should the grudges towards the mother become unending. It is, however, possible to wonder whether the picture for this adolescent was different because issues about instinctual organization, ownership of the body, and object choice had not been finally settled when treatment began.

Discussion

I would like now to examine further the peculiar triangular Oedipal situation in which there is an insistent presence as a result of absence, which was first discussed earlier. In this second case, a situation was created by the concrete absence of the mother. Her absence gives rise to a *preoccupying, as well as a preoccupied*, mother in the patient's mind, who is a figure created out of trying to understand the reasons for the fact of her departure. This explanation is pieced together out of the affective fragments left in the wake of her departure.

I mentioned earlier how this young person seemed to experience the ends of sessions. If we consider this in the light of his fear of his object's contempt and the subjective certainty that he would be rejected without a thought, then I think we can see a similarly distorted Oedipal triangle. This time, however, the internal maternal object is not just lost in a preoccupation, but also, in fantasy, angrily and contemptuously turning away to another unknown figure. Therefore, one point of the Oedipal triangle is taken by a figure created out of the individual's unconscious understanding of the reasons for the missing figure's absence. Hence, there is *no separate and alive* figure outside the control of the individual's imagination to mediate the relationship with the remaining figure and prevent the child being caught inextricably in a dyadic enmeshing with the tormenting figure.

It is clear that the individual trapped in these distorted Oedipal triangles is in a very complex situation to which he/she has no choice but to respond. In younger children, severe disruption to the family constellation through death, departure, or severe mental illness has been linked with the development by latency children of "imaginary companions" (Nagera, 1969) because of the difficulties of mourning the losses caused by these disruptions. Older children and adolescents unconsciously create imagined figures with which to identify, in order to account for the meaninglessness of events. These provide the bases for a self-representation based on a *virtual* object. It is, therefore, not surprising to find such a person reporting a lack of confidence, reminiscent of a false self (Winnicott 1951), because their self-representation is intimately linked to identification with the virtual object, which is constantly being disconfirmed by reality.

At the clinical level, the false self can appear quite convincing, particularly as the only sign that it is a false self is the reported "lack of confidence". But this is not necessarily a "compliant false self", although it may be, which is thought to arise from a premature *over-impingement* by the maternal object. Nor can it be said that it is intended to be deceptive. We are clearly concerned here with *under-impingement* by an actual object that turns into an *over-impingement by a virtual object*. It combined the hostility of the subject and the absence of the object into the creation of the virtual hating mother.

Conclusions

It seems to me that there are implications arising from the consideration of the above cases at the clinical, technical, and theoretical points of view. At *a clinical level*, it is clear that the patient confronted with an unavailable, dead mother is in a very complex situation to which he/she is forced to respond. An unknown something is experienced as preoccupying the patient's mother because the mother decathects the child. Into the psychic hole created by this decathexis is placed a creation, which I have called a "virtual object". This creation is perhaps better thought of as a continuous re-creation. The therapeutic task, then, is to interrupt this continuous cycle, which binds the patient to their dead mother. These virtual objects, created to fill this vacuum of meaning, lead to a "false self" (Winnicott, 1951), because of the inevitable narcissistic identifications.

We could see, in the second case, how in the re-encounter with his actual mother, the terrifying imagined (or virtual) mother was thrown into sharp relief and differentiated from his actual mother. This virtual mother had been created in the space left by the departure of his actual mother and had then powerfully determined his psychic life and, thus, the conscious experience of his life. When he could see that this virtual figure was a product of his own mind, but had been experienced and perceived as if it were a fact of external reality, there was a considerable reduction in his anxiety after an initial profound shock. There was also a radical shift in his capacity to reflect on his own mind and a realization that he did not necessarily know what was in the mind of the (m)other. The minds of others were there to be discovered and did not need to be automatically thought of as frightening or contemptuous. He reported, while these changes were taking root, that he stopped spending time looking at his image in the mirror, which had been an abiding habit. In the first case, he was freer from the power of the projections of his immediate family, which he had adopted so readily because of the difficulties the family had experienced in mourning father's departure.

At the *technical level*, we have seen that there will often be a need for a fairly extended period of holding before surgery can occur, to use the metaphor due to Freud. It is important, it seems, to allow the psychoanalytic setting to develop the frame for experiencing before the psychoanalyst can tackle the presented false selves, which result from the virtual objects. To do this too soon is to risk the patient replacing one set of false selves by another, or taking flight because the equilibrium of their defensive systems has been prematurely shaken. Hence, it is important to allow time for engagement and not be put off by the inevitable early difficulties in engaging. Once established, it becomes possible to work more directly in the transference, which will reflect the phantasies of what is occurring in the mind of the dead mother. This is not easy, and there are many opportunities for error because of the pervasive influence of what is absent as well as what is present. But, with patience, progress can be made.

Green describes what can be experienced by the psychoanalyst as an endless quest to cut off what he calls the heads of the many-headed hydra of the patient's depression. The temptation is to be distracted by the virtual objects filling the psychic hole. This can lead one to regard the emptiness as destructive and aggressive, which will be expressed in enactments" for example, poor attendance, a sense of hopeless and despairing inactivity, a sense of very slow progress, and, once they are established, a feeling in the analyst that the patient never wants to leave and refuses to budge out of the regression. Frustration can tempt the analyst into what are experienced as punitive efforts to interpret the patient's apparent destructiveness.

However, in Green's view, this amounts to tackling the subject's responses to the problem rather than the problem itself, which is the blankness of the psychic hole, which, in his view, is created by the decathexis of the maternal object and the unconscious identification with the child's experience of the dead mother. With this identification come the loss of meaning and the sense of blankness in the countertransference. The virtual objects are the response to this.

The technical challenge is to find one's way out of this paradox in which the patient comes to the analyst to tell them that they cannot help them. Green suggests that it is technically inappropriate to be silent or to interpret the apparent destructiveness of the communication, because this exactly matches and reflects the psychic situation. The silent analyst is reflecting the silent distracted object; the analyst who focuses on the apparent destructiveness of the depression tackles the recathexes filling the psychic holes rather than the psychic holes themselves.

If one is not to be caught up in fruitlessly tackling the subject's responses to the dead mother, what is a useful point of focus of interpretation? For Green, the important level at which to work is the primal scene, for it is via this means, he feels, that the "dead mother" gives up her secret. By primal scene is meant, in this situation, the dynamic going on between the mother and whatever it is that preoccupies her in her mind. Patients like this are locked into this primal scene, as is often revealed by the transference situation, and as a result the psychoanalyst will be deeply involved and implicated once the engagement process has been survived.

Despite the apparently unpromising initial prognosis when working with such young people, it is essential to persevere when treating the young person, who is apparently so bound to their defences that little change appears to occur. Ultimately, the young person may be seeking to make sense of an empty psychic space. We should not, therefore, be surprised to find ourselves experiencing this space in all its despondent futility in the countertransference. But, the young person who persistently maintains the paradox by continuing to attend despite all the apparent evidence and the therapist's internal questioning about "why do they come?" should be thought of as seeking a way out of the futility. The paradox presented reflects the subject's dilemma when faced with the absent mother, who is dead to them. The patient is present with the analyst in body, but part of their mind is somewhere else; as a result, they cannot be helped because "their hearts are not in it". By this means, the patient invites the analyst to experience their Oedipal dilemma. As in the overcoming of all Oedipal dilemmas, their courage deserves our respect.

When working with such young people, I have found it possible, given time, to see them "become subjects" as described by Cahn (1998) and develop a sense of being "real" (Winnicott, 1963). It is as if there comes an uncanny moment when there is an observable change in their being and you feel that that there suddenly really is another, different, person in the consulting room. What Cahn and others mean by "becoming a subject" is the process by which a person appropriates their psychic reality and, thereby, differentiates their appreciation of the external world from that of their internal world. Another way of putting it might be that they have achieved a means of thinking about a relationship from a point of view outside of that relationship. In other words, a triangulated space has been achieved, making it possible to think about experience in a new way.

Last, *theoretically*, we come to the notions of absence, nothing, and nothingness. As we can see, nothingness in this context is a quality that is created by desire and, very definitely, is not nothing. What I think this points to is the question of whether there can be any such thing as a hole in experience. Does nature abhor a vacuum in the mind as much as it does in the atmosphere? The inner subtlety of Green's thesis is, I think, that it poses the question, by implication, of how an individual reacts to the experience of nothingness as a result of decathexis. They have to react because they have no choice. Do they react by developing a sense of *being a nothing* as a result of this decathexis, or face being overwhelmed by their own unrequited desire? By examining decathexis of the child by the mother, he is asking what happens when the child has the experience not only of not being mother's desire, but ultimately the fear of *never* being, having been, or ever likely to be mother's desire. Does this mean, I think he asks by implication, that such a child can never enter, in Lacan's terms, the symbolic order *and thus become a subject?*

This might be the case unless this sense of *being a nothing* then becomes the content of a communication about a sense of empty nothingness, which is then experienced in the psychoanalyst's countertransference. Of course, the Lacanian model makes no endeavour to set itself in developmental terms. Its purpose is to describe the existence of the subject in the tangle of the real, imaginary, and symbolic orders, also known as the Borromean Knot. But, it seems to me that a sense of being a nothing, arising from decathexis, in principle tests the model, because it predicts *that there are circumstances in which the individual can never become a subject.* We seem to find that, if the individual can create a virtual object and can communicate an experience of nothingness, then they can become a subject, even if a distorted and partially false one because of the narcissistic identifications.

Imagine the situation of the child achieving mastery over the comings and goings of mother through the "fort/da" game (Freud, 1920g, p. 15). The trouble is that, for these cases, there is a danger that there is no "da". But, this does not and cannot happen. *Mother's "return" is assured by the creation of a virtual object.* Within this virtual object is the explanation of mother's departure, created out of the subject's omnipotence.

However, we can see from the cases above that the subject's dead mother need not be the actual maternal primary object. In the first case, the family left behind by the departing father could be said to be the subject's "dead mother". In the second case, the subject's "dead mother" could be said to exist as an imaginary figure in his mind, and the virtual object was created within this image of the maternal primary object.

The awful paradox is that the subject creates the virtual object in response to the nothingness of mother's absence, but then dreads the return of an alive mother for fear that she will leave again. This inevitably raises the prospect of an interminable analysis, with no change, which is the initial defensive objective of these subjects and may be the reason for the very slow rate of change. This is the clinical and technical problem created by nothingness.

Theoretically speaking, when can we say that the experience of nothing becomes nothingness? We may answer: when there is desire, by its nature infinite. But, can there be desire without a notion of the future being distinct from the present? We might say in reply that, although there may not be desire, there will be need. But, we are moved by our own desires, whereas we may need someone to help us satisfy our needs. For example, however much the thirsty baby in the desert wishes to destroy the empty glass in his frustration, it is doubtful that he/she will survive unless given something to drink by someone. As we have seen in the cases described above, virtual objects are created in response to an absence. The function of these creations is to convert the nothing of absence, and the consequent sense of being a nothing, into a nothingness. These objects then fall upon the subject's ego so that the subject can defend against the confrontation with nothingness, which is implied by the existence of the virtual object. The sting in the tail is that this closed system is established to defend against "fort" because of the anxiety that there will be no "da". This anxiety does not disappear, despite, and perhaps because of, the creation of the virtual object. The virtual object provides temporary respite, but turns into a closed system if it goes unchallenged by a live object outside the control of the subject's omnipotence.

The effect of these virtual objects is experienced in the transference through the powerful effect of an uncanny sense of absence, or of something missing. I propose that it is by this means that nothingness as it exists in a patient is symbolized and communicated in the transference. The paradox of nothingness is that it is full of desire, but it can appear that the subject communicating nothingness in the transference wants nothing. This gives rise to the paradox of the subject saying "you can't help me", while they continue to come.

Ultimately, it seems that the paradox brought by the patients I have been discussing arises because they, as subjects, are cathecting objects that decathect them. During initial consultation, the psychoanalyst can feel decathected in the countertransference and then may act this out in the treatment decision through a reactive decathexis by judging them as unsuitable for psychoanalytic treatment.

I would like to conclude by proposing that the experience of the nothingness of absence must be classed as an infinite experience (Rayner, 1981). It is this that gives rise to the subjective response of creating a virtual object, which is, in its turn, infinite because it is created out of the subject's omnipotence. It is this quality of infinity which enables the virtual object to be symmetrized with the experience of nothingness in a timeless way. Anything that threatens this timelessness will, consequently, be fiercely resisted because temporality brings with it the sense of the possibility of loss.

This has significant implications for technique, as Green has suggested. One of the most interesting aspects is the question of whether, if the analyst seeks, in his technique, to be infinitely neutral (as a means of accessing the unconscious), he risks condemning both the analysis and the analysand to an exact replica of the patient's response to nothingness, which reflects the infinity of his desire. This is because the patient must experience the analyst as the virtual object in the transference, if the communication necessary to make to the psychoanalyst is to be achieved. Therefore, we may wonder whether, in the face of such infinite experiences, strange phenomena appear which test our notions of subject, object, and psychoanalytic neutrality in technique.

Notes

1.   Lacan (1954) uses the notion of the virtual object in a discussion of Optics in his seminar entitled "The topic of the imaginary". Thus, he says,

> Optical images possess a peculiar diversity—some of them are subjective, these are the ones we call virtual, whereas

others are real, namely in some respects behave like objects and can be taken for such. More peculiar still—we can make virtual images of those objects which are real images. In such an instance, the object which is the real image quite rightly has the name of virtual object. . . . There is in truth something, which is even more surprising, which is that optics is founded on a mathematical theory without which it is absolutely impossible to structure it. For there to be an optics, for each given spot in real space, there must be one point and one corresponding point only in another space, which is the imaginary space. This is the fundamental structural hypothesis. It gives the impression of being overly simple, but without one cannot even write one equation, nor symbolize anything—optics would be impossible. . . . Here too, the imaginary space and the real space fuse. [p. 76]

2.   Winnicott had two notions of omnipotence. I shall confine myself in this discussion to the meaning of omnipotence as an experience essential to the first experiences of the "me" and the "not me", which belong to, and rely on, dependence. His second meaning of omnipotence related to hopelessness about dependence, which may be closer to what Bion intended to describe.

References

Balint, E. (1963). On being empty of oneself. *International Journal of Psycho-Analysis*, *44*: 470–480.

Cahn, R. (1998). The process of becoming a subject in adolescence. In: M. Perret-Catipovic & F. Ladame (Eds.), *Adolescence and Psycho-analysis* (pp. 149–160). London: Karnac.

Damasio, A. (1999). *The Feeling of What Happens: Body and Emotion in the Making of Consciousness*. New York: Harcourt Brace.

Freud, S. (1900a). *The Interpretation of Dreams*. *S.E.*, *4–5*. London: Hogarth.

Freud, S. (1905d). *Three Essays on the Theory of Sexuality*. *S.E.*, *7*: 125–243. London: Hogarth.

Freud, S. (1915e). The unconscious. *S.E.*, *14*: 159–216.

Freud, S. (1917e). Mourning and melancholia. *S.E.*, *14*. London: Hogarth.

Freud, S. (1920g). *Beyond the Pleasure Principle*. *S.E.*, *18*: 4–67. London: Hogarth.

Green, A. (1986). The dead mother. In: *On Private Madness*. London: Hogarth Press and Institute of Psychoanalysis.

Green, A. (1999). *The Work of the Negative*. London: Free Association Books.

Kennedy, R. (1998). *The Elusive Human Subject*. London: Free association Books.

Laplanche, J., & Pontalis, J. B. (1973). *The Language of Psychoanalysis*. London: Hogarth Press and the Institute of Psychoanalysis.

Laufer, M., & Laufer, E. (1984). *Adolescence and Developmental Breakdown: a Psychoanalytic View*. New Haven: Yale University Press.

Matte-Blanco, I. (1975). *The Unconscious as Infinite Sets*. London: Duckworth.

Nagera, H. (1969). The imaginary companion: its significance for ego development and conflict resolution. *Psychoanalytic Study of the Child, 24*: 165–196.

Rayner, E. H. (1981). Infinite experiences, affects and the characteristics of the unconscious. *International Journal of Psychoanalysis, 62*: 403–412.

Rosenfeld, H. (1987). *Impasse and Interpretation*. London: Tavistock.

Russell, B. (1903). *The Principles of Mathematics*. London: Routledge.

Sartre, J.-P. (1943). Translated as *Being and Nothingness*. London: Methuen and Co., 1958.

Wilson, P. (1991). Psychotherapy with adolescents. In: J. Holmes (Ed.), *Textbook of Psychotherapy in Psychiatric Practice* (pp. 443–467). London: Churchill Livingstone.

Winnicott, D. W. (1951). Transitional objects and transitional phenomena. In: *From Paediatrics to Psychoanalysis*. London: Hogarth and Institute of Psychoanalysis.

Winnicott, D. W. (1963). On communication. In: *The Maturational Processes and the Facilitating Environment*. London: Institute of Psychoanalysis and Karnac, 1990.

CHAPTER TEN

Couples, doubles, and absence: some thoughts on the psychoanalytical process considered as a learning system

James S. Rose

Introduction

The fundamental therapeutic aim of psychoanalysis is to enable an analysand to learn about themselves in the context of the presence of an other. As a consequence, I think we can say that we all work within a learning system, which we create when we start a treatment. This chapter seeks to explore some aspects of the psychoanalytic learning system. By aspects, I specifically mean the concepts of the couple, the double, and the presence and absence of the psychoanalyst and patient from one another, which I shall try to define as characteristics of the relationship between psychoanalyst and patient in the psychoanalytic process. Let us begin with the notion of the couple.

Essential to this learning system is the fact that two people—psychoanalyst and analysand—meet regularly in a particular setting that to the outsider seems to vary as little as possible. Seeing these two *as a couple* does not in itself seem very remarkable. But, in so doing, there is the obvious implication that they occupy distinct *complementary roles* in a system whose task it is to learn about the analysand. Hence, the notion of this couple, exploring their differences and experiencing their presence and absence from one another, gives the "couple" a context capable of bringing the concept to life. When stated like this, it can make psychoanalysis sound like a cognitive process, or simply an exercise of consciousness which, of course, it must, in part, be. This is because there is something missing—the unconscious. To my mind, we need to be able to conceptualize how one unconscious can communicate with another if we are to capture the essence of psychoanalysis. Of course, this is not to say that there is no reference to this in the psychoanalytic literature. However, its conceptualization is not, perhaps, as systematic as it could be. Without this, psychoanalysis can appear to the outsider to be a purely cognitive exercise, rooted in consciousness. This suggests that we need something more descriptive of the psychoanalytic situation. More, that is, than the couple.

In this chapter, I wish to discuss the impact on the work of this psychoanalytic couple of what Cesar and Sara Botella (2005) call "working as a double". This seeks to describe the moments of identification of the psychoanalyst with the analysand. I want to explore the idea that countervailing tensions between what I will refer to as (following the Botellas' conceptualization) the heterosexual *couple* and the homosexual *double* are a powerful driver of the psychoanalytic learning system. My hypothesis is that this is because the couple and the double set an antinomic tension upon one another. This is because the notion of the couple places difference in the foreground, whereas the double is, in essence, a phenomenon of identification. I call it antinomic because both phenomena occur and, while they are conceptually mutually exclusive, each has a claim on the truth of describing what happens and can occur contemporaneously.

I will further propose that this antinomic tension is triangulated by the iterating presence and absence of the psychoanalyst and analysand from each other, because this, of necessity, changes the form of identification with one another. The alternating presence and absence of the psychoanalytic couple from each other provides an impetus to learning because this accentuates the conflict between difference and identification. It is this iterative presence and absence that makes it possible to disentangle difference and identification. The fundamental reason for this continuing tension is the fact of the constantly creative and active quality of human perception, which is partly due to the pressure of unconscious drives, and partly, the exigencies of the situation.

My exploration of these matters will take the following route. I will begin with some thoughts deriving from Freud's paper, "Constructions in analysis" (1937d). The main point is to use the distinction he makes between *intervention* and *interpretation*. From there, I will move to discuss the Botellas' (2005) concept of "working as a double". I will then discuss a clinical case in which the emergence of a grudge in the material seemed to be a defence against an unconscious guilt, which seemed to demand what might be called a "construction" to prevent the analysis from becoming interminable. I will argue that this came about as a result of my becoming aware of the presence of an absence in the transference. My purpose is to illustrate how these three concepts, the couple, the "double", and iterative presence/absence go together as a dynamic description of the psychoanalytical learning system.

Constructions in psychoanalysis

I will begin with a quote from Freud's paper, "Constructions in analysis" (1937d), written towards the end of his life in response to criticism that psychoanalysis was essentially suggestive.

He wrote,

> What we are in search of is a picture of the patient's forgotten years that shall be alike trustworthy and in all essential respects complete. But at this point we are reminded that the work of analysis consists of two quite different portions, that it is carried on in two separate localities, that it involves two people, to each of whom a different task is assigned. [p. 258]

Thus, he seems here to invoke the idea of the patient and the analyst being a couple.

A few lines later, he asked,

> What then *is* his [the psychoanalyst's] task? His task is to make out what has been forgotten from the traces which it has left behind or, more correctly, to *construct* [my italics] it. The time and manner in

which he conveys his constructions to the person who is being analysed, as well as the explanations with which he accompanies them, constitute the links between the two portions of the work of analysis, between his own part and that of the patient. [*ibid.*]

Interestingly, later in the paper, he said,

If, in accounts of analytic technique so little is said about constructions, that is because "interpretations" and their effects are spoken of instead. But I think that "construction" is by far the more appropriate description. Interpretation applies to something that one does to some single element of the material, such as an association or a psycho-parapraxis. It is a "construction" when one lays before the patient a piece of his early history that he has forgotten . . . [p. 261]

Freud's paper was a response to a criticism of psychoanalysis, which was that the patient has no option but to agree with the analyst. This is because, if he disagrees, then all he is doing is resisting or being in some other way defensive. At the conclusion to the paper, Freud's response to this criticism of suggestion is that a patient's agreement or disagreement with the psychoanalyst's intervention—be it interpretation or construction—cannot be thought of as a simple matter of "yes" or "no". The criticism of analysis was that the position of the psychoanalyst towards the patient is one of "heads I win and tails you lose". However, what this criticism fails to take account of is the fact of the human subject's resistance and defence. In other words, the human subject reacts to being studied. Freud's response was that this reflects the assumption on the part of this kind of critic that the psychoanalytic learning system works through a process of simple incremental and linear accumulation of knowledge.

The two phenomena I would like next to discuss are, first, the phenomenon of the double, and second, some aspects of the clinical impact of absence on the human subject.

Working as a double

In their recent book, *The Work of Psychic Figurability* (2005), Cesar and Sara Botella seek, as Michael Parsons puts it in his introduction, to address the question of experience "that will not go into words". The word "figurability" is a neologism coined to translate the German word *darstellbarkeit*, usually translated as representability. *Darstellbarkeit* was one of the components of Freud's conception of the dream work, the others being condensation, displacement, and secondary elaboration.

The point of coining the neologism, however, is to emphasize that the processes that permit the apprehension of that which is *readily representable* are not the same as those that permit the apprehension of that which is only *indirectly or partially represented*. The latter will emerge in the clinical material in different ways. For example, they may become apparent through repeated enactments or reversals in the transference and to discern them requires the psychoanalyst's free-floating attention and, as some put it, their negative capability—or what some have called the capacity to see what is not there.

The experience of this in everyday clinical work will, I think, be shared by all, even if it might be conceptualized in different ways. It emphasizes, however, the importance of free-floating attention. The Botellas suggest this is because, in the encounter with the unrepresentable, the psychoanalyst picks up at an unconscious level of awareness, *the patient's experience of non-representation*. Being in the presence of something, by its nature non-representable, can bring a sense of a void and a sense of a threat to one's survival or existence. This is because it represents (a word I use advisedly) a challenge to one's ongoing sense of the continuity and intelligibility of experience. One might think of it as the unconscious knocking on the door of consciousness.

A description by the Botellas (2005) of these clinical moments is as follows:

> When in borderline situations, quite unexpectedly and involuntarily, the analyst's thinking regresses beyond the state of free floating attention and his word-presentations tend to be disinvested, an *accident of thought* may occur, a rupture with the world of representations. Equivalent to the traumatic state of non-representation, the "accident" supposes a retrogressive movement of convergence–coherence, tracing new links in the simultaneity of the varied and multiple fields of the session: the patient's discourse of acting out, the transference / counter-transference, as well as the whole variety

of "actual perceptual material" ranging from sensory perception and momentary bodily impressions to the "sensory remains" of earlier sessions. It is the psychic capacity of such a movement that we call *figurability* and its accomplishment, the *work of figurability*. Its result is a "'figure' common to representation and perception" (Green, 1993). The retrogressive movement of the analyst's thought opens the session to an intelligibility of the relation between the two psyches functioning in a regressive state. The outcome of this *mode of working as a double (travail en double)*, so to speak, reveals that which already exists in the analysand in an irrepresentable state, as a negative of the trauma, and can at last have access to the quality of representation. [p. 49]

The Botellas (2005) further propose that psychoanalysis, as conceived by Freud, sprang from his experience of his relationship with, first, Fliess, and then, Jung. They proposed, therefore, that two couples were involved in the creation of psychoanalysis as a science of subjectivity. However, they felt that Freud's creation required both the contact with, and then the breaking away from, these relationships. What the Botellas are suggesting is that, within these couples, there was what they call a homosexual transference at work because there were moments when these couples functioned as what they call "doubles". This creation probably would not have been achieved by the individuals comprising those couples by themselves, but the experience of the couple as a double enabled Freud to make his ideas emerge. The Botellas hypothesize that:

the "materialisation" of the double, with the aid of the hook of homosexuality, offers a protection against the vertigo of thought, the price to be paid is the adhesion of the collage of thought to the double, the sacrifice of differences. And it was the transition *from* the relationship to a "material" double, *to* the relationship to an autonomous, internal double, as a result of analysing homosexuality, that would give Freud's thought all its originality. [p. 68]

As we will see below, I do not think that they are here referring to a genital homosexuality.

To describe this in more prosaic but, perhaps, plainer words, we might imagine the experience of these two couples reaching for a description of experience (*and, thus, being able to think together about the unthinkable—despite the implied "vertigo of thought"*) and being excited by a sense of the mutual recognition—in each other—of their emerging ideas. In reaction to the excitement of these moments of identification might inevitably come the discovery of differences "in the cold light of day", as one might say. Nevertheless, the amazing revolutionary thought that needed the context of the double to flourish was the realization that what we see, what we treat as objective, is partly a function of our drives—truly a Copernican moment, because the full impact of the subjective upon the "objective" becomes apparent. This might be enough to rattle any rationalist because it seems to tend towards the equation of the "first person view" with objectivity. For this reason, we can see why it was that such an idea had to emerge from a discourse between two people in the first instance.

It is my impression that it should be noted that what they mean here by homosexual transference is not what we British usually mean by it: that is, *inter alia*, negative Oedipal process or a defence against the anxieties of heterosexuality. I think their meaning of homosexuality is more akin to the concept of a primary homosexuality (or thinking of homosexuality as manifesting a drive towards identification) rather than solely as a defence, which is how it is more commonly thought of in this country. Fain and Marty (1960) put forward a theoretical argument explicating a view on aspects of homosexual cathexis in the positive transference. This may, to British ears, sound rather surprising.

They said,

Here again, in fact, the principal basis on which the classical and therapeutic concepts described are founded, was established by Freud.

When the subject, said Freud, comes up against a painful reality for the first time, he begins by denying it and hallucinates a satisfaction. This defence is only temporary and the subject is led to recognize an external world, losing at the same time his sense of omnipotence. The lost omnipotence is then projected on the object, which becomes his first ego-ideal. In this statement, Freud provided a striking schema of the mechanism essential to ego-maturation. The qualities and the richness of the individual's successive ego-ideals are the moulds in which his personality is formed. The ties which unite the ego to its ideals, Freud tells us, are built up by an essentially homosexual libido.

If the relationship is to be set up correctly and constructively, three conditions must be present:

a.   There must be a certain frustration which reveals the full reality of the object and, in particular, bestows on it new and hitherto unperceived qualities.

b.   The frustration must be compensated by a climate of affection.

c.   There must be a certain pressure exercised by the object as ego-ideal, which tends to direct the subject in a progressive sense, whilst satisfying his passive and receptive desires.

These three conditions are fulfilled in psycho-analytic treatment when a positive transference is established. *The homosexual nature of this transference is obvious.*

Neurosis is, basically, established in infancy by the dominance or absence of one of these three conditions, according to whether the ego-ideals are deficient or incapable of playing their part correctly. The ego structure is then profoundly modified by fear and guilt. The id perseveres in the hope of encountering valid ideals, or turns destructively against the whole personality. [pp. 403–404, my italics]

The psychoanalytic couple functioning as a double

At this point, I think it may be helpful to describe a clinical incident as an example of what the Botellas seem to me to be describing as "working as a double". When I first read their work, it seemed to me that they risked criticism of being "wild" in their analysis because their interventions seemed to come directly from their intuition. But then I realized the importance of their recognition of the regressive and identificatory features of this aspect of their work. The psychoanalytic couple thus becomes a double in which the boundary separating one from another and defining differences somehow seems to become increasingly permeable. It involves a regression and an identification, but once achieved, a new kind of emotional contact is possible, albeit with its attendant difficulties, distastes, and even terrors. Its importance, in the Botellas' view, is that "This mode of thinking reveals, in particular, aspects of the analysand's infantile history with which it has not been possible to work: hence, its importance, its necessity, in the analyses of borderline patients" (p. 71).

To give an example from my own experience, I recall an incident in the treatment of a young adult woman, who had come for help with abiding feelings of a lack of confidence. Very often, I find, these patients are wrestling with a profound sense of feeling unwanted. While this provokes an angry reaction, this anger is vigorously repressed because there is a belief that expression of this anger will be further grounds for their not being wanted by their objects. Thus, they are in consciousness left feeling afraid, as a result of this repression, or lacking in confidence ,which maintains an uneasy *status quo* from which it is not easy to escape. Because it is a fact of their daily experience, or, one might say, an assumption upon which they build their relationships with others, it remains indiscernible and, thus, cannot easily be reflected upon in consciousness.

I shall not go into her history, except to say that she came from a family of middle-class professional parents and had an older brother who had become a rather spectacular disappointment to them. This had become an abiding preoccupation for them. I had a sense that he had never forgiven his sister for being born and that he expressed his disappointment in being displaced by being a disappointment. Gradually, what seemed to be described was a family depression, resulting from this preoccupation. She seemed to have developed a belief that she could, and ought, somehow to bring them out of it, and this eventually came to be seen as a way of describing her depression. Unconsciously, she saw this depressing obligation everywhere in social and work contexts, but she was quite unable to see this replication because the force of this "duty" was so profound.

One day, towards the end of a session, as she was describing her reluctance to go home and yet, at the same time, her misery at being away from her family, I found myself experiencing an impulse to hug her as a father might hug his daughter. At a certain level, it seemed that a much more direct way of responding to her distress was to be a receptive father; as a result, I think I experienced what the Botellas (2005) mean by *working as a double*. On the one hand, I was a listening psychoanalyst (part of the couple), and, on the other, a loving and receptive father (part of the double). In itself, this was an antinomy—that is, the co-existence of mutually exclusive ideas, each with a claim on the truth.

At a certain point, I said it seemed that in addition to her wish to help her family out of their misery, she also perhaps hoped for a loving hug. In the intensity of the moment, I said that I was not going to give her a hug, which I think was my reaction to the antinomy. She looked at me with tears in her eyes and asked if she could go (i.e., before the end of session). Thus, there was an enactment in the transference that captured her internal predicament. I have to say that in the moment this surprised me, and I replied by saying that I thought it would not be right to end the session before we had understood what had been so unbearable about what I had just said to her, which led her to want to terminate the session. With a struggle, she said that what was so unbearable was her father's reluctance to give her a hug when she went home. Then the session ended, bringing an experience of her absence, and I worried if would see her again. In other words, had she found the last few minutes so unbearable that she would not return?

Thinking afterwards about why I had said that I was not going to hug her, I reflected that I had been anxious lest the reference to a hug might be taken as an indirect expression of my concrete desire. It might be asked whether it needed to be said at all. But, I knew from her history that a male teacher had been felt by her to be a little too close in his interest in her. This had embarrassed her in front of her school friends. What I felt, at the time, was that her need for a hug needed to be described because it immediately gave status and recognition to both the dutiful young woman in her and the little girl desperately anxious about whether she mattered. However, it was equally possible that she experienced my statement as meaning that I wanted her to go away. This could have been a reflection of a belief, on her part, that her father's reluctance to hug her meant that she should go away and not come back because he was not interested in her.

Thus, I wondered, do we see in this instant an enactment of an antinomic traumatic tangle that had been abidingly disturbing for her? In other words, in saying that I was not going to give her a hug, I had unwittingly enacted an aspect of her relationship with her father that deeply troubled her. It must be mentioned that I would not have said it had I felt it was not necessary. But I do not think that I can say that it was a matter of conscious deliberation. Was I, therefore, simply "wild" in this moment, because, in saying that I would not hug her, I was implying that I might or could and was, therefore, in some way rejecting her? In my thought that she might not return, I clearly felt that something horrifying had happened and I did not know what it was except that I was implicated.

In the event, she did return for her next session so my anxiety was not borne out. Nevertheless, I felt that I had accurately experienced her desire for a hug, which seemed to her to be painfully unattainable. However, my experience in the countertransference, based, as it must have been, on an identification, captures in the moment the experience both of what she had desired and her fear of the consequence of that desire. I, in turn, experienced this as my fear that I would not see her again. Hence, we can see the power of her desire and the force of its repression—and all this takes place in moments before the end of the session and consequent absence. Thinking about this incident in terms of the couple and the double, one might wonder whether the experience of wanting to give her a hug was an identification *or a phenomenon of the double*. But, in order to retain some capacity to reflect on this painful predicament, I had felt that *the separateness of the couple* needed to be re-established in order to be able to reflect on the situation. The trouble was that it was experienced both by her and myself as rejectingly clumsy.

Absence in the transference

At this point, I would like to turn to the phenomenon of absence in the transference and its links with a particular form of depression whose origins seem to be found in the experience of decathexis in the manner described by André Green in his paper entitled "The dead mother". To remind you briefly of his thesis, he proposes that what he calls the "dead mother complex" arises when, in the child's early life, the mother is, or becomes, chronically preoccupied with something that takes her away from her child. As he says, "the mother cares for the baby but her heart is not in it". Hence, the dead mother is most certainly not a mother who has actually died, but one who plunges her child into a premature Oedipal triangle made up of her child, herself, and whatever it is that preoccupies her and takes her away from her child, making her perhaps "dead to the child". It is this that comprises the complex, which is, as he puts it, a revelation of the transference. .

It has been my repeated observation that there is often an enactment of decathexis in the transference in treating these patients. This can take the form, for example, of a patient who steadfastly keeps coming to tell you that the therapeutic task is pointless. Thus, in the countertransference, one easily feels decathected, but I think it is a mistake to regard this statement as destructive.

Of particular concern has again been my repeated observation that what may superficially appear to be destructive attacks on the psychoanalytical enterprise very often turn out to be desperate efforts—by an enactment in reversal—on the part of the patient to communicate the nature of their depression. It is the difference between seeing the "dead mother" as an object and seeing the transference situation as a complex. Failure to make this distinction has the implication that interpretation of the apparently destructive as simply destructive intent on the part of the patient drives them deeper into despair. The countertransference experienced is often one of a dispiriting feeling that all efforts to help will fail and the patient will either terminate the treatment prematurely or forever continue telling you that you are useless—a position from which it does not seem they will budge. In these moments, I think we can propose that one is experiencing the full force of decathexis.

The very term *decathexis* seems to assume that it necessarily means the loss of cathexis. In other words, the child is initially fully cathected but then something happens which creates an abiding preoccupation in the mother that takes her from the child. However, some years ago, I asked André Green what had given him the idea of the dead mother complex. He said that it came from the experience of treating a young man who had been a replacement baby for a child that had died in infancy. I think it is not difficult to imagine that, in these circumstances, it is hoped that the arrival of the new baby will enable the bereaved mother to "get over" her tragic loss. Alas, experience shows this often to be a vain hope because, if the mother has not fully engaged with her mourning of her dead child, the danger is that the new arrival becomes a persecuting reminder of the child who has died. The shadow of the dead sibling thus falls on the emerging subjectivity of the new child and they run the risk of being forever entangled in it. I think one can easily see that if one grows up within a dead mother complex, one is likely to feel constantly compared to something without knowing quite what it is and fear that one can never match these implied ideals and aspirations. We might imagine that *decathexis* here means that while the child is cathected by the mother, they are not cathected as they feel they are in themselves.

However, when I first began thinking about the paradoxical situation in which a patient persisted in coming to see you to tell you that you are useless, I came to the conclusion that an understanding lay in seeing that these patients could do no other than cathect objects that decathected them. Indeed, they could not help but do just that because the search was driven by a desire to resolve a particular kind of guilt—the guilt of not being what their mother apparently wanted. This guilt seemed to arise from feeling that they must have done something to cause their being decathected, but that they had not the first idea of what it was. Yet, I have found in the course of treating such cases that sometimes something unexpected—uncanny even—happens that permits the patient to see that their perception of their situation is to be questioned. This can be when they see the predicament of their decathecting object in a new way. This causes them to experience their object not as a rejecting demon, but, in fact, as a tragic figure. When this happens, one can sometimes witness dramatic change and what can seem like a cure that touches one's heart.

Decathexis is inevitably associated with the idea of absence. Those that live with the experience of this kind of decathexis experience a particular kind of persecuting solitude. However, you will no doubt see now why absence appears in my title, because I think that patients who live with this kind of solitude will bring it to the experience of the couple—analyst and analysand—and communicate a powerful and *apparently* destructive decathexis in the transference. And, while I agree with the Botellas that there is an emergence of a double from the couple, enabling profound communication, I would like to propose that the apparent merging identification implicit in the notion of the double must be *triangulated against the experience of an absence*.

It is this absence that permits the maintenance of the creativity of the double. We could say this results from the inevitable *après-coup* or *nachtraglichkeit*, but, however we term it, I would like to propose that this absence creates a third which places a dynamic tension on the double/couple. The corollary must be that if this absence is in some way refused, denied, or in some way is disavowed, then there could be two consequences. The first is that the dynamic tension is removed, possibly to the relief of both parties in the couple because it permits in fantasy the continuation of the double. However, the implication of the elimination of the third could also be that the need to identify the meaning of what is absent is obviated. The couple/double can continue in immaculate union, safe from disturbance or intrusion, with the result that the essential psychoanalytic work in *nachtraglichkeit* is side-stepped.

Now, in the context of a double, absence has a different significance from its ordinary everyday meaning that something is not concretely present. It is clearer in the context of a couple, but the experience of the double is both internal and external and, thus, it can be carried away at the end of a session despite the concrete separation. Because it can be carried away, and often is, during intense periods of an analysis, the work will continue *in absentia* in one way or another. The psychoanalytic process works as much in the *après-coup* (the concrete absence) as in the here and now (the concrete presence)—if not more so. Therefore, absence, in the context of the double, means essentially a sense in which separateness and difference are maintained in, and co-exist with, the presence of the capacity for intuitive identification in what Fain and Marty (1960) called the homosexual transference of the double. Thus, a patient can say "I was thinking about what you said last night" the following day. We will know that this is a complex statement both about our absence from them and the discourse they have with us, as they create us in their minds, in our absence. As a result, we see ourselves in the transference when we are absent from them.

It will be clear that this is an antinomy in the sense that the recognition of difference and identity has a subjective reality, each with a claim on the truth, however contradictory this appears to be. It is essentially this that I mean by the double being triangulated against the experience of absence; that is, the creation of a sense of difference. This is not always easy to achieve, because, for some patients, the insistence on difference of perspective can feel like an experience of their murder or the murder of their minds. Understandably, they fight tooth and nail against such intrusions and threats to their view of the world because they unconsciously detect an effort to ram something into their consciousness or construe it to be so. As they will experience it, this is likely to be the reason they have created in their minds to explain their object's absence, that is, what it is that they know they do not want to know.

Clinical vignette: a patient exhibiting a dead mother complex

I would now like to consider a patient who suffered from the effects of decathexis in her childhood. What I want to focus on is the work directed at reconstructing the meaning of a particular phenomenon in the transference, which was against the intuitive understanding of the patient concerned. This phenomenon was the development of a grudge. This patient, thus, arrived at an unexpectedly different understanding of the meaning of her object's decathexis which was, none the less, convincing to her. One might say that, in these instances, the bitter accusation and recrimination towards her object—with all the consequent implications for the maintenance of unconscious guilt—gave way to a radically different understanding both of herself and the plight of her object.

Her problems seemed to derive from her being a child conceived as a replacement for a loved "beautiful" brother, who had died of a cot death in very early infancy. Being a girl, it seemed that her mother had been unable to attach to her as a girl and throughout her childhood had related to her as if she were, in fact, the lost beloved boy, while at the same time berating her for not being the boy—a paradoxical experience, to say the least of it. Her mother's short-circuited mourning, therefore, effectively meant that the patient was cathected by her mother as a boy, but actively decathected as a girl. In response to this paradoxical situation, the patient had complied with her mother's wishes and trained in the occupation assigned to her by her mother, with the result that she felt that she had been forced into something that was not her. The abiding consequence of this disturbance was that somehow—as she put it—she did not feel real.

The patient had entered treatment in her late twenties and became strongly attached to her psychoanalyst, who eventually had to terminate the treatment as he was retiring. Not surprisingly, this was very distressing for this patient, and he recommended that she enter treatment with me. This move was not at all easy for her because she had found emotional attachment opened her to great anxiety. For quite a time, she held me at arm's length. However, after some time, it was clear that her attachment and trust in me was increasing, as her anxieties receded in the light of the ongoing experience of the treatment.

But something quite uncanny was to occur with this patient as her treatment progressed. The analysis of her decathecting maternal object had been comparatively easy to describe, as had its connection with the loss of the much loved sibling. However, my patient began to develop a way of relating to memories of her mother that seemed to be destined to turn into an everlasting grudge, threatening an interminable analysis. It suggested that the grudge indicated an unconscious guilt that could not be analysed.

As this progressed, I began to entertain the possibility that, as this grudge developed, I was becoming a decathecting object that would not (that is, refused to) help her. The troubling question for me was—would not help her with what? You will see that I began to ponder with myself at some length about this predicament in moments that might be called my *après-coup*, based on an identification with her in her absence from me. In some sense, the situation called for thinking my way into her plight and, in this manner, experiencing it *from the point of view of a self representation in the double*.

Then it gradually began to dawn on me that there was possibly an absence being indicated. This time it was the absence of her father. In swiftly impregnating his wife soon after the loss of their son, it seemed that he had short-circuited the process of mourning such tragic loss. However, in the transference situation, I found myself listening rather passively to her constant complaints about her mother and could have made rather pointless and aimless interpretations of her complaints towards me that were being deflected on to her hapless mother. Thus, I came to a hypothesis that in the transference I was a rather helpless husband, who felt helpless in the face of his wife's distress, and a rather helpless father who could not, or would not, help his daughter understand her distress and difficulties with her mother. It was this conscious perception of my helplessness that led me to consider that she was making an *uncon-scious communication of having an absent father.*

Possibly, the emergence of the grudge represented an identifica-tion with a mother holding a grudge against her. To this might be added the possibility that her mother could not forgive herself for the loss of her son and had been locked in an interminable self recrimination. It seemed there was a breakdown in an essential triangulation because one of the points of the triangle was absent—that is, father. The presence of this absence was revealed by the endlessness of the patient's recriminations and *my experience of help-lessness.* Because I suspected that this grudge maintained an attach-ment to her mother, and because I suspected that the grudge obscured an unconscious guilt, then there was the following ques-tion. Is this structure being maintained by the grudge, which, in turn, perpetuates an *unconscious* guilt? I felt I saw a structure tying itself into a kind of psychic Gordian knot, which would be incap-able of undoing itself by itself.

It seemed to me that the situation called for an intervention a little more active than simply waiting for the correct interpretation of the maternal transference to suggest itself—in itself an experi-ence of waiting for something absent to turn up. Without con-sciously deciding to do so, I found myself progressively thinking with her about her mother's plight. We built up a picture of her mother's terrible distress at the loss of her baby son. It was going away from the immediacy of the transference in the presence of the creation of the grudge, which was, it seemed to me, a self-defeating defence against her unconscious guilt for existing at all because of her belief that her very existence was a persecuting reminder to her mother of the loss of her son.

I was conscious that in this work I was stepping back from the immediacy of her persecutory anxiety. Furthermore, I was intro-ducing an idea of her mother that was in contradiction of her view—which raised the question of whether I was simply suggest-ing something to the patient. However, over time, it was clear that this reconstructive work of imagining the reality of her mother's plight gradually enabled her to see her mother as a complex but tragic figure, rather than simply a terrible persecutor. But what was most important was a gradual development of a feeling for her mother's tragedy. This was not some intellectual archaeological dig into the past. When she thought of mother's plight, tears came to her eyes, and she felt a new-found experience of sympathy for her.

In confirmation of this view, she brought one day to her session three newly discovered family photographs. One was of her mother and a friend at the christening of her dead brother. She noted how happy she looked—confirmation that she had once been able to be happy. Then, there was a picture of her mother alone with her brother in her arms, and she noted how peaceful and serene they seemed to be together. This was a picture taken by her father. Finally, there was a picture of herself with her mother at the age of about three months. She felt her mother had a slightly dazed look and that she herself looked as if she was somewhere else. But, the fact that she could see that her mother had been once capable of happiness meant that the loss of her son—the patient's brother—must have been tragic for her. This radically altered her picture of her mother from someone irremediably cruel to one who had been desperately unhappy. She could, as a result, see herself from a quite new perspective. In her mind, she changed from being a freak (i.e., a girl who was not a boy) to someone who had had a grievously unhappy mother.

Now we come to the uncanny incident. In the year preceding this incident, she had moved into her own flat. She had lived for many years with another, older, woman. She was, therefore, in a space of her own, which she could make her own place without having to accommodate herself to the other woman. This relationship had a kind of mother–daughter quality and was not an explicitly homosexual relationship, although it possibly served the purpose of avoiding heterosexual relationships. As part of her homemaking, she had acquired two kittens—a male and a female—and became quite devoted to them.

Shortly after she showed me the pictures described above, and was gradually getting in touch with her mother's agony, the male cat strayed and did not immediately return. A more direct resonance with her mother's agony was hard to imagine. She admitted the temptation to get a replacement cat so that her remaining cat "would not be lonely", but then could see the repeat of history and desisted. She feared the return of her depression that had afflicted her for years.

Now, I call this incident uncanny because it had an obvious relevance to the unconscious issues being worked through in relation to her mother and the effect of her father's inaction. We could say that it was an extraordinary coincidence that so soon after a change in her feeling towards her mother, an event occurred which led her into a direct replication of her mother's experience of the loss of a child. It is possible to make many speculations about the reason for this occurrence, which might concern the extent to which the incident was unconsciously determined; all I can report with any confidence are my patient's reactions to the experience as I witnessed them.

After about a week, some neighbours responded to notices about her missing cat and he was returned, to the enormous relief of all concerned. The extraordinary replication of her experience with that of her mother in the context of having so recently shown me the photographs of her mother had a decidedly uncanny feel. Thus, not only had her conception of her mother changed from one of her being a tyrannical bully to one of being a tragic figure, but she had experienced an event that approximated to her mother's tragedy.

In Freud's paper, "The 'uncanny'" (1919h), he concludes that "an uncanny experience occurs either when infantile complexes which have been repressed are once more revived by some impression, or when primitive beliefs which have been surmounted seem once more to be confirmed" (p. 249). My purpose in describing these two clinical episodes above has been to examine two somewhat uncanny experiences and to discuss how they emerged. In so doing, I wish to think about the notion of the double and the notion of absence against which the double can be triangulated. By this means, I think we can add greater meaning to the notion of construction in psychoanalytic treatment.

The psychoanalytic process as a learning system

We can think of the case just described as an instance of depression as a reaction to decathexis—an initial failure on the part of the mother to cathect her new child because of an abortive mourning of her previous child. In this case, there was evidence of an unconscious guilt developing in reaction to this decathexis. Because this guilt remained unconscious, her mother was *in consciousness* condemned to the point of being the object of a grudge, which served to defend against the patient's guilt and, thus, held them both—subject and object—in a state of *unconscious persecutory* guilt. Thus, a self-sealing system was created from which there was little hope of escape unless somehow the unconscious guilt could be successfully revealed and worked through, because that held the key to the self-sealing system.

What seemed to bring about a change in this patient was the entry of a new perspective created by the development of a third position, arising from seeing the significance of an absence in the transference. In this case, I propose that I saw a presence of an absence in the transference through an experience in the counter-transference of helplessness: the helplessness of her father. Now, in this experience of helplessness, I propose that I was working as a double in a manner akin to that described in the first case, that is, becoming aware of something that the patient yearned for but dare not request. I was becoming aware of something from my patient concerning the experience of helplessness of everybody in the family resulting from the cot death. In the alternating presence and absence from each other, I could have a place to ponder my own helplessness and see an absence in it.

As soon as we add the significance of perceiving the presence of absence, we are adding to the requirement of observation of what can be perceived in the immediate *hic et nunc*. This concerns the impact of the patient on the psychoanalyst's *après-coup*, or how the psycho-analyst conceives their patient in the patient's absence. In working with this patient, it seemed to me that, in developing a construction out of my response to the emergence of a grudge, I was actively doing something that ran against the grain of my patient's view of the world. Some might say that I was side-stepping the interpretation of my patient's destructive omnipotence in the creation of the grudge. And yet, I think that what I was doing was using the inevitability of my *après-coup* and becoming a conduit for the absent—either the absent object or the absent experience that had never been directly experienced, but had been the cause of the grudge.

Freud's paper on constructions must, I think, be read with the understanding that the expected duration of psychoanalytic treat-ments was then much shorter than seems to be the practice today. Further, his objectives were not the same. I doubt that all would agree with his definition that I quoted at the beginning of this paper. These days, I think we seek, if we can, to do a full character analysis—a reassembly of all the introjected and projected parts—rather than reconstructing a patient's history, however convincing it might be to the analysand concerned. I think that, as a result, we have tended to become less active and interventionist than Freud might have been.

In my title, I refer to the idea of the learning system implied by psychoanalytic treatment. I think that what Freud is proposing in his paper on constructions is that the psychoanalyst must work both in immediate emotional proximity—*hic et nunc*—to the patient and, at the same time, be building up a picture or perspective on the patient which requires standing at some distance—*alibi et tunc*. By this means, both interventions and interpretations are made possible. Freud refers to the different responsibilities of the psychoanalyst and the patient. If the purpose of the treatment is for the analysand to learn about themselves, then part of the psychoanalyst's task is to learn from their experience of themselves in relation to the analysand and to use this learning to assist the analysand learn about themselves. The advantage that the psychoanalyst has, compared with the patient, lies in the fact that the psychoanalyst is better placed to observe the patient's internal process and to see the impact of absences in the transference and in his countertransference. The discourse between the two is, thus, at more than one level, and the two are contemporaneously separate and together, proximate and distant, present to and absent from one another. This is a complex learning system, but it behoves us, in these days of prospective registration and competence definition, to be as articulate as we can be in its description. This chapter is an effort to try to understand its complexities.

References

Botella, C., & Botella, S. (2005). *The Work of Psychic Figurability*. London: Brunner-Routledge.

Fain, M., & Marty, P. (1960). The synthetic function of homosexual cathexis in the treatment of adults. *International Journal of Psychoanalysis, 41*: 401–406.

Freud, S. (1919h). The 'uncanny'. *S.E.*, 17: 217–252. London: Hogarth.

Freud, S. (1937d). Constructions in analysis. *S.E.*, 23: 255–270. London: Hogarth.

PART IV

SOME METAPSYCHOLOGICAL SPECULATIONS AND SOME TECHNICAL CONCLUSIONS

Reflections and summary

How can we be objective about subjectivity? This was the question posed at the beginning of this book, and we have been considering various ways of approaching this problem from the conceptual and clinical/technical points of view. One of the main difficulties, as we have seen, is that experience is both unique to the individual human subject and, partly, at least, determined by their unconscious drives. Another difficulty lies in the representation of that experience to another human subject, because this is the *sine qua non* of communication between experiencing subjects.

If there are such difficulties in capturing subjective experience in terms that make it possible to approach being in some way "objective", are we setting ourselves an impossible task because we are trying to be able to predict something when we can only have a limited knowledge of all the relevant variables? If we set ourselves the task of predicting experience—as opposed to events—with the technology of the quadratic equation or the multivariate regression equation, can we expect that the error will overwhelm the reliability and validity of established results when these results are applied in the so-called "real world"? Is the quest to be objective about the subjective worth the many candles burnt when sitting up trying to achieve it? Some might say no.

Yet, there is something about our subjective experience that we, as humans, seem to want to understand, to represent, and, thus, be able to communicate to others. Otherwise, how can we understand the fact that artistic endeavour—in all its many forms—is universal to all cultures, both now and in the past? Now, is this too mystical, or sacred even, to sully by trying to be "objective" about it? Are we doomed to be always chasing something just out of reach because the essence of subjective experience is that we can never quite or fully know what it is that we will experience in the next instant? Or, could it be that if we try to understand more about how and why we experience, or, indeed, *why we do not experience*, then the result might be that we will come to be able to experience that which is unimaginable without such enquiry? To the twenty-first century subject, the idea that what we see and experience is not necessarily coincident with the objective is readily available, even if its consequences are not. The issue is that this dilemma of seeking to be objective about subjectivity brings us to what Paul Whittle called a philosophical fault line. If Freud stood astride this philosophical "fault line", he did it by creating the psychoanalytic method as a means of studying subjectivity.

But there are other fault lines. I can think of few concepts that divide British psychoanalysts more than the concept of time or the diachronic–synchronic fault line. For some (the synchronists), the notion of chronological time is essential because, being based on the irreversibility of physical and psychological processes involved in growth, it permits the notion of development and enables psychic development to be tied to physiological development. For others (the diachronists), more interested in states of mind, such considerations are unnecessary. Bion, for example, recommended that each psychoanalytic session be approached by the psychoanalyst without memory or desire. Yet, Bion's notions of memory and desire are, to my mind, about time, because they concern the past (memory) and the future (desire). How far it is actually possible for a psychoanalyst to approach a session totally empty of themselves is a very moot point. Such a position makes no room for the reality of the psychoanalyst's unconscious and, hence, how the unconscious of analyst and analysand can communicate with one another.

Furthermore, it is hard to envisage learning without the ideas of time and repetition. As was proposed above, psychoanalytic treatment implicitly involves the creation of an iterating learning system based on the sequential presence and absence of the analyst and analysand from one another. One way or another, the learning in one session feeds forward and becomes input into the next session. This iterating feature is what makes possible the link with what has perhaps been rather romantically called "chaos theory". Chaos theory emerged from the need to understand the circumstances of the behaviour of iterating systems, for example, the growth or decline of species populations in differing environmental conditions. With this effort came the recognition that the differential equation was limited in its capacity to be an adequate model for complex, dynamical, non-linear systems. When a different equation was used to model these phenomena, it began to be possible to predict when the linear relations between input and output began to break down, leading to apparent "chaos". These matters were further thought about in the second part of this book.

Another concept that divides psychoanalysis, but less obviously, concern what has been called "the theory of mind". The problem lies in how to use, and apply technically, the implication that each of us has a theory of mind, regardless of whether we are consciously aware of it. Fonagy (1999) has said that this derives originally from the work of Brentano, who is thought by some to be the harbinger of phenomenology through his concept of the intentionality of consciousness. This is reflected by the development from Descartes's position of "cogito ergo sum" (I think, therefore I am) to "ego cogito cogitatum" (I know that I know), or a consciousness of our consciousness. This implies that we all have a theory of our own minds even if we are not aware of it: that is, it can be unconscious. However, the recognition that we cannot come to know our own minds without an interaction with others brings with it new questions about how we establish or achieve our subjectivity. When applied in psychoanalysis, does it carry an implication of the avoidance of personal responsibility for one's destructiveness?

It is indisputable that the idea of the intentionality of consciousness leads to phenomenology, finding its way through phenomenology to existentialism. I think I am right, however, that Sartre had great difficulty with the notion of the unconscious because he saw it as a means of absolving oneself from personal responsibility. Thus, we psychoanalysts are brought by Brentano, the teacher of Husserl, and his successors to a much deeper gap, which is gathered up in the debate about subjectivity and intersubjectivity. Although this is raging in the USA, the ripples have yet to reach our shores to disturb the tranquillity of our object relations gentleman's club. Thus, I think the British Psychoanalytical Society finds itself geographically situated between the subjectivity–intersubjectivity debate from across the Atlantic and the challenge to the notion of the object by the concept of the *other*, which comes from the European continent, which embraces the same issue but out of the perspectives created by phenomenology. Thus, at least two, if not three, gaps exist. I think we need to address these because they have profound implications for the development of theory and practice.

This conceptual "research", based on philosophical considerations of what we mean by mind and consciousness, may seem far beyond the scope of psychoanalytical thinking. However, I think for me this is essential work. Partly it is because it is fun, but also because I think it is the essential part of becoming a "psychoanalytic subject", in which we think about how we know what we know. Becoming a subject in this sense, of course, involves coming to know one's own mind. The philosopher Marcia Cavell has said that it is essential to this process that there is a triangulation created by the discourse between oneself and another's mind in relation to something. I further contend that this is something that occurs over time in a process we might call progressive triangulation. The psychoanalytic process, originated by Freud, models this process and achieves this by making the subject of discourse the relationship as it emerges and unfolds between the subject and the other mind. But, because this discourse occurs over time and is subject to the continual process of *nachtraglichkeit*, the system created by these two actors becomes an intersubjective learning system. This formulation has two consequences.

The first is that that this learning system, because it is an intersubjective one, has all the necessary characteristics of a complex dynamical system, which is modelled by the mathematical model underpinning chaos theory—specifically, the logistic difference equation. The second is that the intersubjective relationship is relative to something, which might be called objective reality. When aspects of this reality can be operationalized and then measured, we can start to get a lever on subjective experience by relating it to measured reality. In the study of psychology, this approach was started by Fechner, and later Wundt, with the development of psychophysics. Life becomes a little more difficult when this starts trying to describe the reality of experience or psychic reality. As psychoanalysts, however, we must do this, or our efforts to understand experience become dissatisfying.

But, if we keep Cavell's intersubjective formulation in mind, we can start to see why the principle of triangulation is so important, and particularly its extension into *progressive triangulation, which brings in the temporal dimension*. This is because we can use features of the environment, which are comparatively unambiguous, to triangulate the discourse of two subjects—an analysand and their analyst. This book has sought to explore how this can be done.

The first four papers reproduced in this book introduced and explored the ideas of what we mean by the objective and the subjective. In essence, they seek to work towards Marcia Cavell's proposition that in order *to know our own minds, we require discourse with another mind about something external to both parties* to the discourse. This is the essence of the triangulation necessary to establish an experience of our own subjectivity and to experience someone else's subjectivity in relation to something external to both of us.

Having established that triangulation is an essential feature of how we can come to know our own minds, the way is open to think about how this applies to the psychoanalytical endeavour, because it may be thought of as a process designed to help someone come to know their own mind. Taken as a generalization, this is all very well, but the fact is that few patients seek help because of a desire for speculative exploration of their minds. In my experience, matters are usually much more urgent than that, with the result that the calm detachment of enquiry is overcome by a sense of something that demands satisfaction. This provides the psychoanalysts of patients (also known as analysands) with an early introduction to their experience of the pressure of their drives.

But, before getting into a discussion of clinical material, it seemed important to think about the various ways in which the concept of triangulation might be used to think about or support the psychoanalytical psychotherapeutic endeavour. It is for this reason that the next two papers were included. The first concerned the use of psychometric instruments in the preliminary assessment of someone's difficulties and in the process of monitoring the impact of their treatment. Three data points are used: the patient concerned, a significant "other" they nominate, and the treating psychotherapist. Measurements are taken as the treatment proceeds. Thus, we can have an impression of the impact of the treatment process as it proceeds from three different points of view. This immediately introduces the importance of the *temporal dimension*, which is intrinsic to thinking about psychotherapeutic effectiveness and psychic change.

The other paper on chaos theory—or the characteristics of iterative systems—was included to introduce the idea that the iterative quality of the psychoanalytical process creates an impetus to exploration involved in coming to know one's own mind. This is because, in and of itself, an iterating process has the potential to create both disturbance and containment. The basic point, however, is to think about the psychoanalytical process as an *iterative learning system* that will, because of its iterative quality, provide the disturbance, making it possible both to see the potential for psychic change and the containment to make such changes without being overwhelmed by anxiety.

This iterative quality means that we can think of the process of psychoanalytical psychotherapy as being one in which the results of the first encounter between psychoanalyst and the analysand partly form the input into the next session, and so on. But, the various reflections that have occurred to both parties between the sessions in *nachtraglichkeit* - sometimes translated in English as *afterwardsness*—also play a part.

From this way of thinking of the psychoanalytical endeavour as an iterative learning system, we moved to four papers looking at clinical material in an effort to think about the application of these ideas. The first of these sought to look at the development of communication between the psychoanalyst and the analysand, because the iterative quality of the encounter permits the observation of the characteristic sense of time that is brought by each patient to the endeavour.

The three final papers in this group are concerned with how the iterative quality of the process permits the emergence of what has been unrepresentable. For example, the iterative quality of the encounter permits the observation of the characteristic sense of time that is brought by each patient to the endeavour. Secondly, by thinking about the experience of absence in the transference, we can start to think about paradoxical situations in which patient keeps coming to say that psychotherapy will not help them. This sets the ground for thinking about the antinomic (i.e., apparently contradictory, but coincidentally true) presence in the transference of *identification* of patient and psychoanalyst with one another and *the experience of their inevitable differences* of perspective and role in the iterative learning system is *triangulated by their iterative presence and absence from one another*.

I hesitate to list a catalogue of conclusions to this book, because I think each reader will develop their own based on their experience and interpretation. This process I do not wish to pre-empt. However, I do think that the extraordinary characteristic of Freud's creation of the psychoanalytical method was that he developed a means of investigating the irreducible subjective quality of human experience in such a way that took full account of the triangulated quality of the human subject. As the human subject develops a sense of their past, present, and future, and, thus, situates themselves in time and space, the unique quality of their subjective experience and its difference from others' experience become readily apparent, and for some, possibly, problematic to the point of being intolerable. It is this that brings patients to seek help and which renders, for some, the prospect of being helped seeming to be impossible.

If, in the course of writing this book, any one characteristic of the psychoanalytic endeavour has impressed itself upon me more than anything else, I would have to say that it was the significance of the temporal dimension and the consequent significance of the iterative quality of the psychoanalytical learning system. I say this because triangulation might *seem* above all to be associated with relating objects to one another in spatial terms. Hence, I have introduced the notion of progressive triangulation to incorporate the essential contribution of the temporal aspect of psychoanalytical process.

But, as soon as we introduce the fact of the human subject's experience of past, present, and future, we gain an entry to their development of hopes and anxieties that are uniquely their own concern and with which many feel hopelessly, even horrifyingly, alone. Psychoanalysis, perhaps, might be thought of as a means of emerging from the potentially solipsistic quality of human experience, and to do so seems to demand going beyond the "here and now". Even if it seems that only remaining in the "here and now" will satisfy the requirements of being objective, it seems that such a position can never embrace the psychic reality of the human subject. Because the human subject is situated temporally, the experience of past and future are inevitably open to exploration and interpretation in idiosyncratic ways unique to their subjectivity.

Returning to Molnos's (1995) statement about the essence of psychoanalytic psychotherapy,

> In order to do psychoanalytic psychotherapy, one has to create a special place in which the past can reappear in the here-and-now, a place in which past emotional conflicts are relived and understood with clarity, and in which new solutions to old problems are found . . .

she seems to describe a situation in which past, present, and future are coincidentally and simultaneously experienced. By this means, perhaps, a new subjectivity emerges. Because of the experience of reflection on the past, acceptance of the present, and anticipation of the future a sense of oneself as a being that knows that its experiences can inform a new sense of being and can engage with others in new way. A temporally triangulated being emerges, free of the exigent pressures of the "here and now" because of a newly won power of reflection based on the achievement of temporal triangulation, bringing with it an experience of being experienced.

We seem to have reached a position such that an answer to the question about how we can be objective about subjectivity lies in thinking about triangulation, both spatially and temporally. It is no accident that as humans began to be able to situate themselves, or, more plainly, "know where we are", they were able to do so by creating criteria that were agreed upon and could, thus, be used to create points of rendezvous, which were effective. At a very basic level, triangulation is essential to communication. That was the achievement that enabled us to place ourselves in external time and space.

Triangulation also makes possible the experience of insight when the temporal dimension is included. The iterative quality of the psychoanalytic process draws on this experience and allows us to situate ourselves in internal time and space in new ways. By this means, we can come to know "who we are", or, at least, to achieve a good enough approximation to see that we are not condemned to an eternal solipsism. By this means, we can know that there will always be a "first person view". The inevitable existence of others' views need not be a threat to our existence but what it is that makes life possible and potentially joyful. This is readily observed when a child points to something and says "there".

References

Fonagy, P. (1999). Memory and therapeutic action. *International Journal of Psychoanalysis, 80*: 215–223.

Molnos, A. (1995). *A Question of Time*. London: Karnac.

INDEX